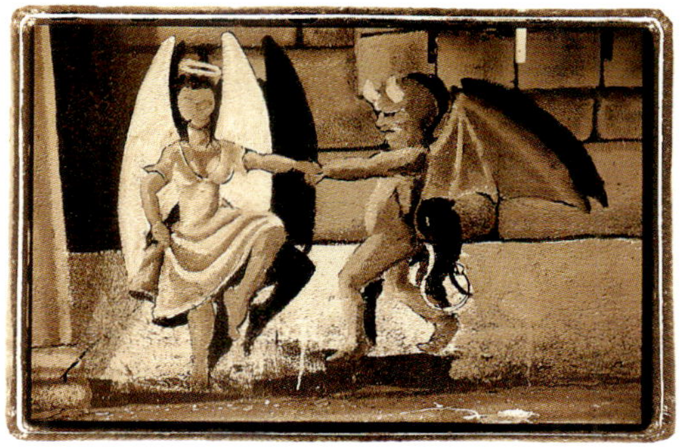

**wings of peace**

new york city – lower east side graffiti

“Peace is not constituted by the absence of war. Peace is a virtue, an attitude of mind, an inclination toward benevolence, trust and justice.”

Baruch de Spinoza (1632–1677)

peace is being happy
peace means no fighting
peace is being calm

**katarina**
philippines

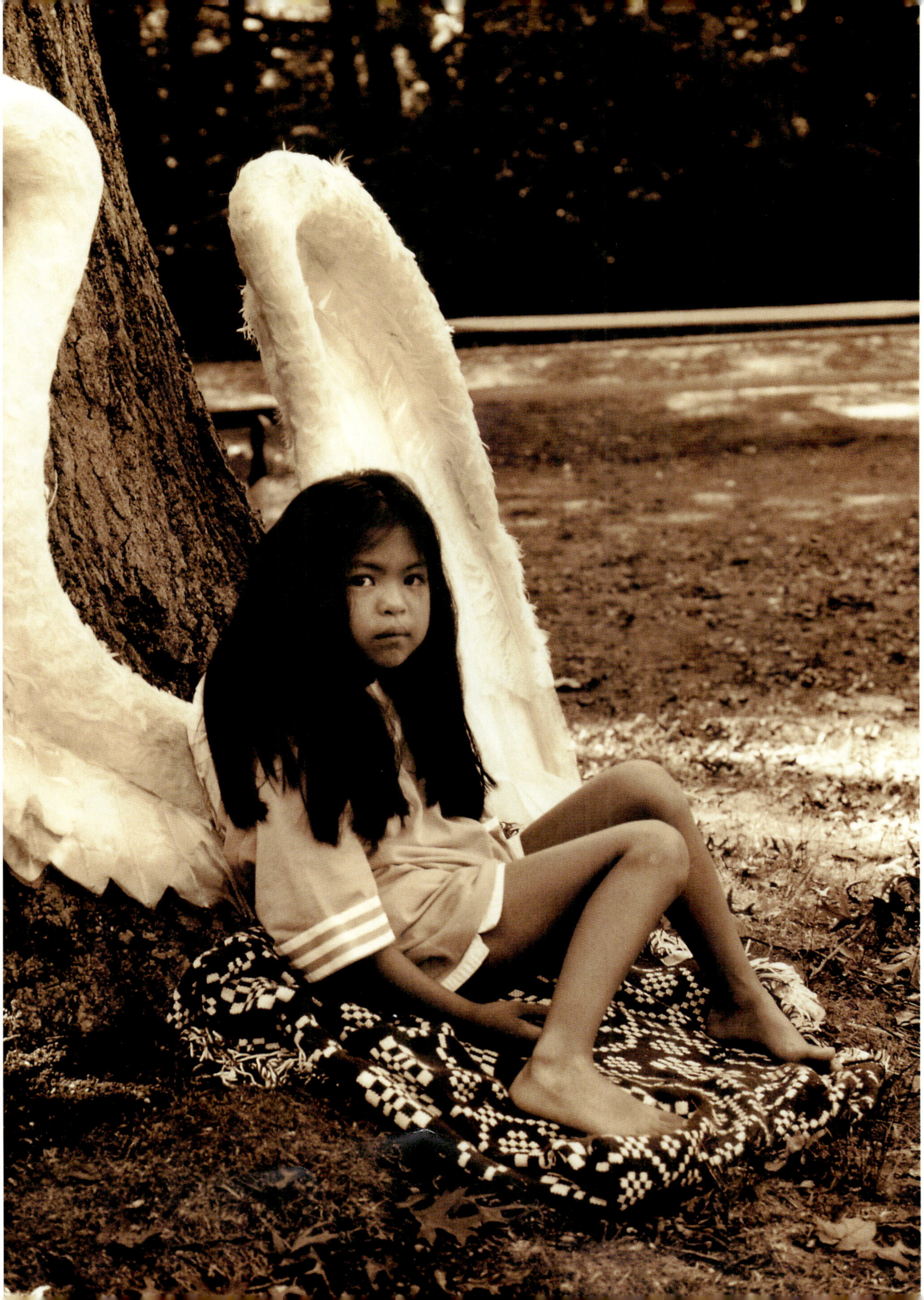

peace means sharing
two countries who are sharing
are not killing each other

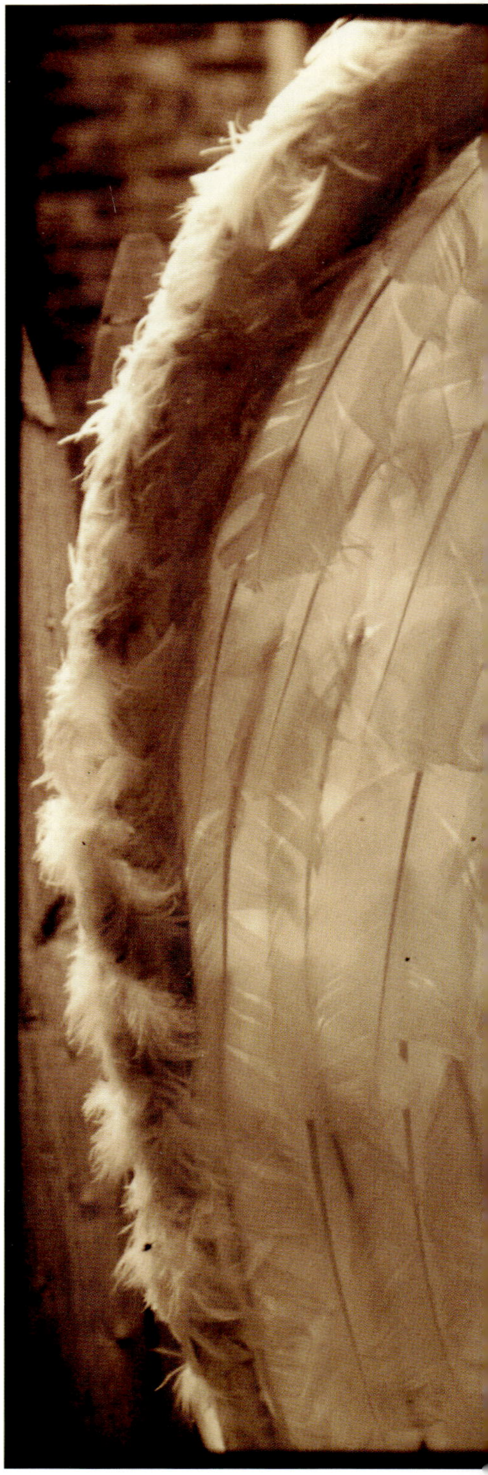

**john**
palestine

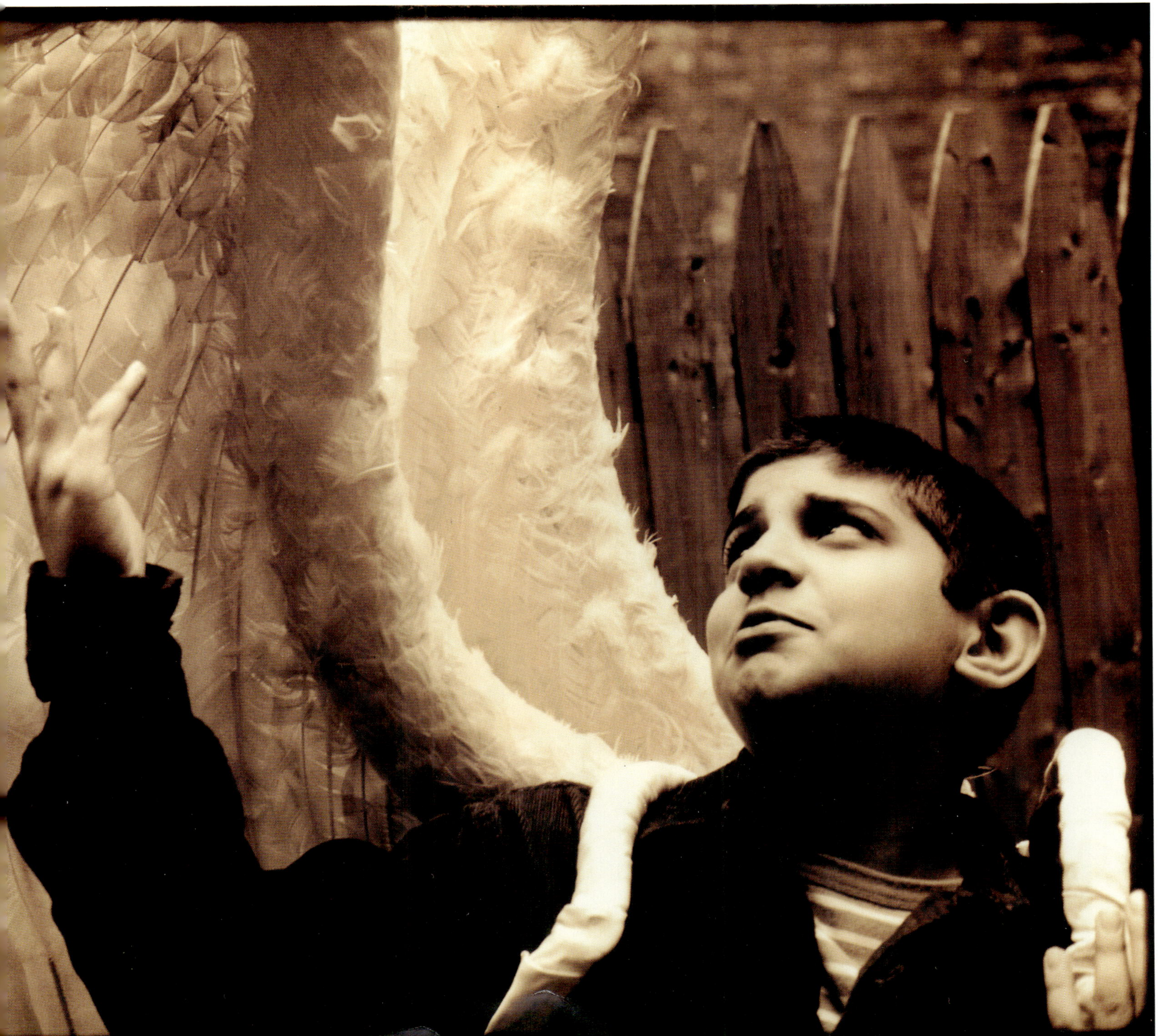

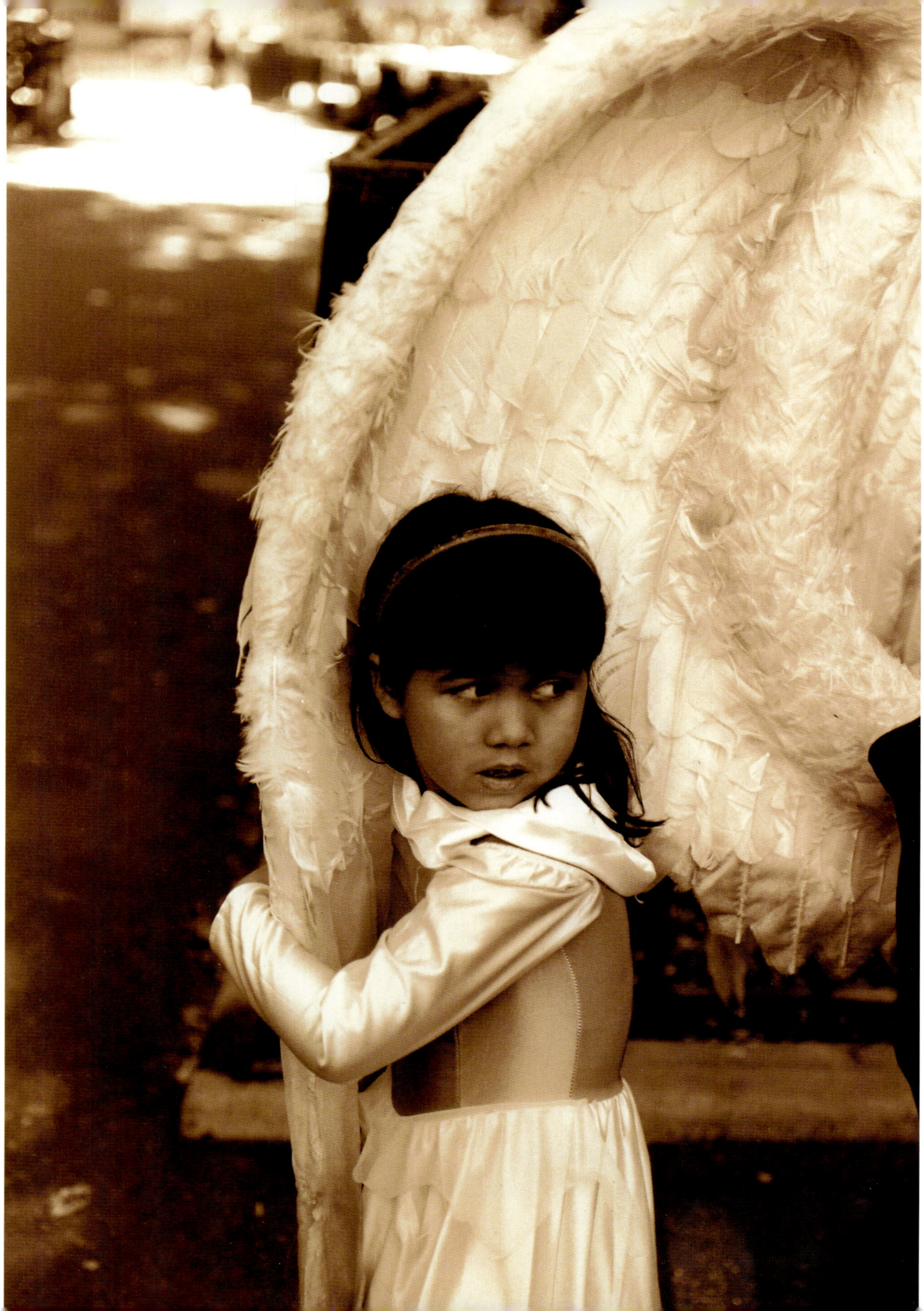

**iliana**
puerto rico

panja jürgens

# wings of peace

foreword
udo lindenberg

KNESEBECK

Harry N. Abrams, Inc., Publishers

## Phoenix – Angel – Astronaut

Rise up. Fly out to where your eye finds wide open spaces and the path that leads to where you are on the pinnacle of time, where time is already the future where today already lives in tomorrow.

Overcome the petty stumblings of your everyday, stressed-out, chased-around, kicked-around victim of the rat race. Leave it behind, the tangled confusion in your daily management of banal crises in your little world, stuffed so full with futile vanities and so barricaded with fences and boxes that you can no longer recognize the wide world beyond, while you burn yourself out for a mini-role as an extra in your ridiculous puppet theater, and sell yourself for a measly petty top-billing as a melancholy clown in the marionette culture which has never taken in a single line by Brecht, not even the one that's been said a thousand times to make sure it wasn't said too seldom "let us renew the warnings, even if they have turned to ashes in our mouths" to those who in full public view are preparing the next war.

And rise out of the ashes like the PHOENIX with the eternal flame which burns in his heart: "… he does not forget the dead, and warms the unborn." (From the poem PHOENIX, written for me by Heiner Müller in 1986.)

Fasten your wings, be the one to bring the good news, the messenger with good science fiction, ASTRONAUT who looking from afar comprehends our beautiful fragile little blue planet in its entirety (and knows that it needs our protection).

Be the PHOENIX, who without missing a beat of his wings takes off time and again to a new life, to a new start, and calls: “Peace at last, for everyone, for all people!”

This is possible, it must be possible, the globe can now be taken in at a single glance after all! Real peace, and no more promises that it will all be better someday somehow.

No, now! Let’s have an end to spin-doctored soundbites and the lukewarm lip-service politics that conceal the backroom arms trade.

The times they are a-changin’, and the time is NOW!

Be the ASTRONAUT who after his flight to the stars returns to his town in Gronau or Kentucky and sees the restrictions, the constrictions, the one-way streets, and the weakly glowing screens that seek to dull his vision. THE ANGEL, THE PHOENIX, THE ASTRONAUT. High in the air, up there, the home of better thoughts, and the wider view, and the law that bans all war, now. Peace, love = world-love, freedom. Where no one asks any longer which is the only true god. There’s room in heaven for many gods. Where no one asks any longer which country is “the most powerful”. When you soar high above everything, you see a country that is the whole Earth. And all people have at last understood that war and hate belong on the scrapheaps of yesterday. Angels with a lofty mandate – Phoenix in flaming feathers – Astronauts stretching over the horizon – Panja’s wings fire our fantasy and drive our determination.

Udo Lindenberg

peace is an inner balance
a harmony that must be
achieved individually

**evelyn**
cuba

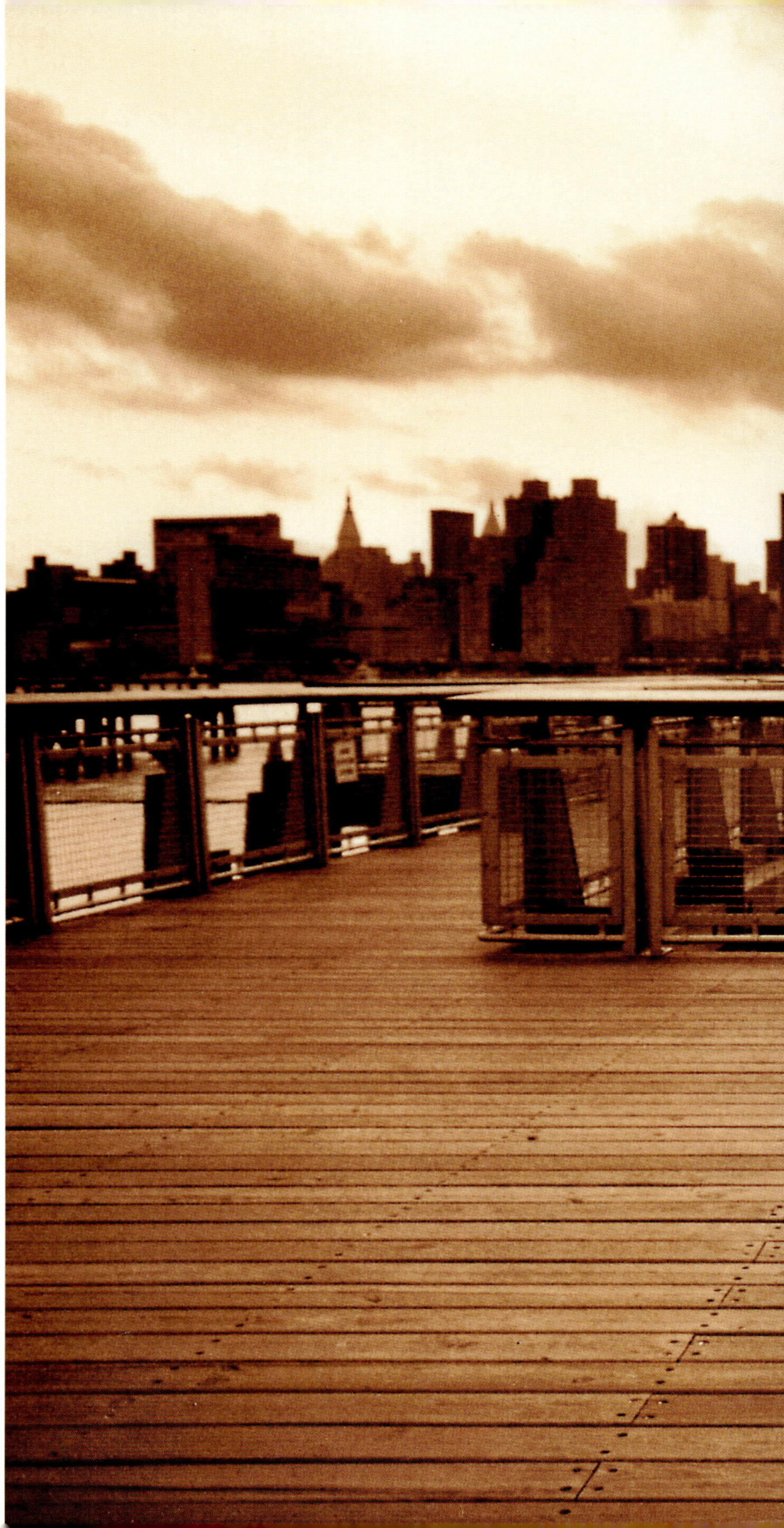

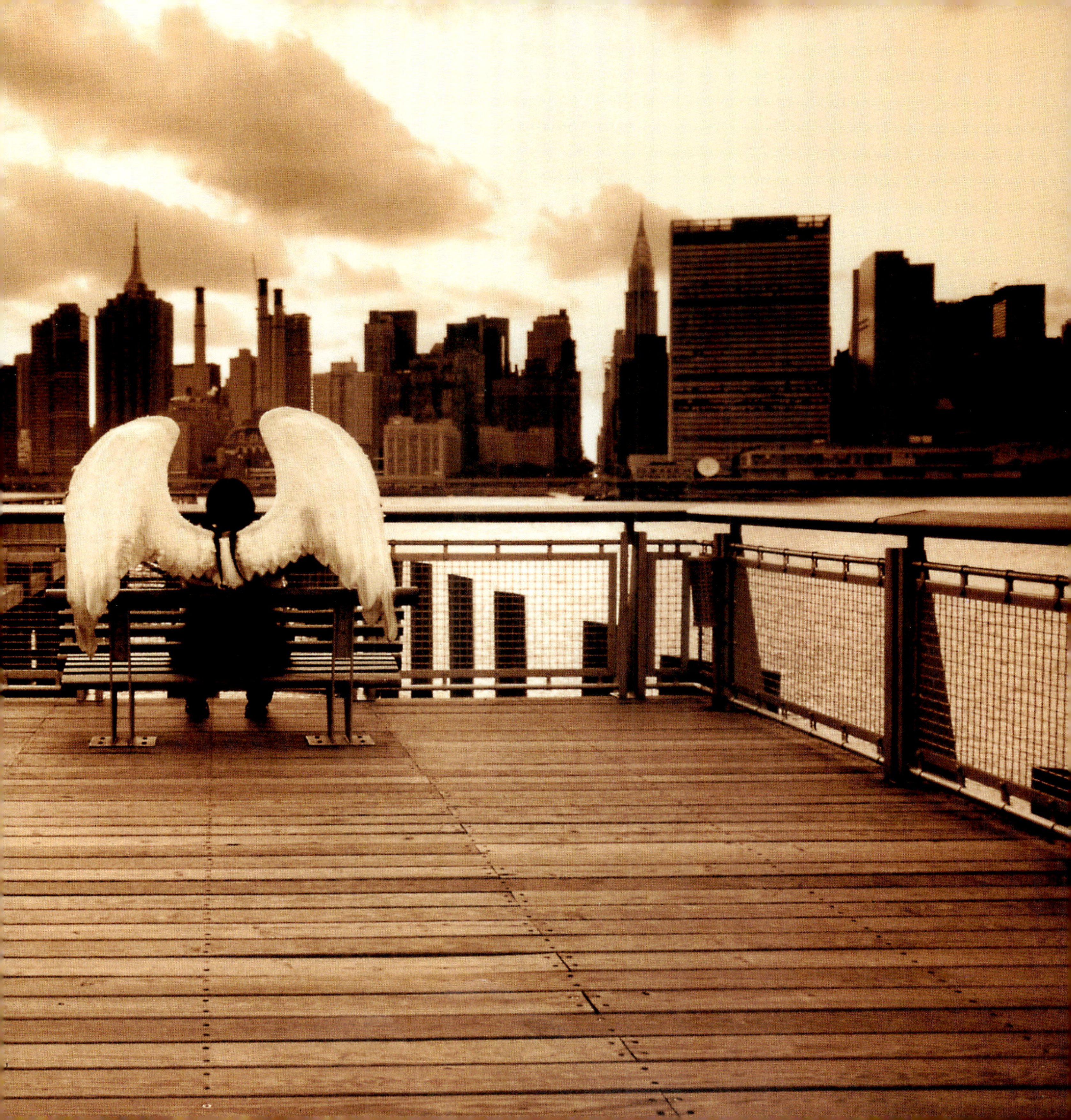

i believe
peace
is a choice
but unfortunately
it's not always an option

**brian**
poland

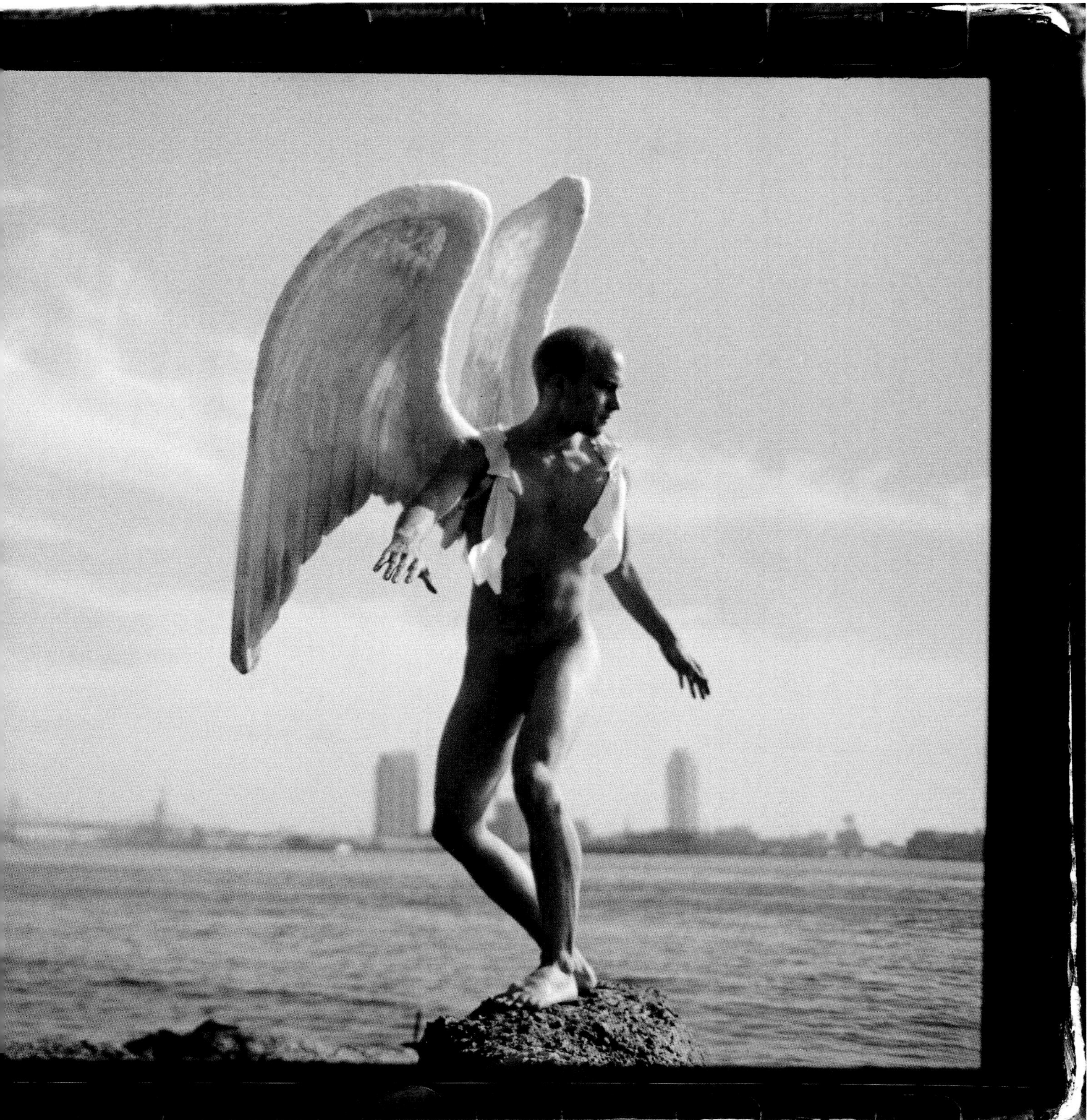

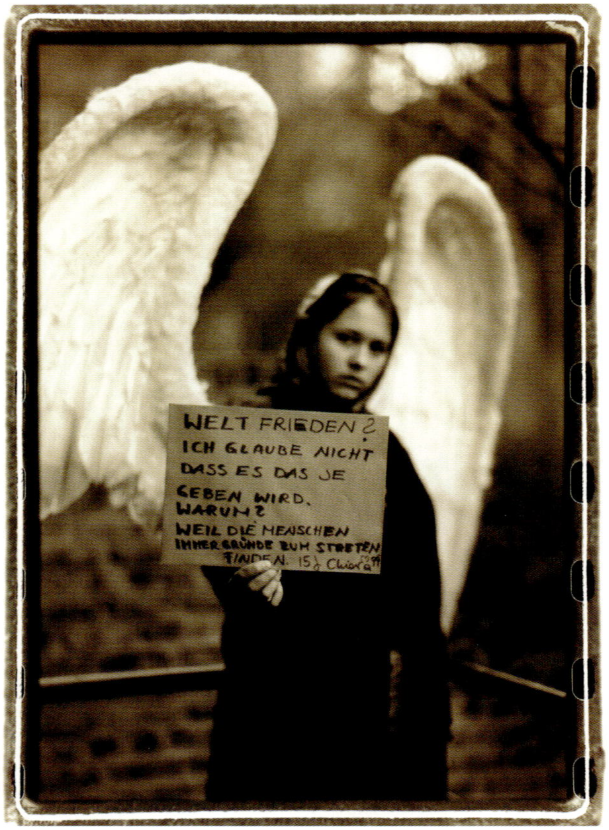


**chiara**

armenia

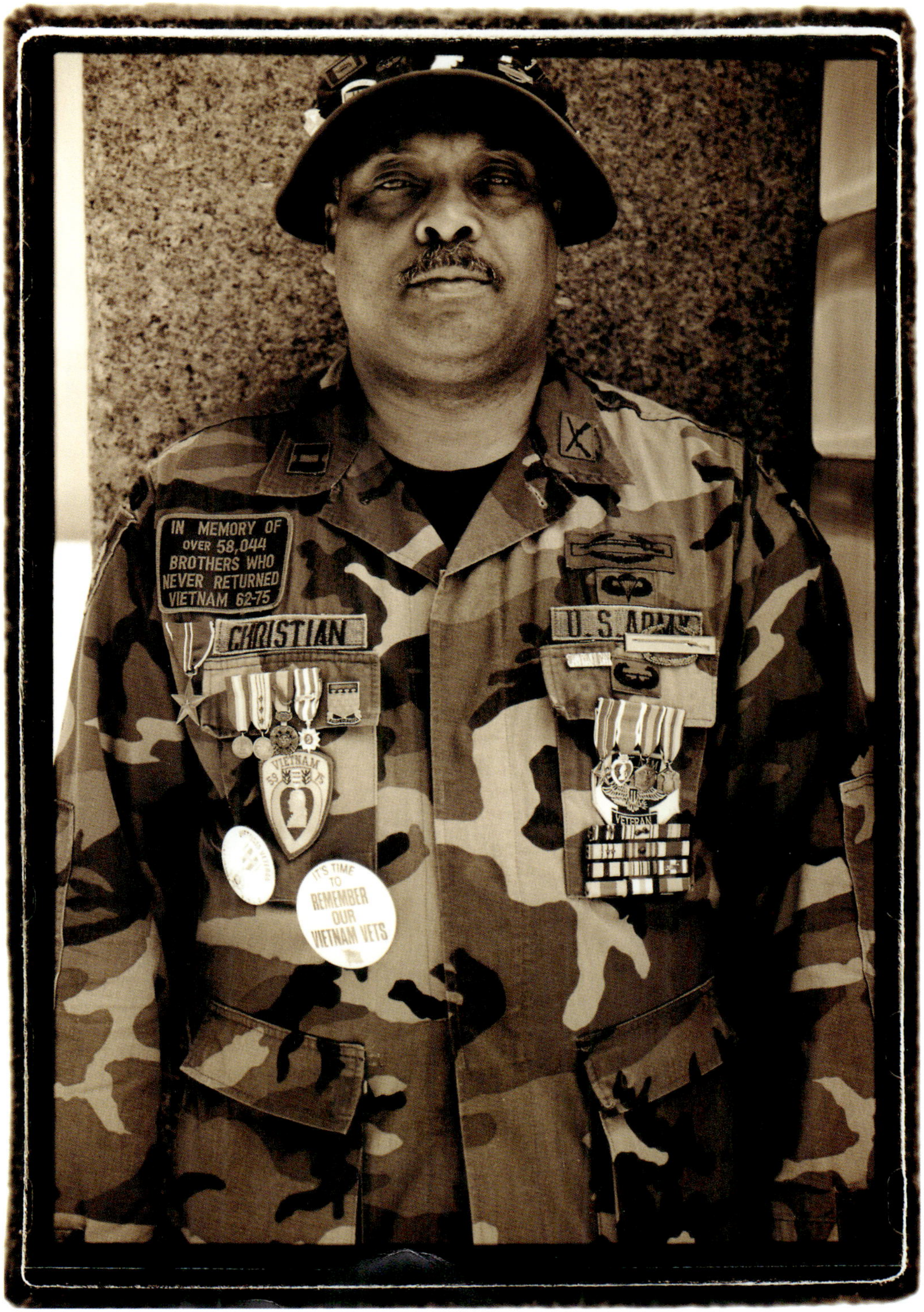


**christian**

new york city

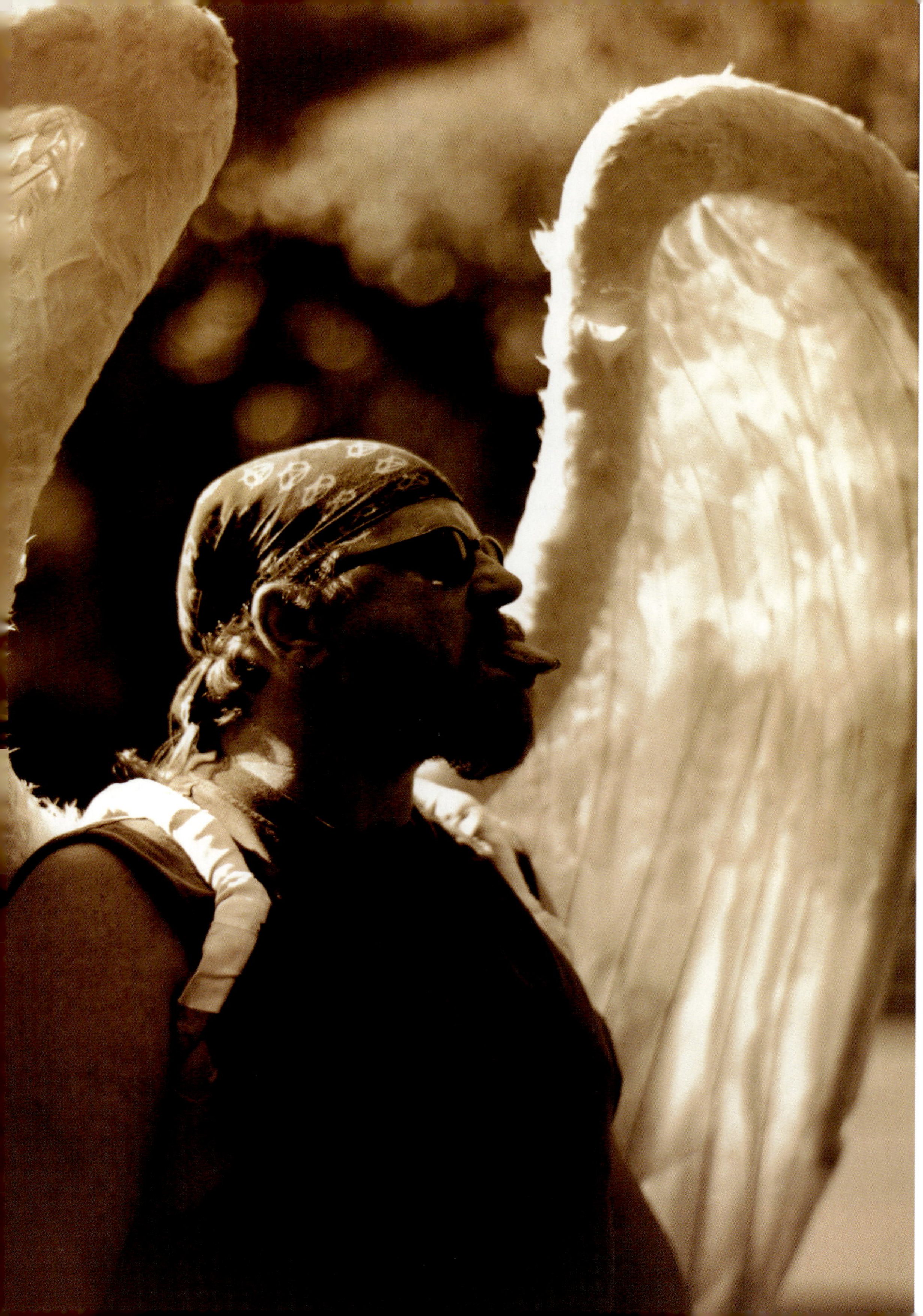

the angel
stands alone
in the chaos
as the warlords
try to tear him apart
but they may as well
rip him to the bone babe
'cause they can't
kill the peace
in his heart

**pat**
norway

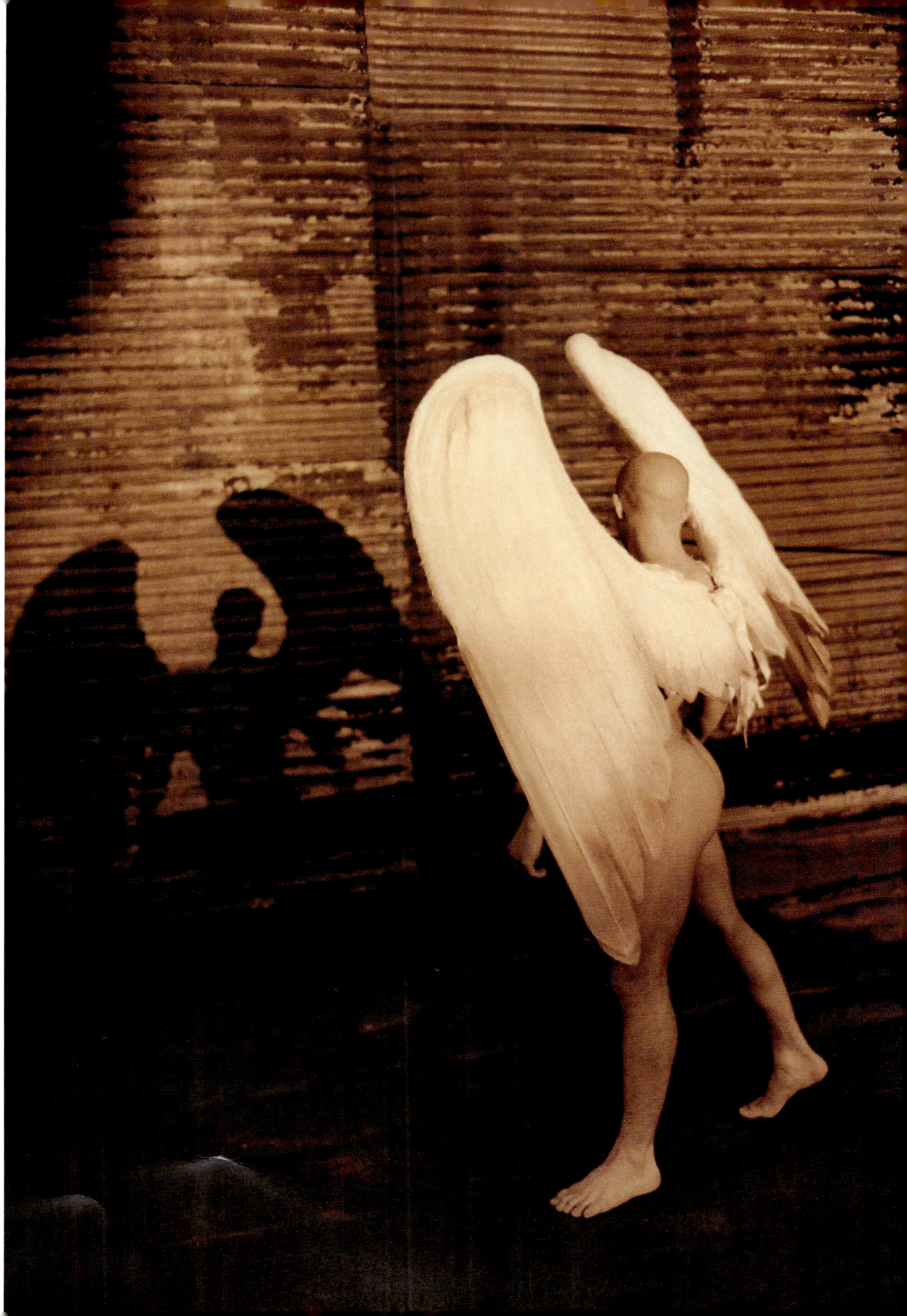

**troy**
ireland

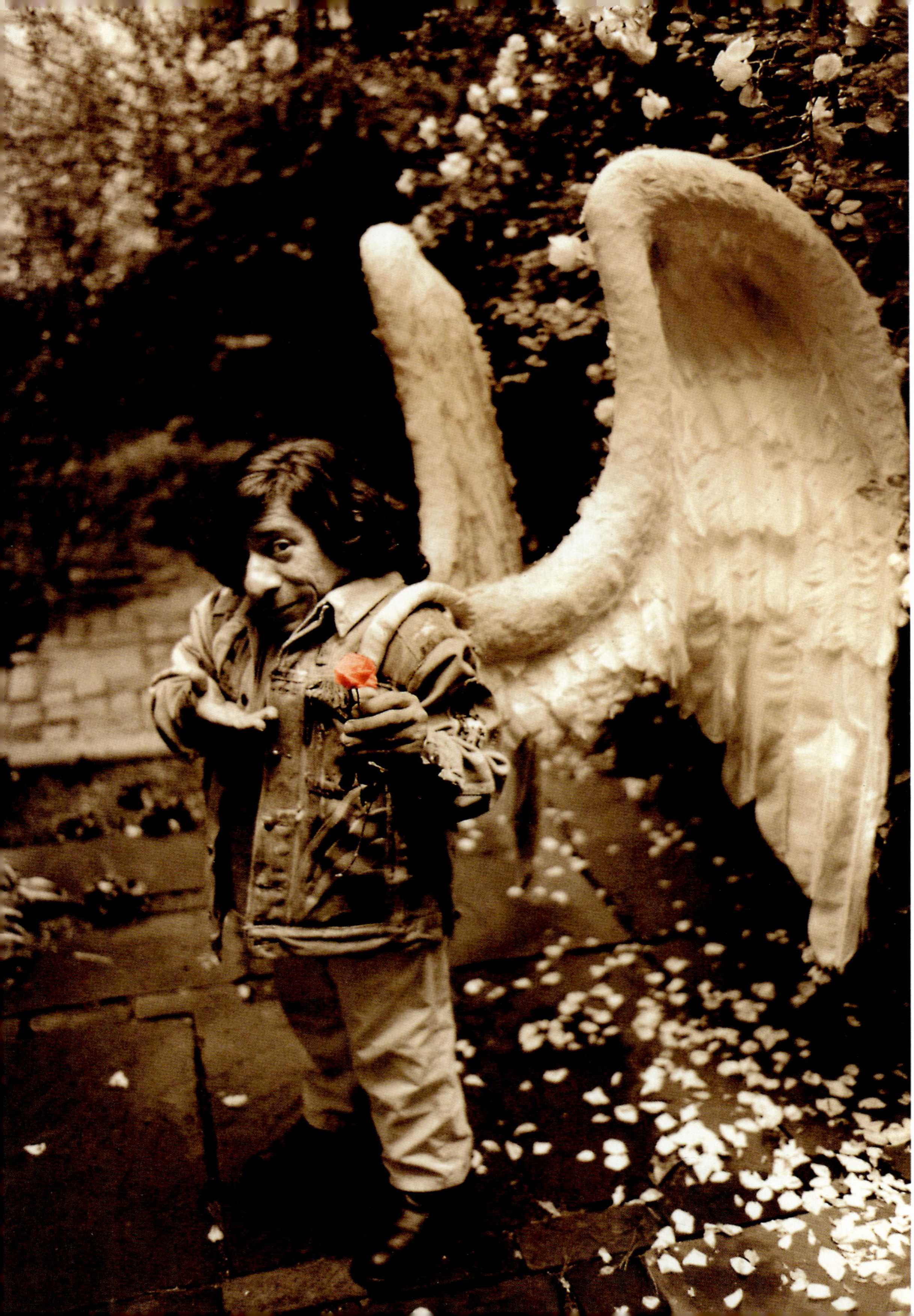

it takes love
to find peace
it takes patience
to keep peace

**bobby**
italy

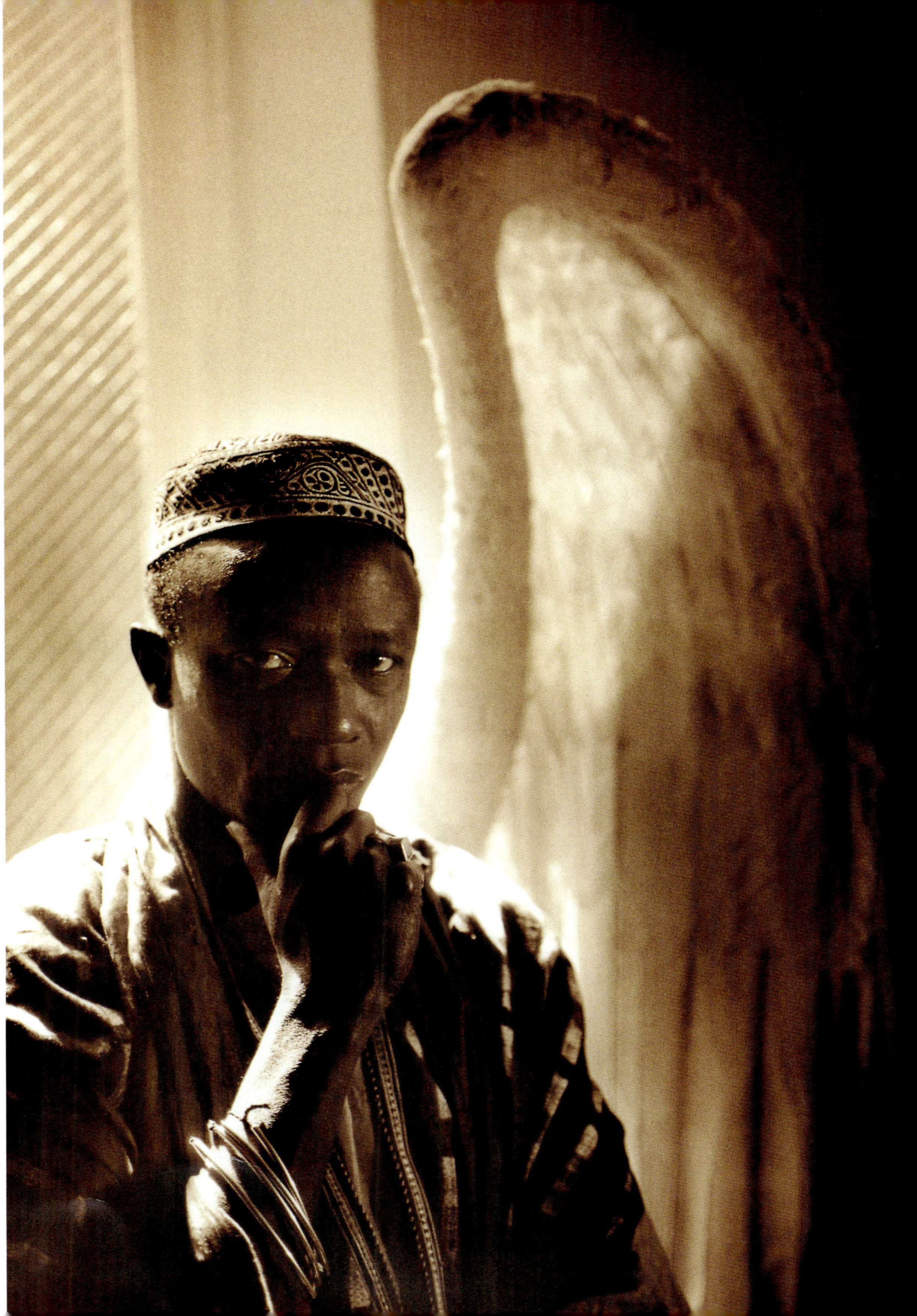

**moussa**
senegal

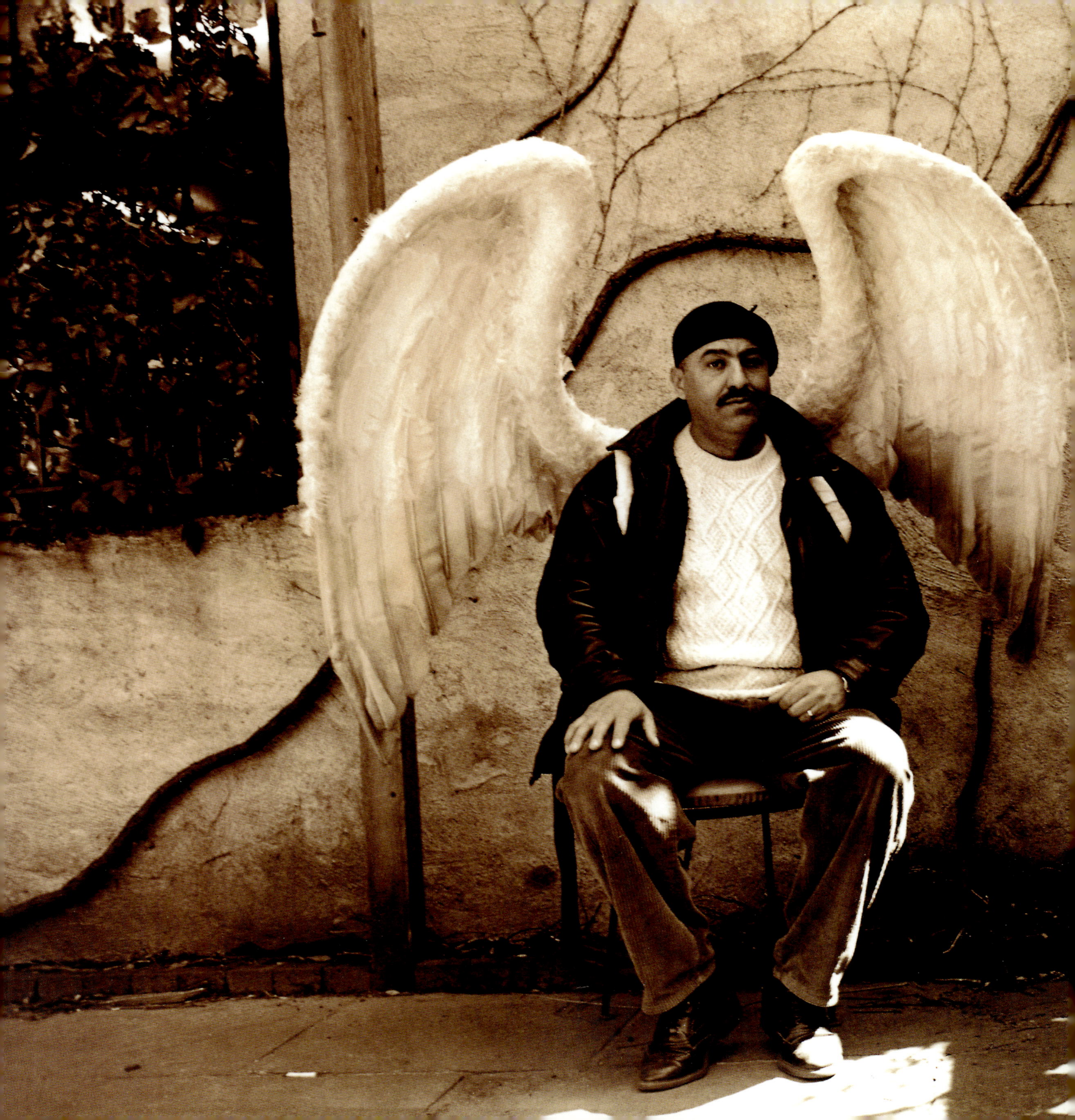

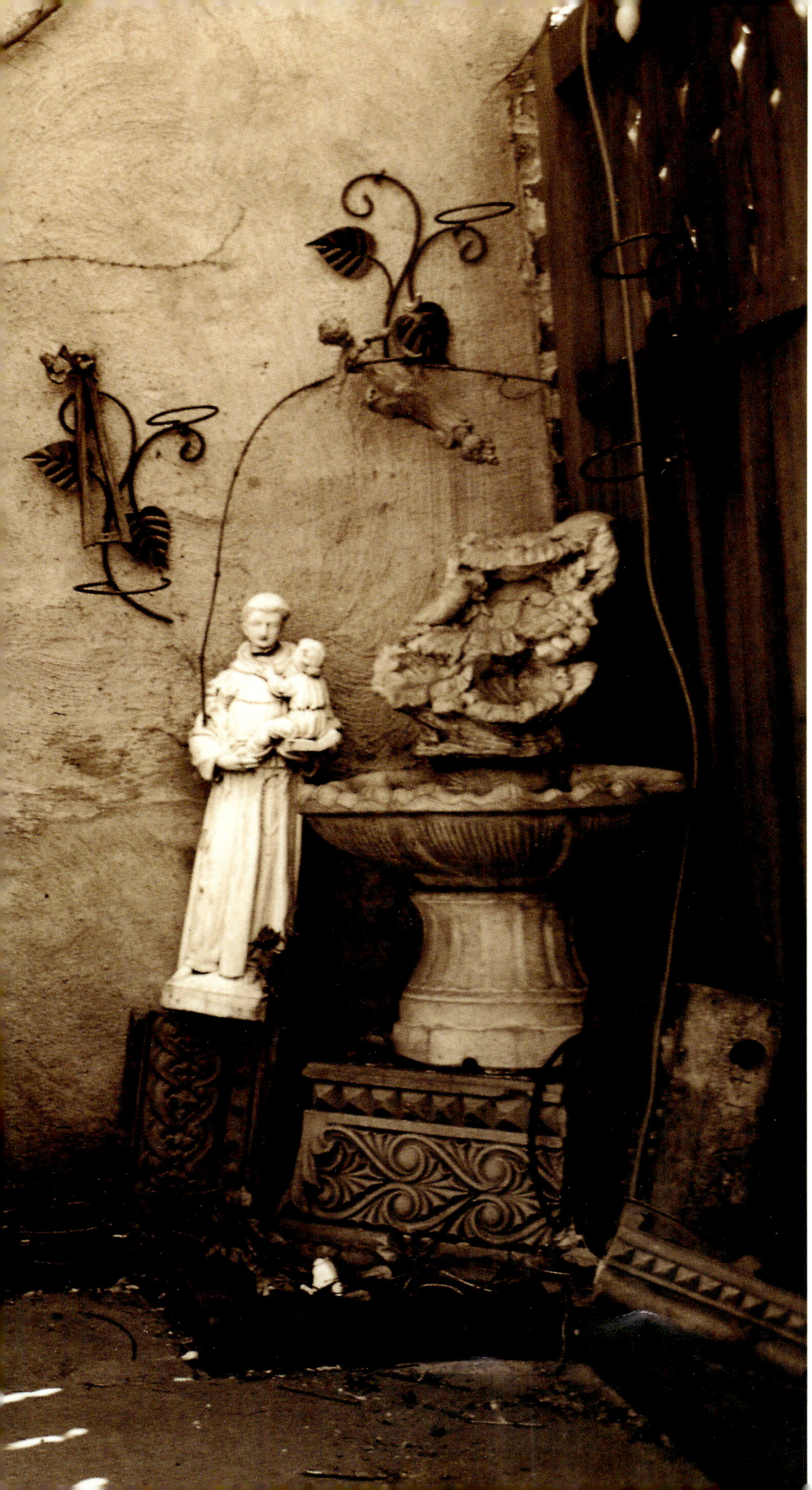

we fight every day for peace
in our religion the name of god
*al-salaam* means peace

**nasser**
jordan

peace is the grace of god
in which we are
fortunately given
the chance to achieve

**ninfa**
philippines

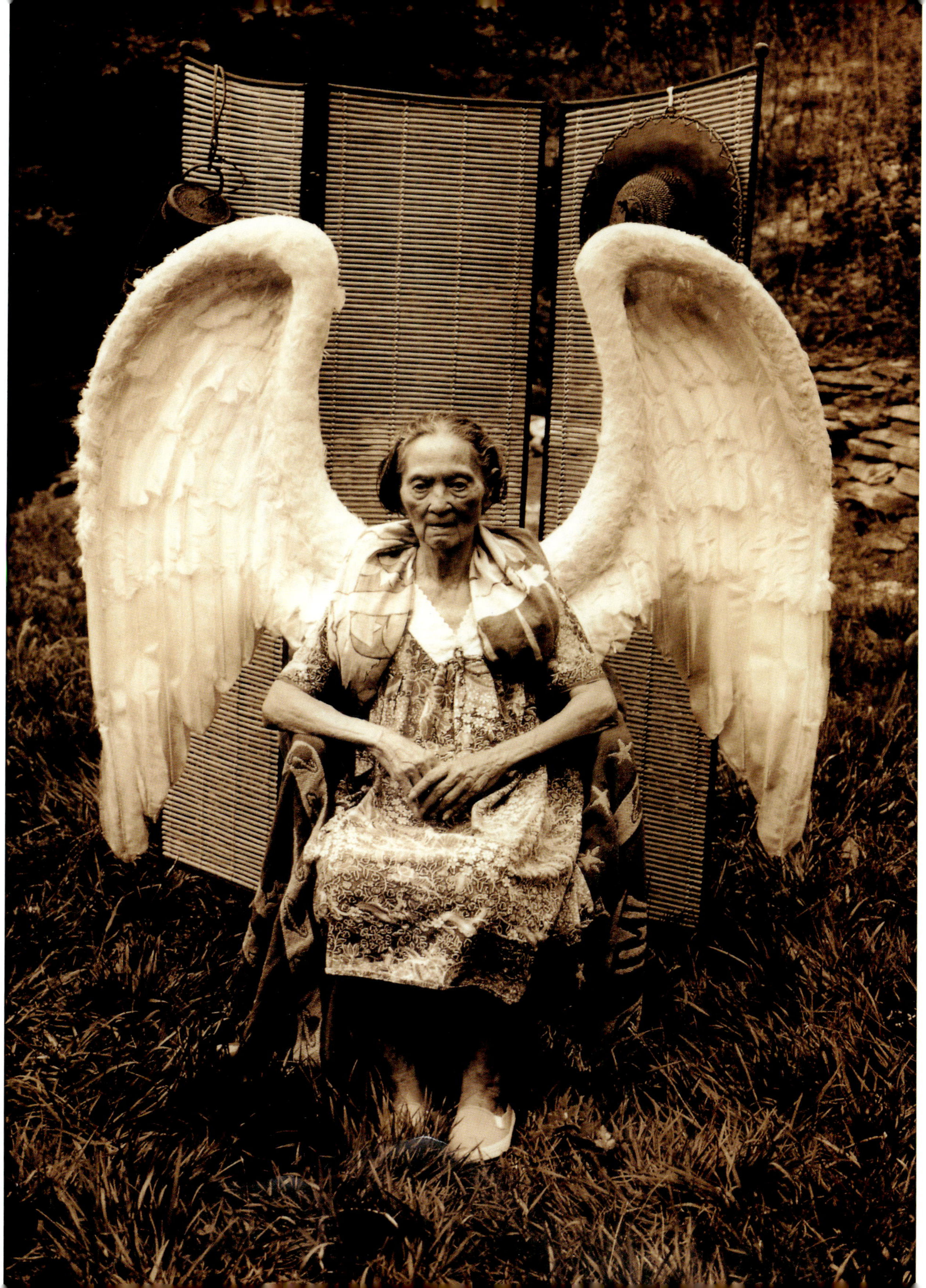

peace is the courage
to seek out the kingdom
within yourself

**emanuel**
ecuador

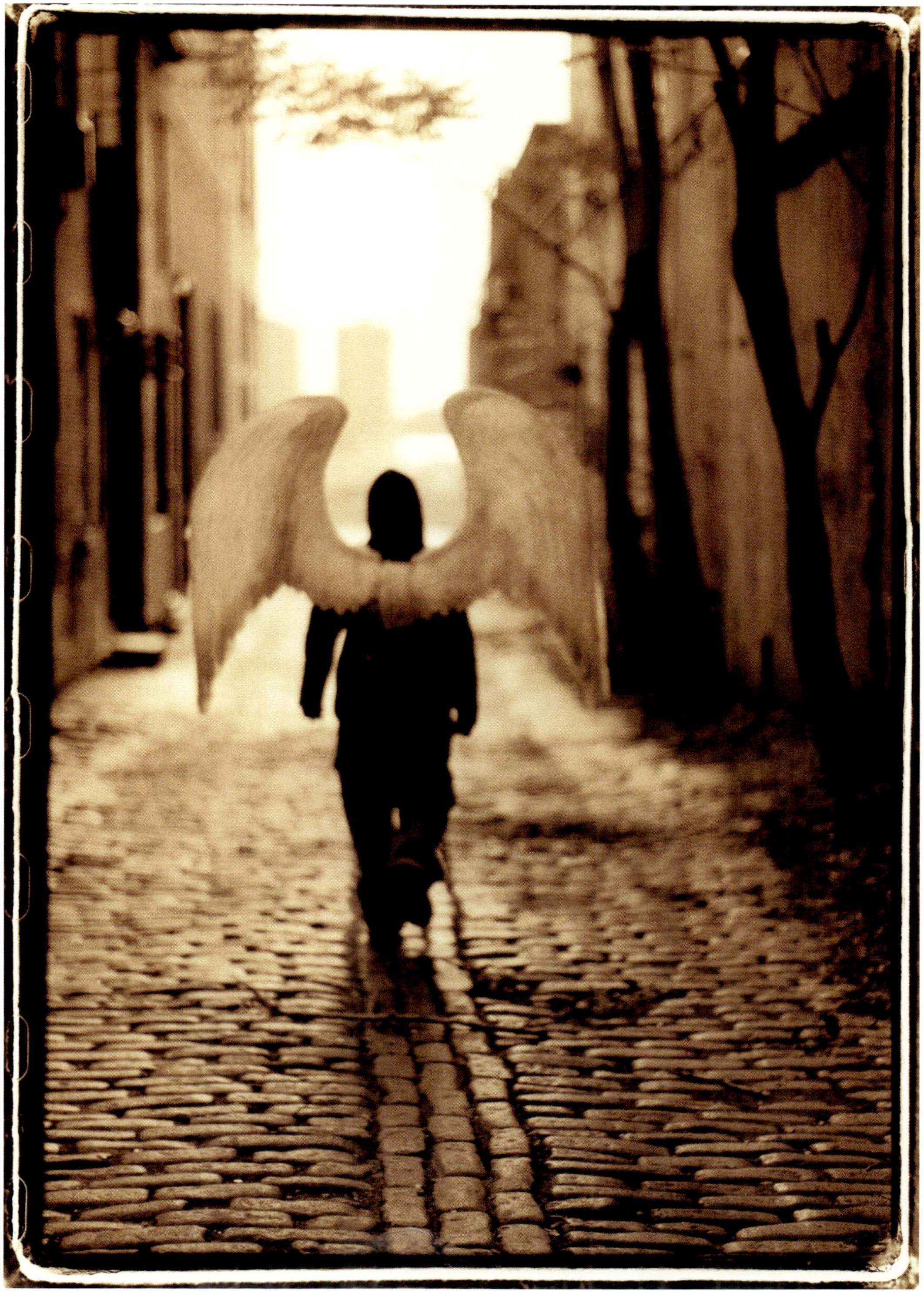

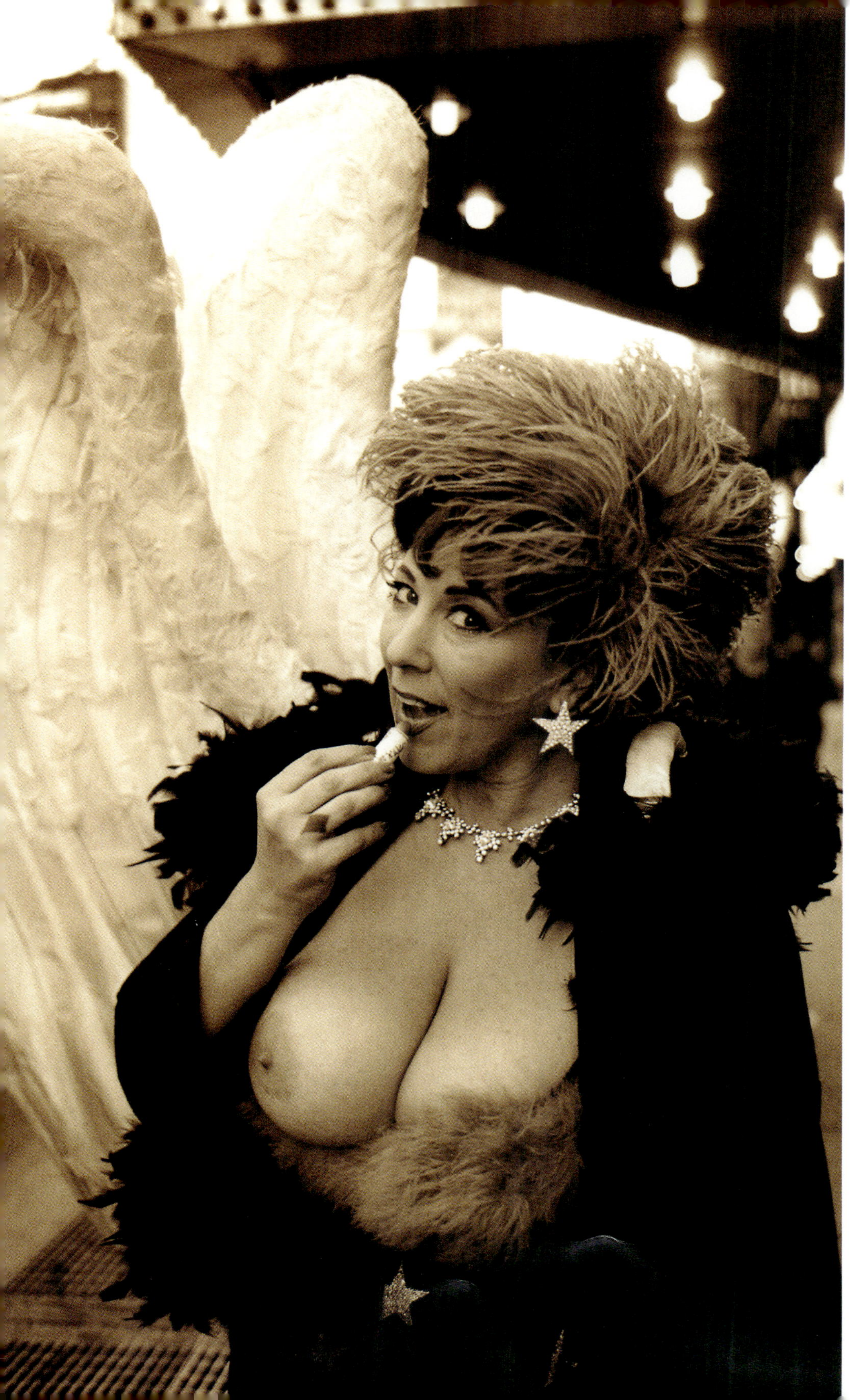

peace is a skill
that can be learned

**annie sprinkle**
russia

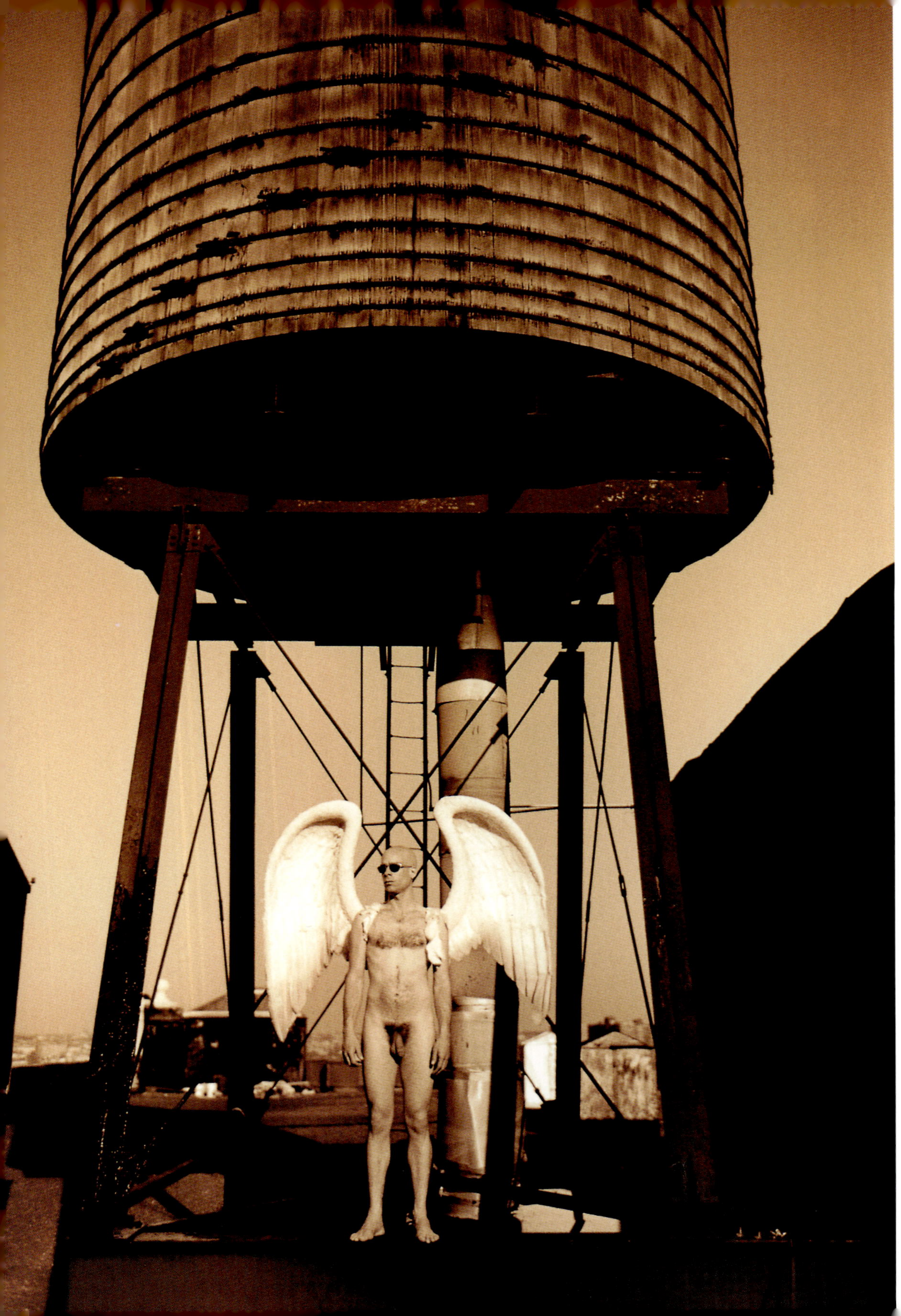

**brainhard**
norway

if you are
at peace with yourself
peace is everywhere

**kevin**
usa

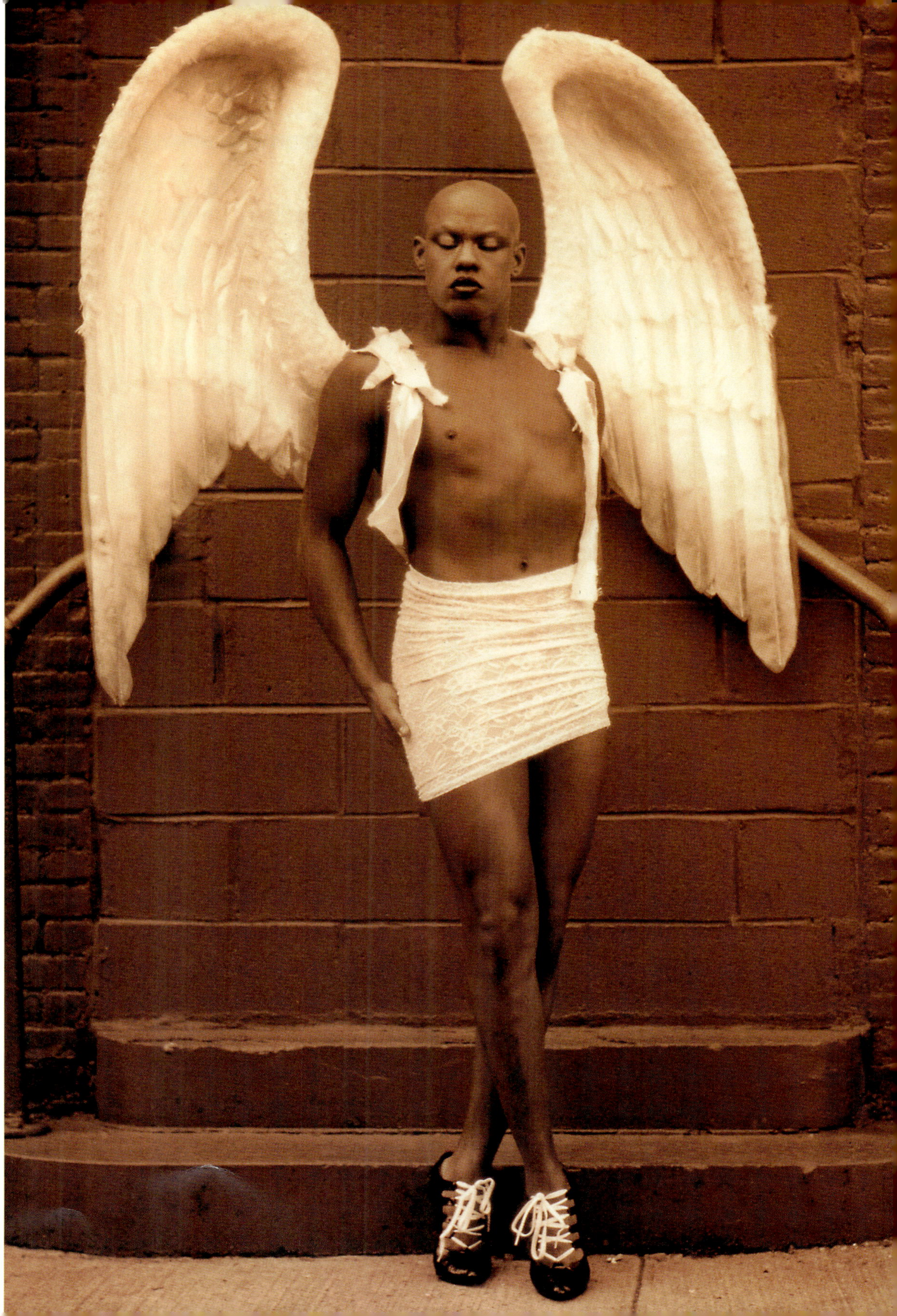

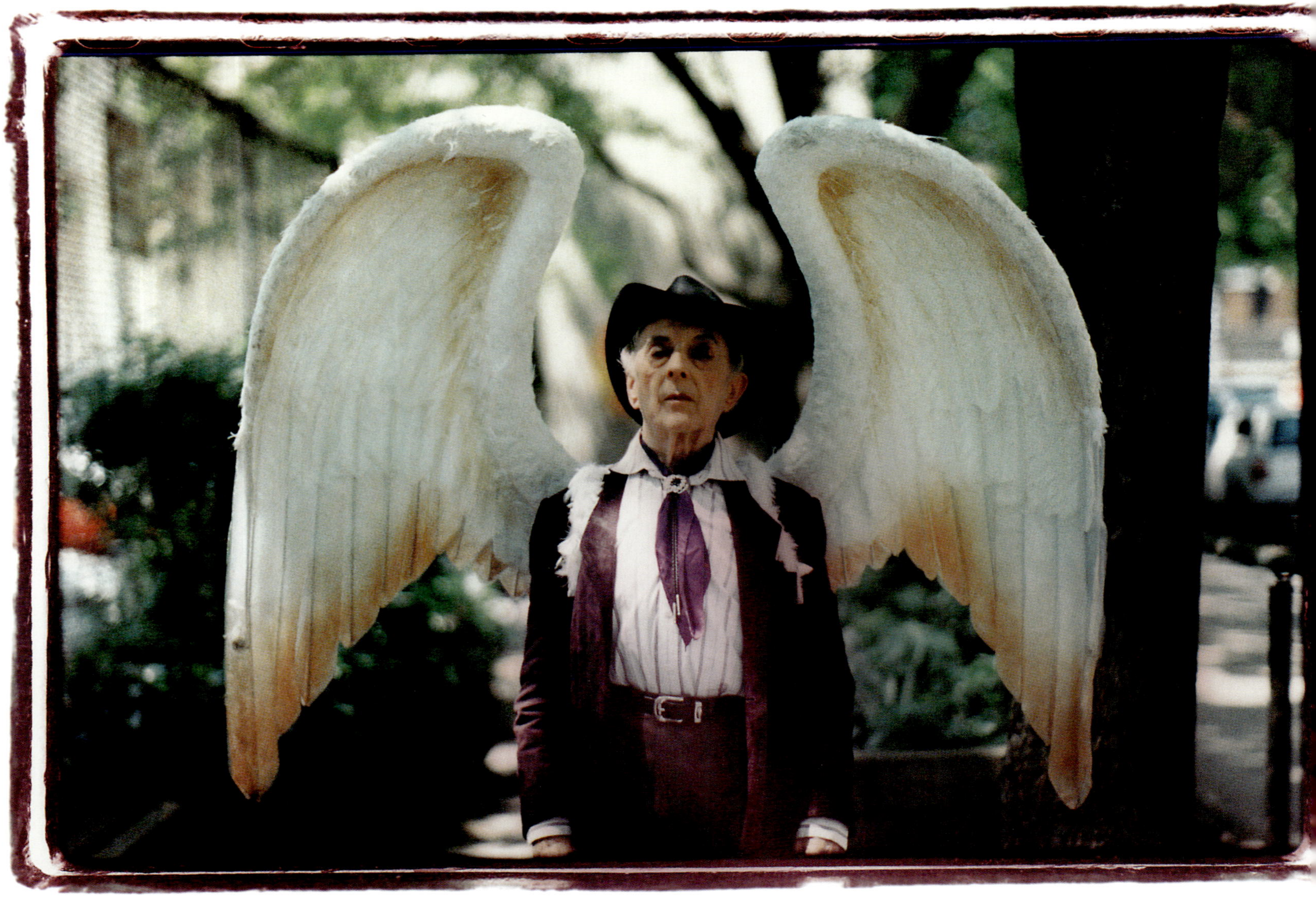

**quentin crisp**
great britain

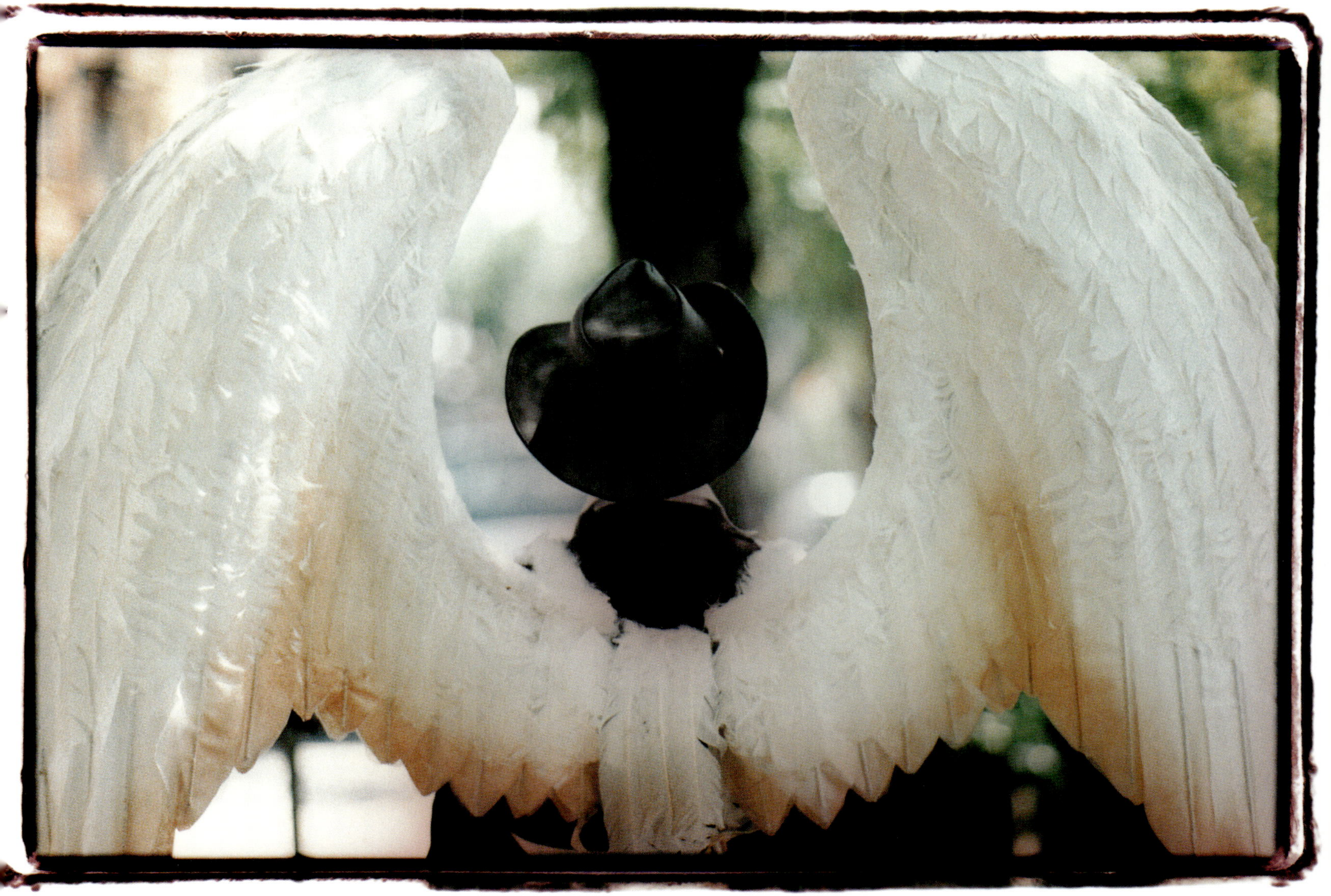

i like to think that i have earned
my wings but we all believe that
as for endorsing the idea of peace
i'm less certain
war has its uses

yet in this chaos
peace is a pretty elusive thing
when i think about peace
i gotta think about war

**emily**
sweden

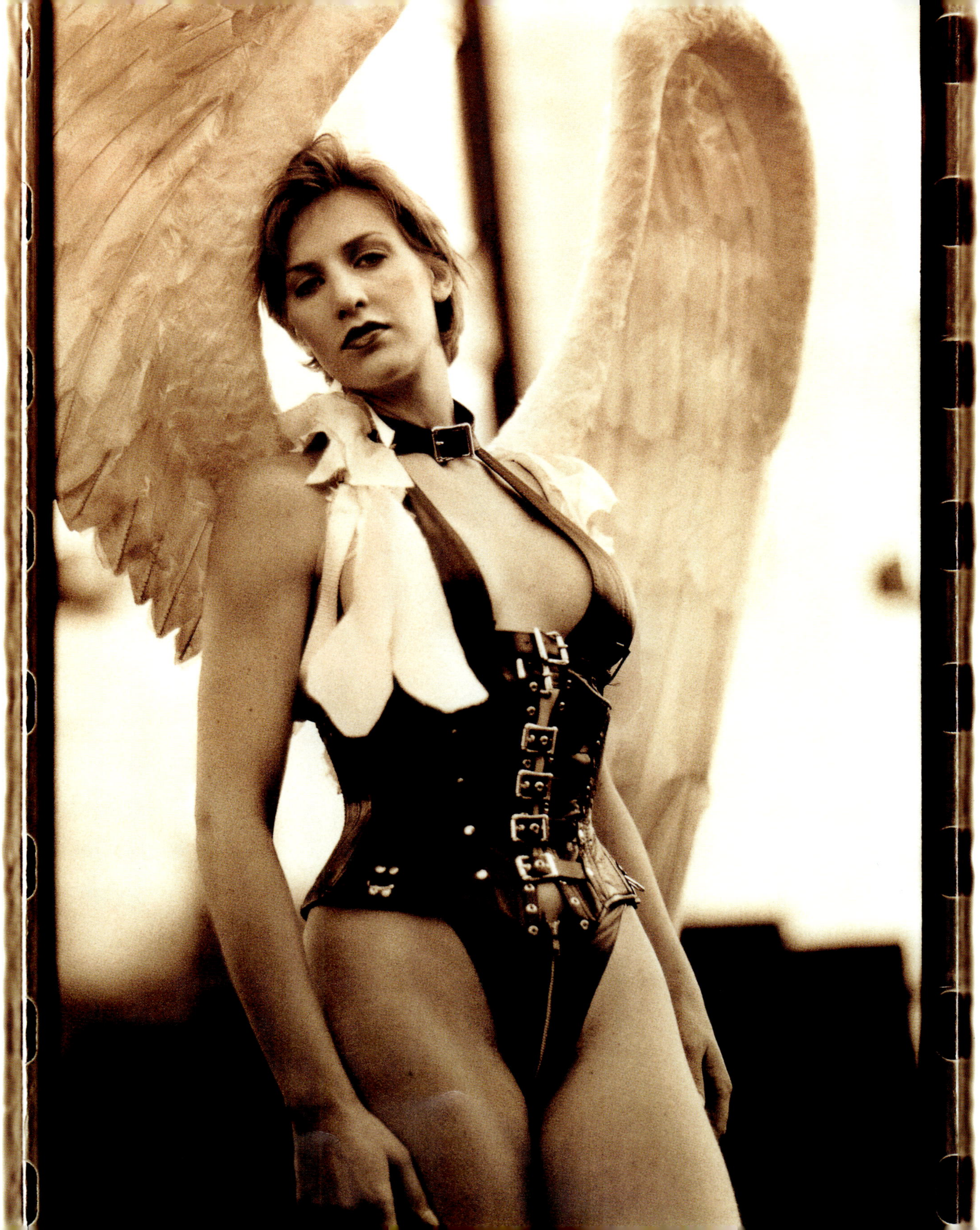

peace within us
peace outside us

**arjan**
india

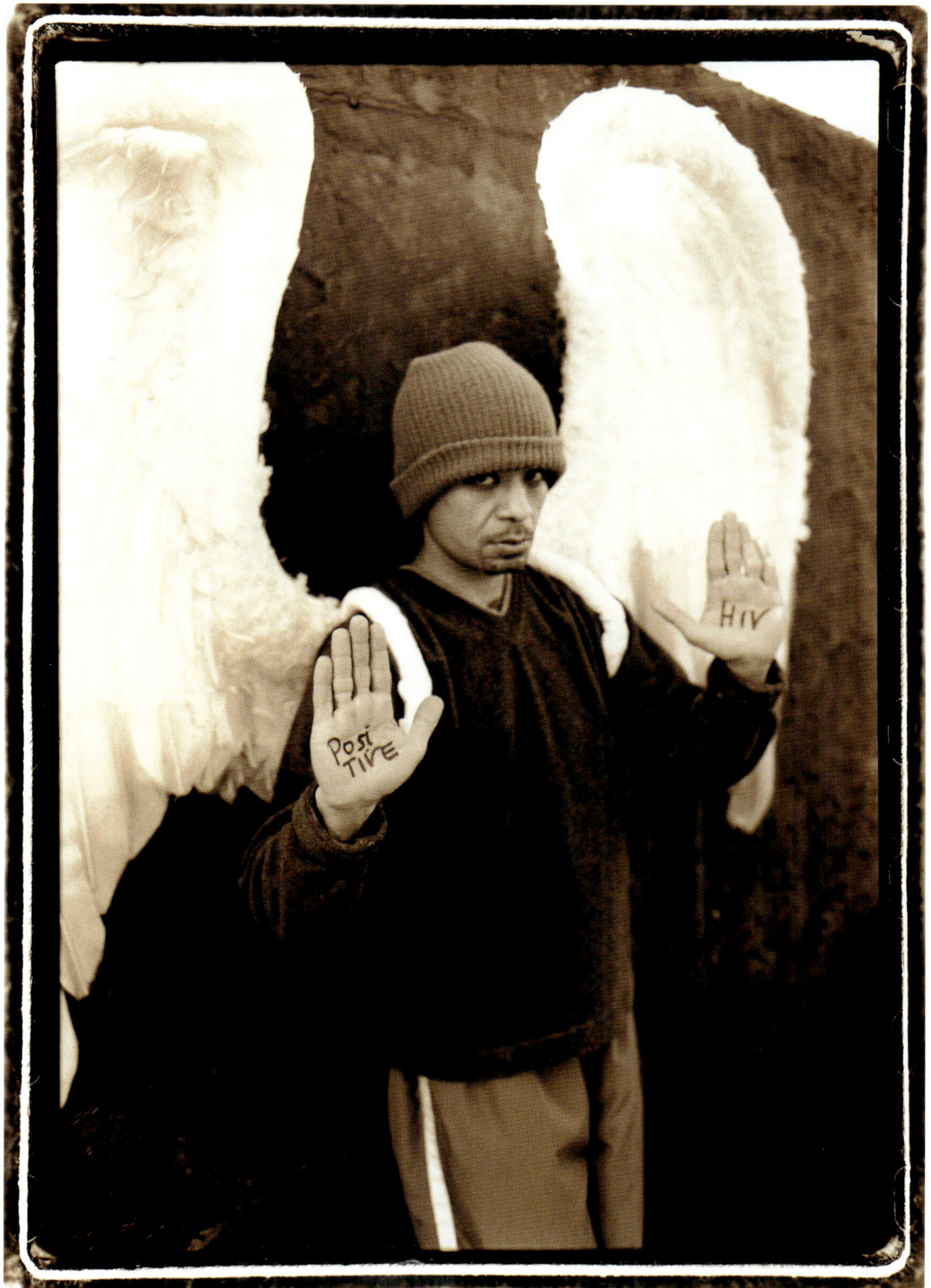
HIV
POSI
TIVE

we are all angels
we all put on the wings
at different times

**grego**
singapore

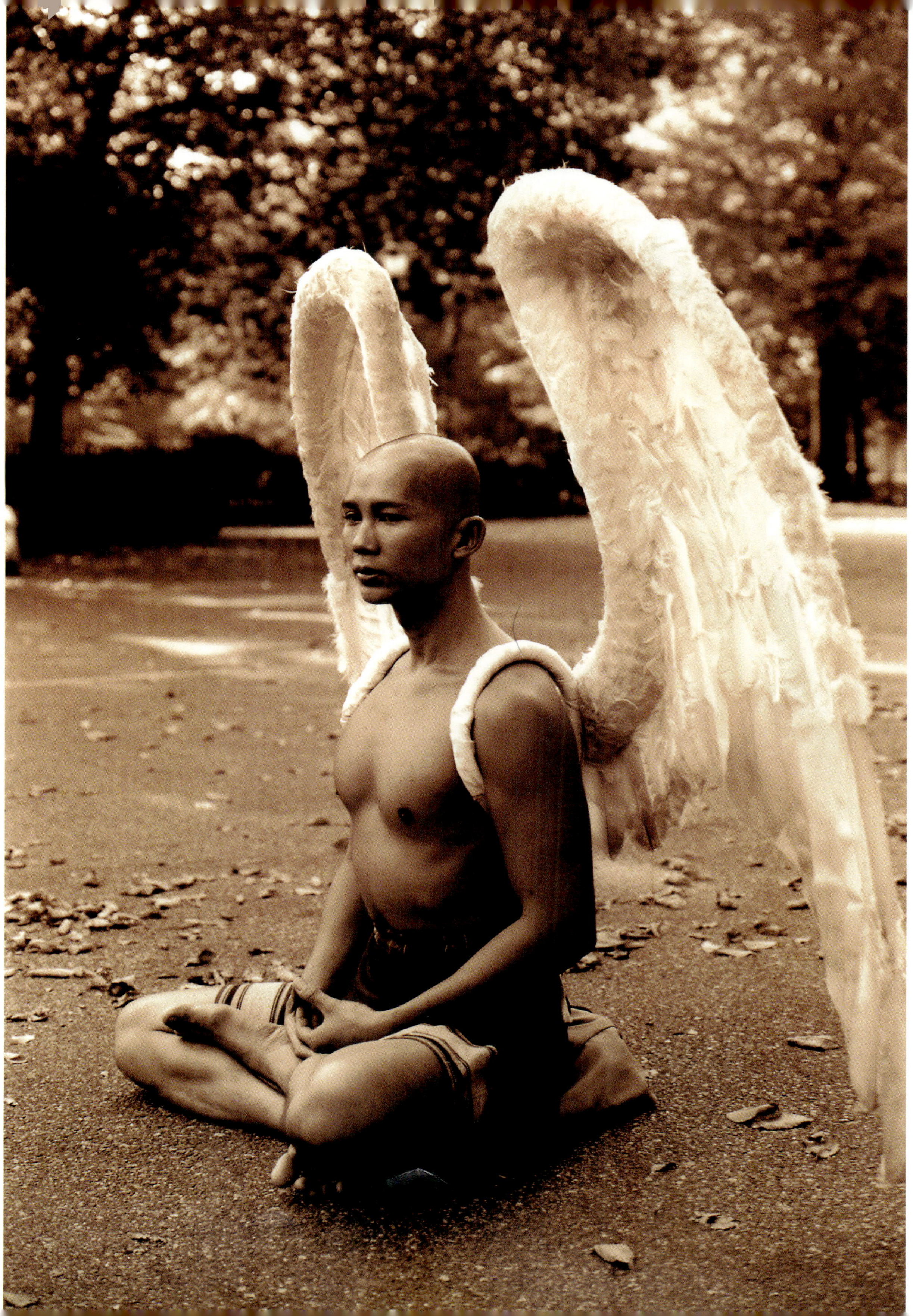

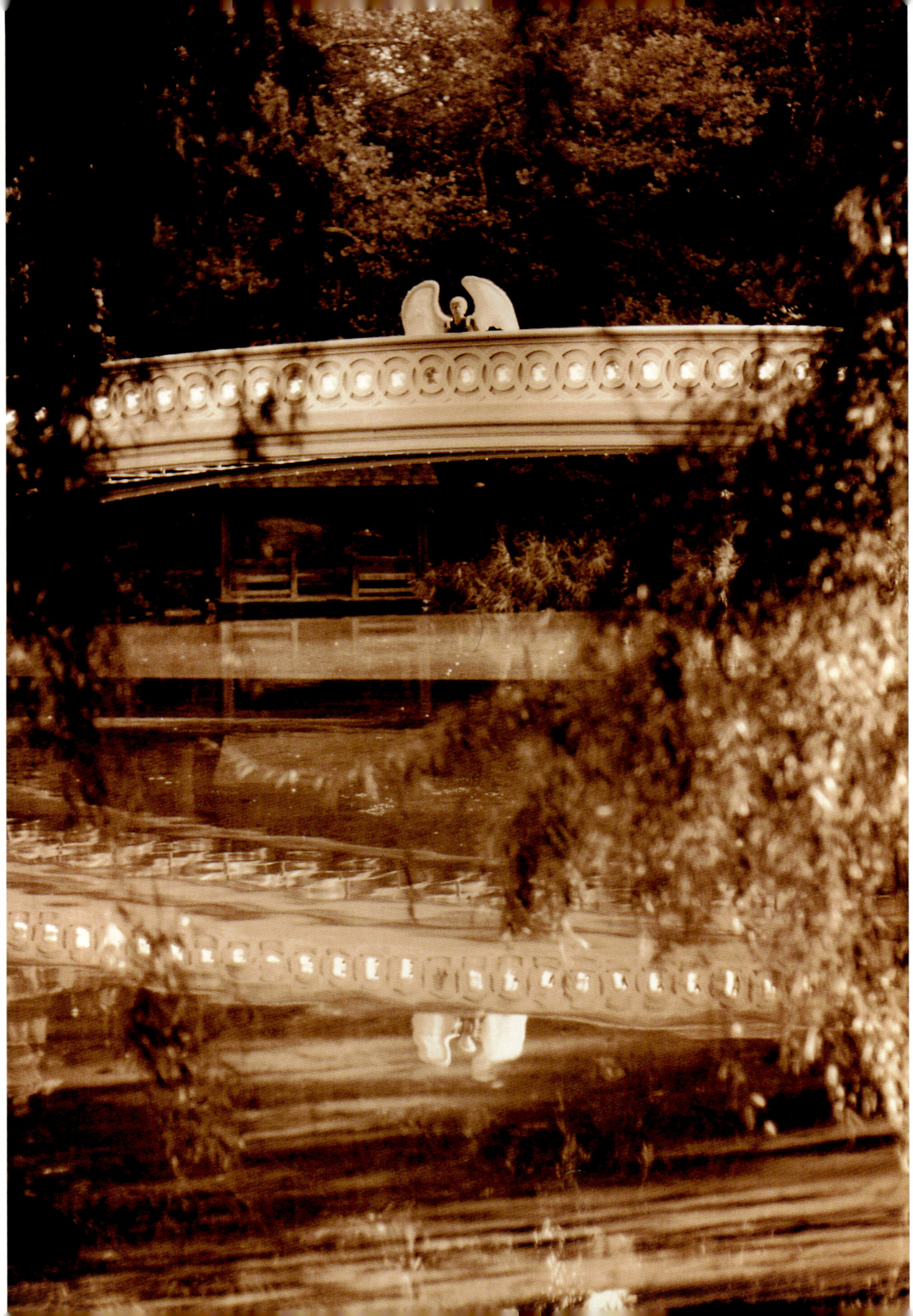

**norma**
cuba

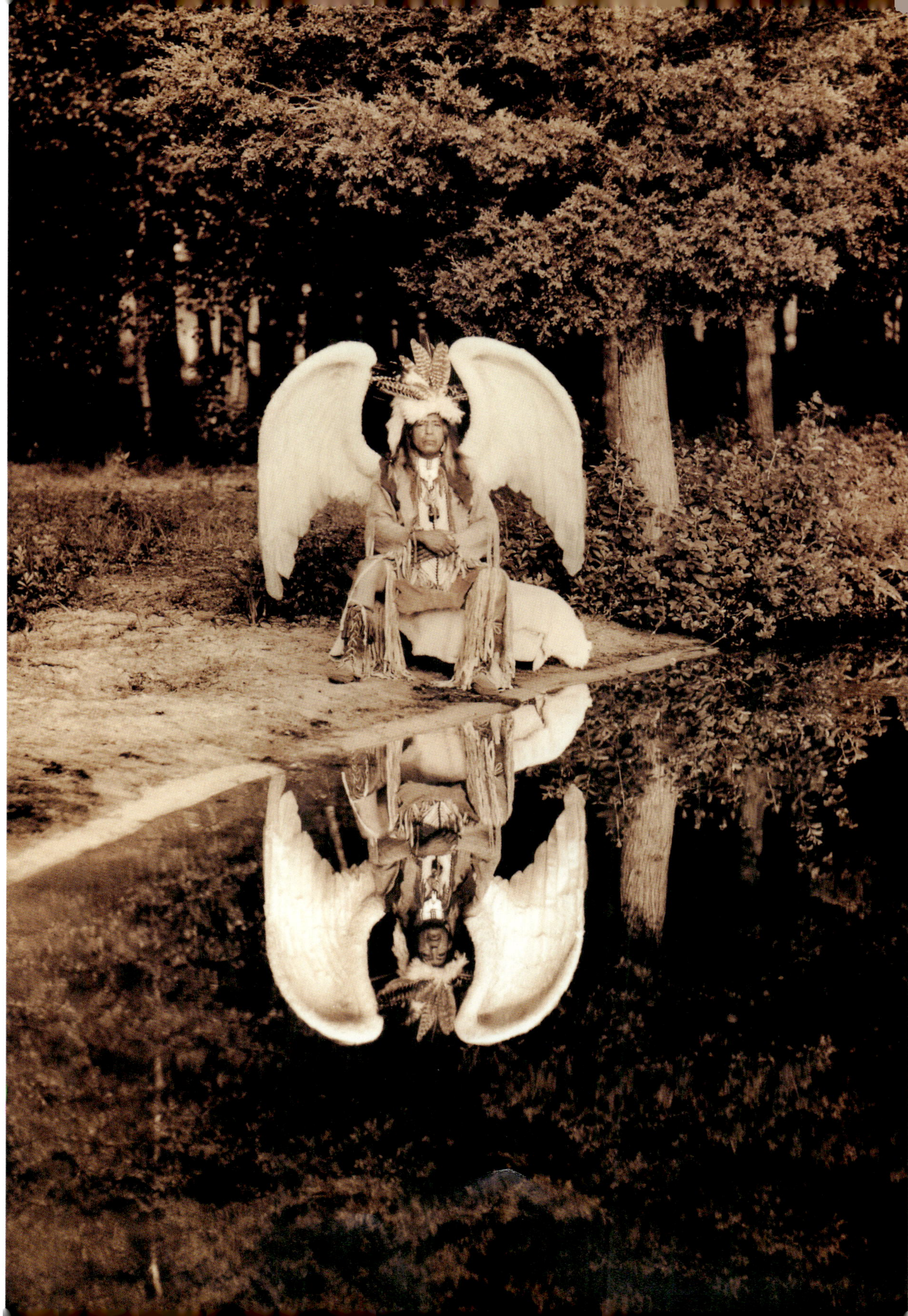

we all have
the same
mother (earth)
and the same
father (sky)
we are all
related
peace is
when our heart
gives love
to all life

**little hawk**
canada

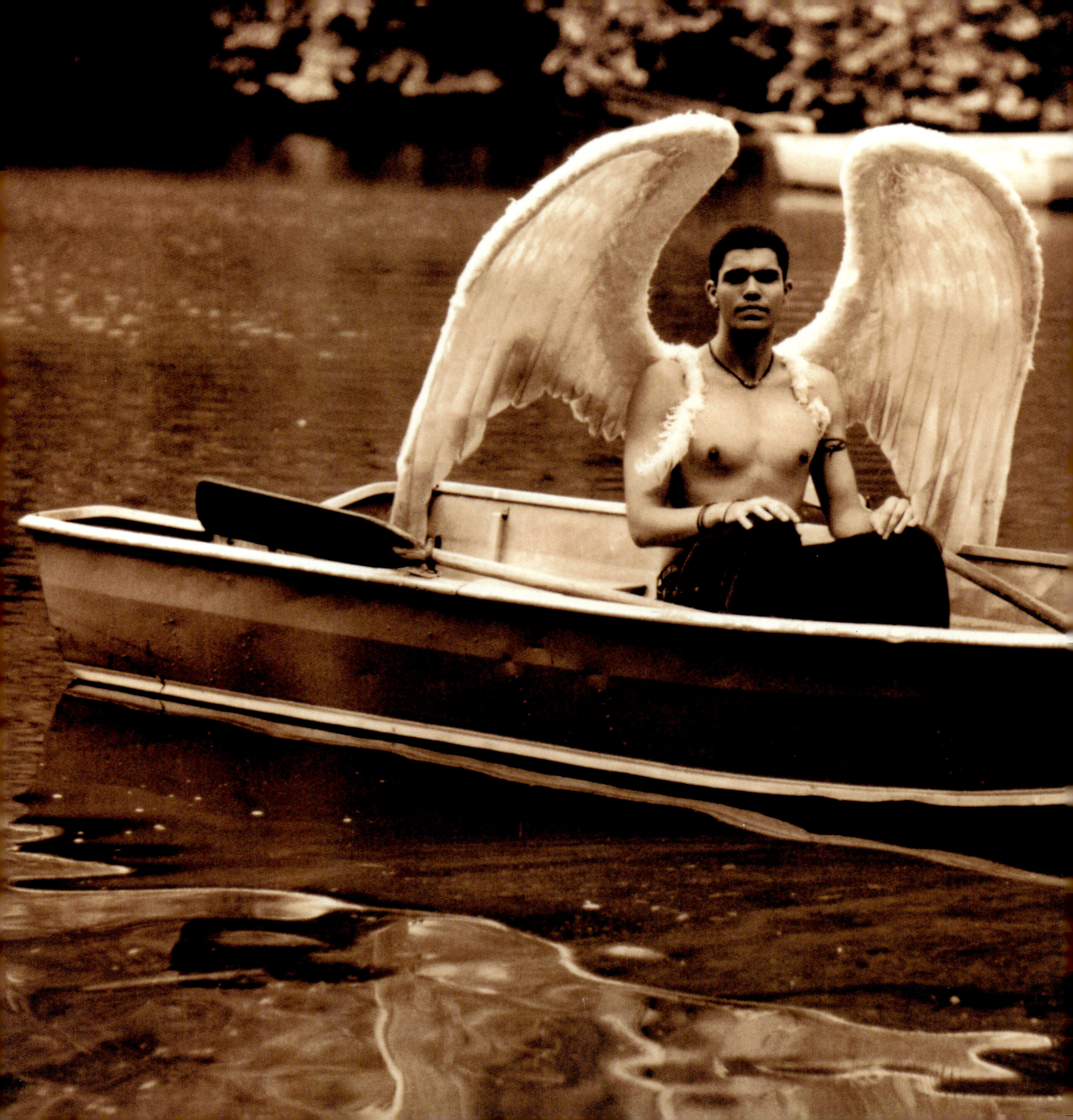

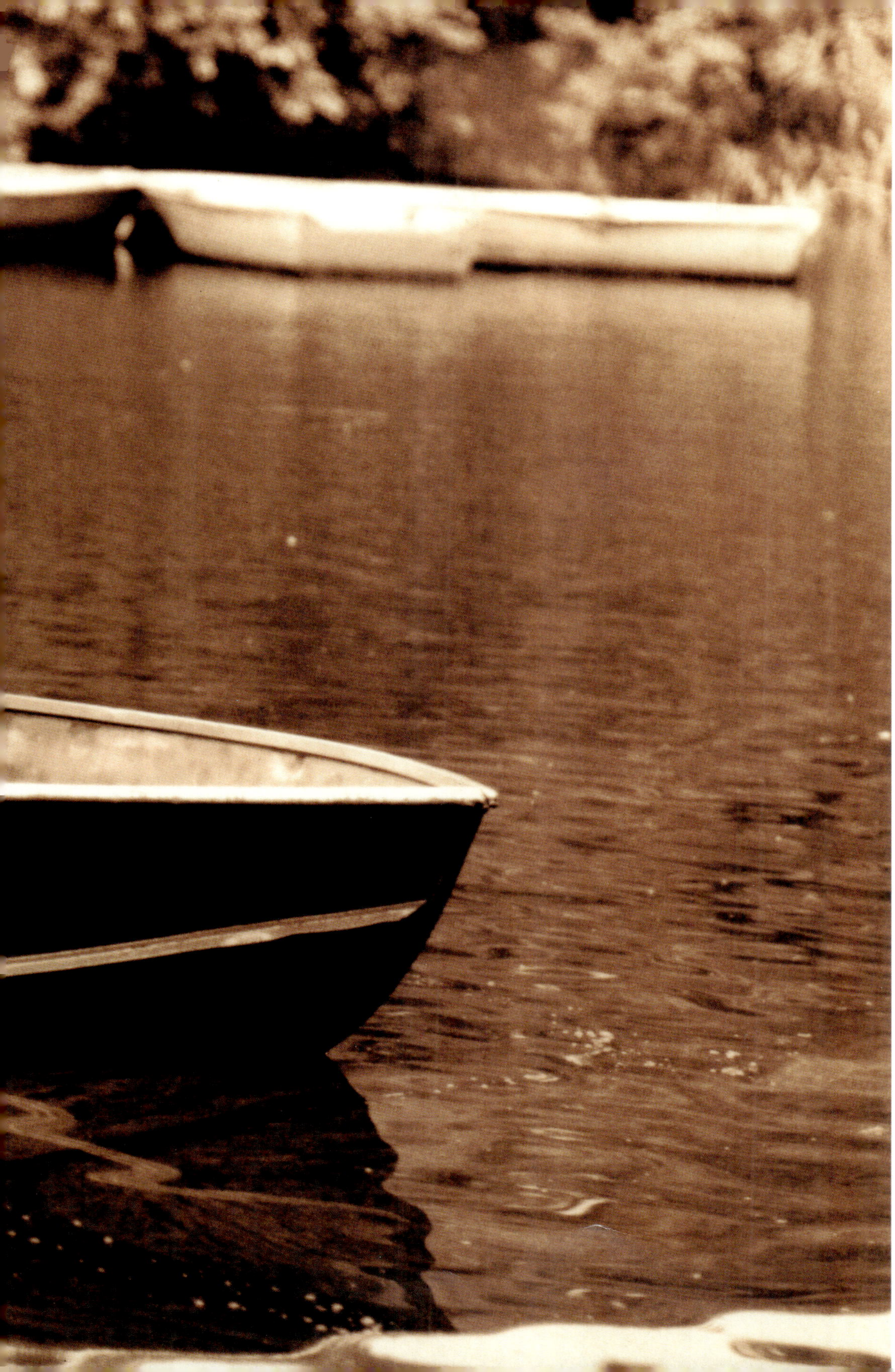

we must all work
to lift the veil from our eyes
and look at the world

**j. p.**
cuba

aria bactra
khoransan
the brits named
it afghanistan

**leeza & lida**
afghanistan

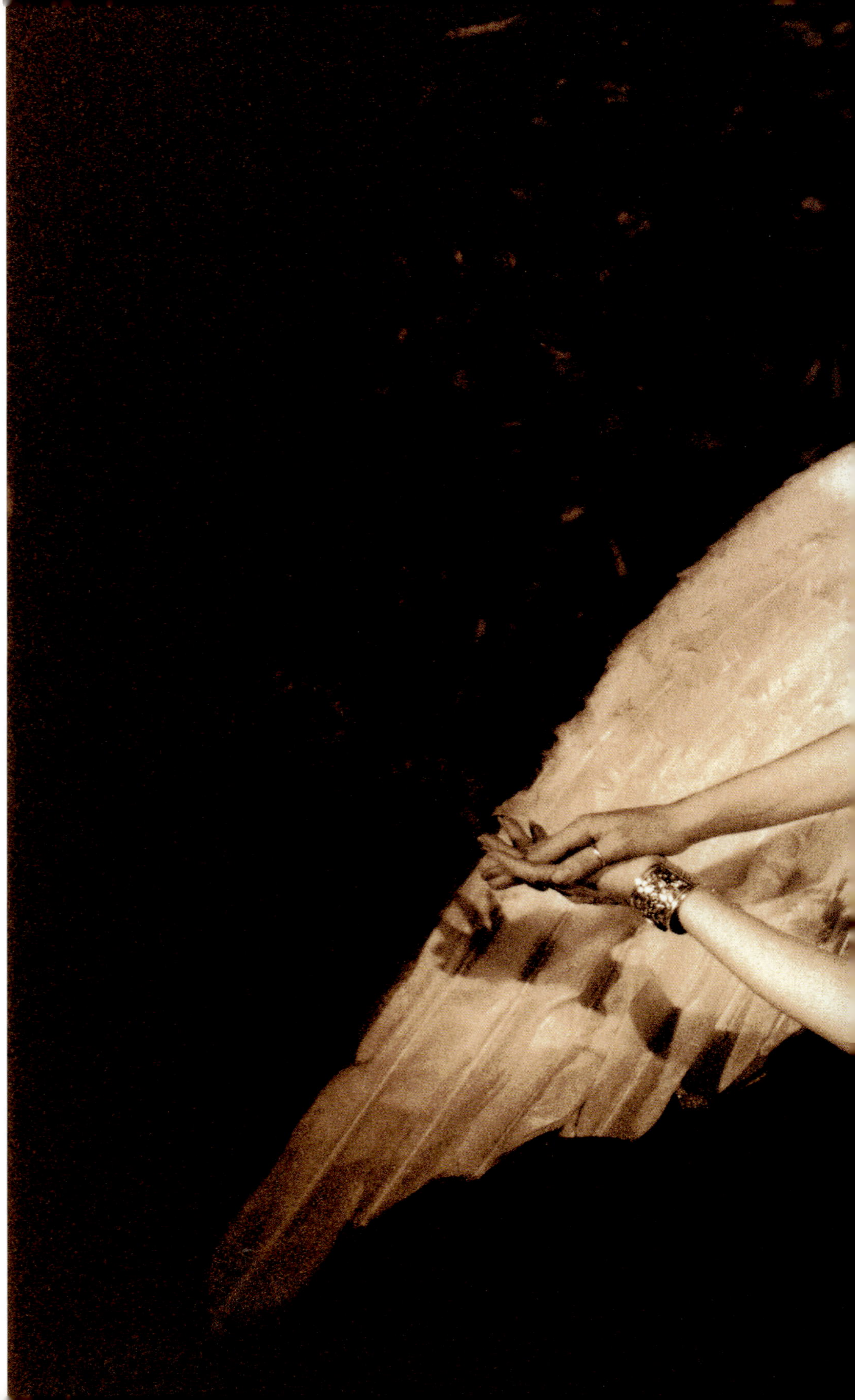

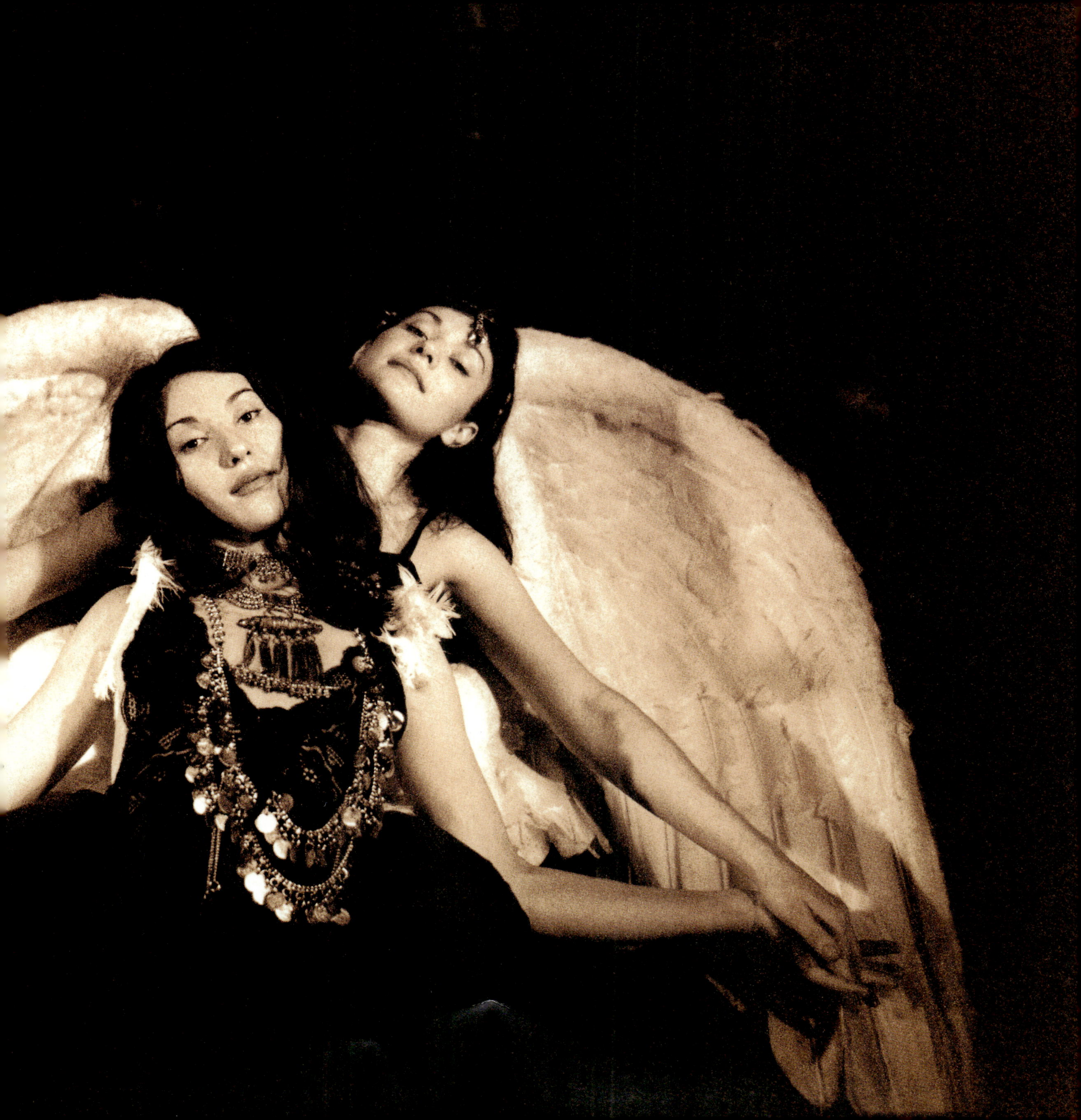

when politicians say
they want to make peace
they actually mean let us kill peace

**bina**
pakistans

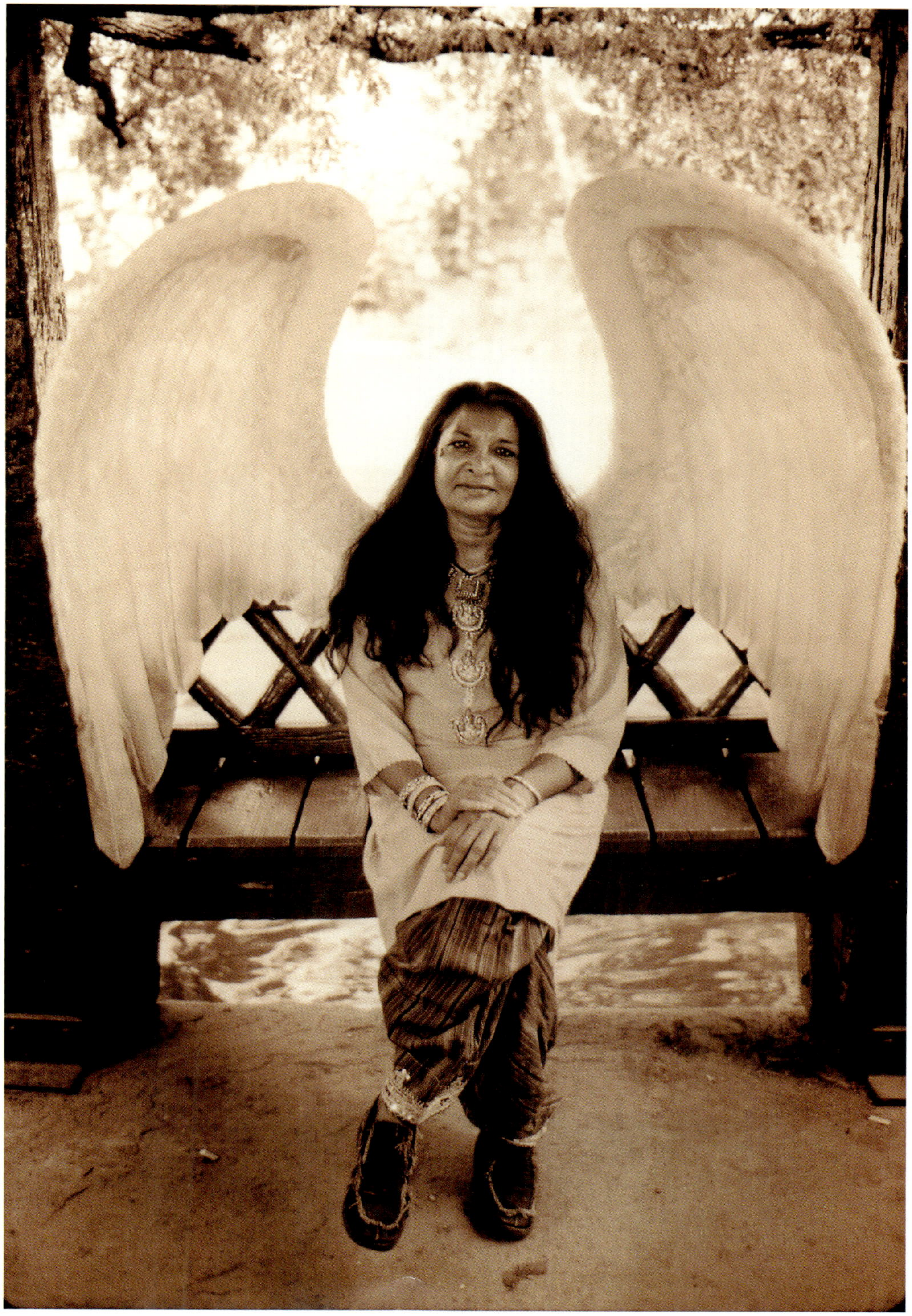

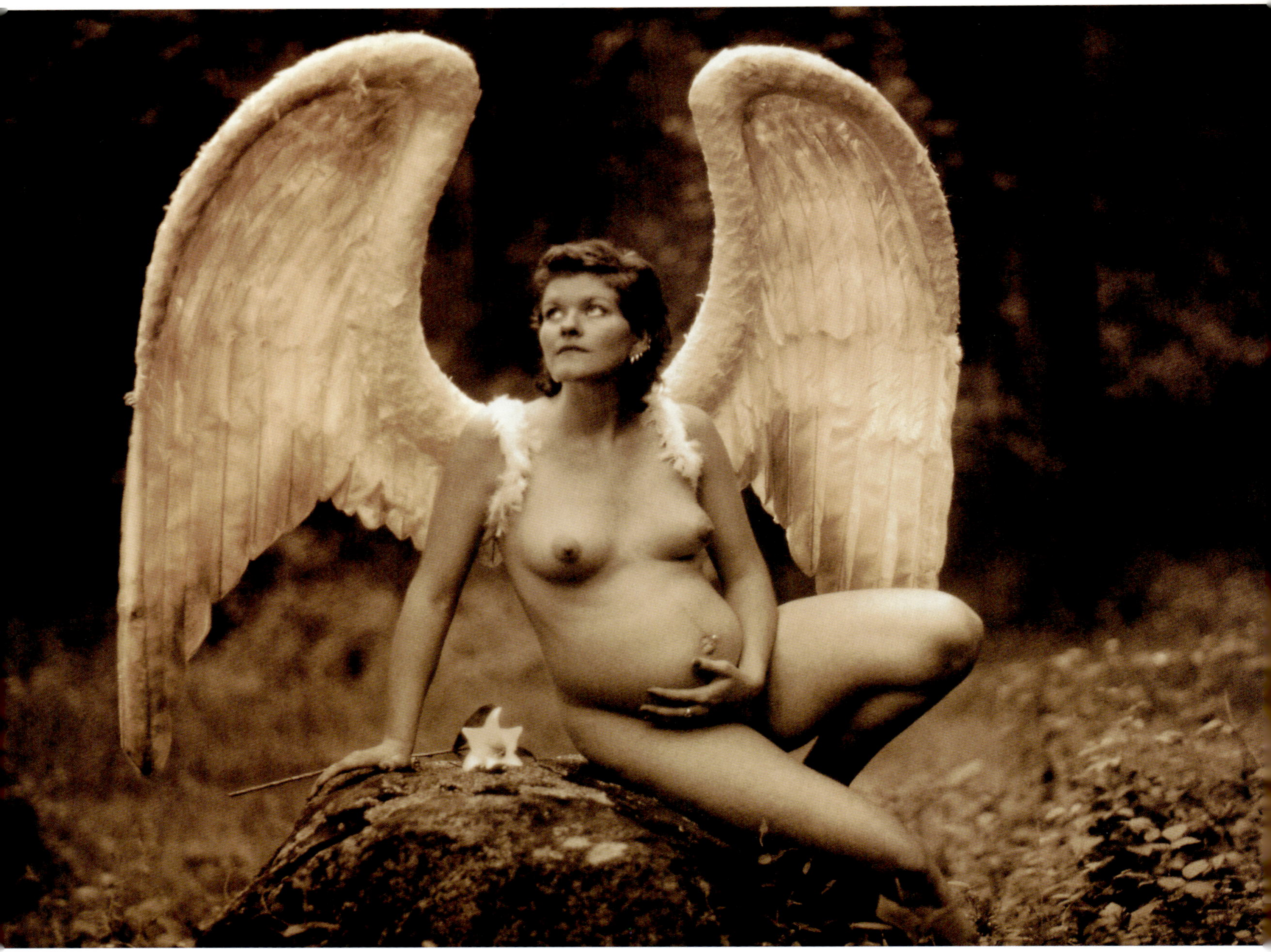

**kelly**
ireland

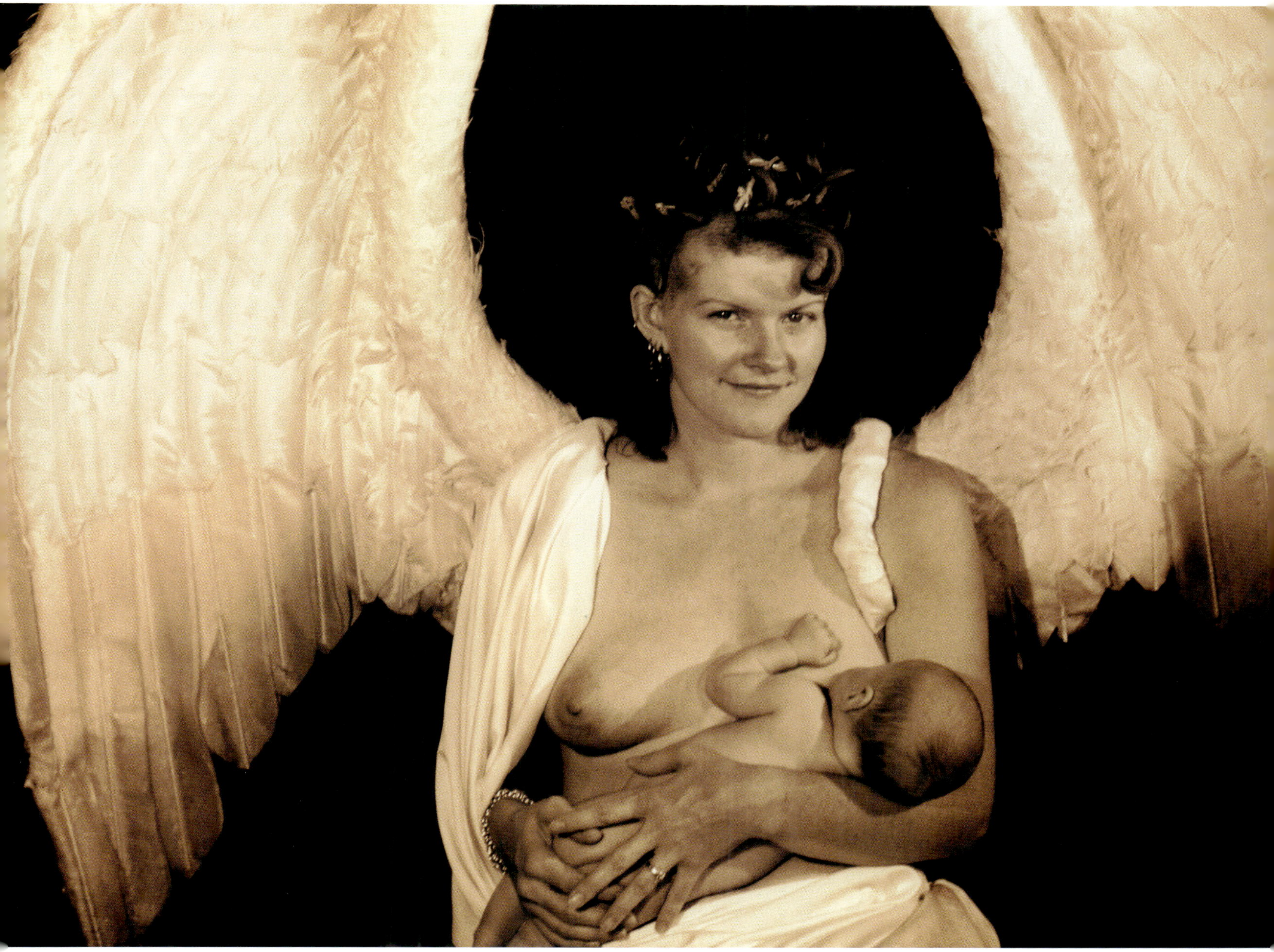

i am worried about our future
about humanity's future
when will there be peace
throughout the world?

**kelly & daniel**
ireland

i guess peace
to me is a state of mind
an emotion
that is not necessarily tranquil
but sometimes deep in turmoil
striving to reach my goals
standing up for myself and others
while staying true to myself
brings me peace

**tom**
wales

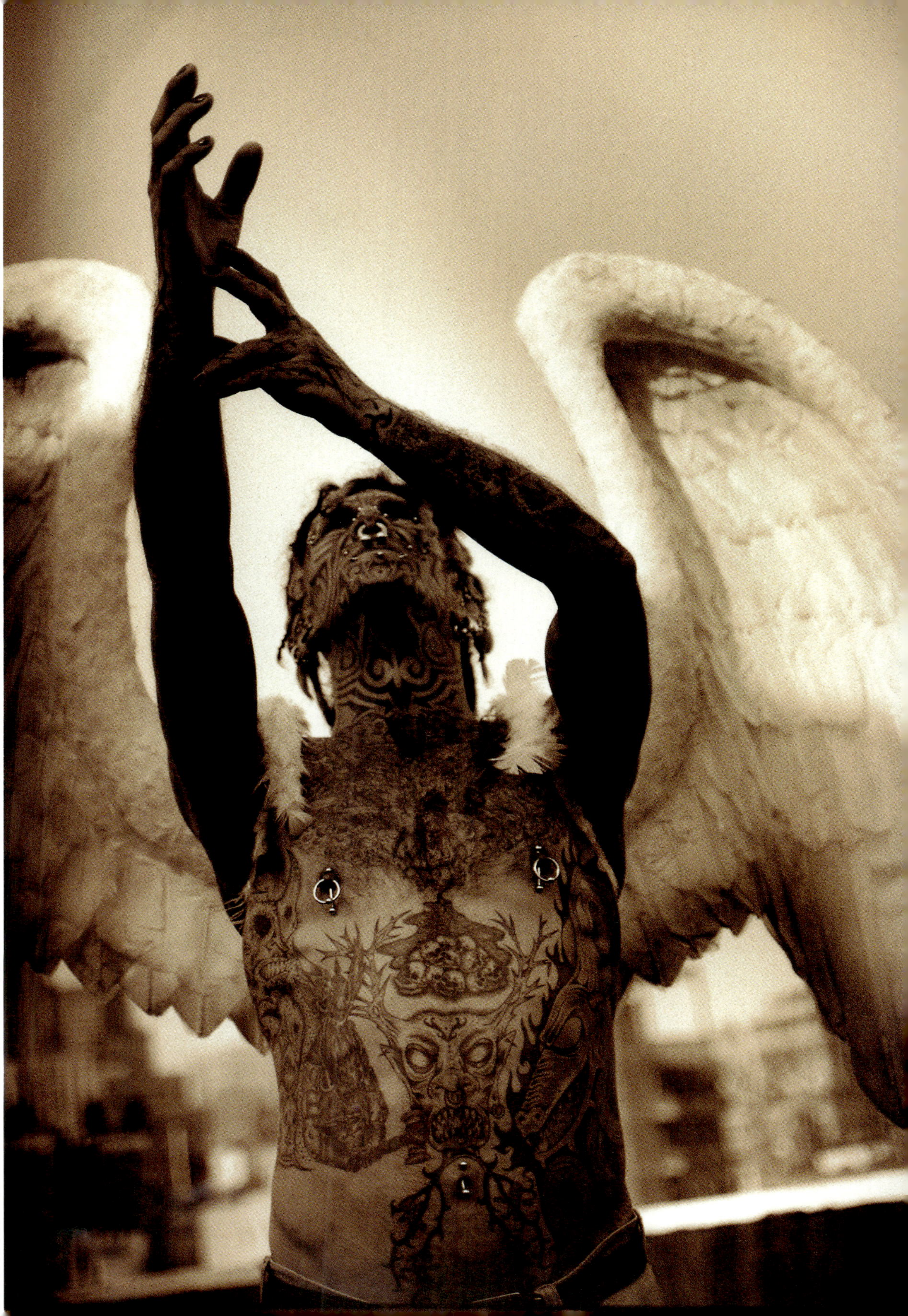

perspectives of emptiness
and of nonexistant objects
a universe of tender volumes
and perfect passions
this atmosphere
of fluent shades
composed the peace
that desire took away from me

**claudio**
brazil

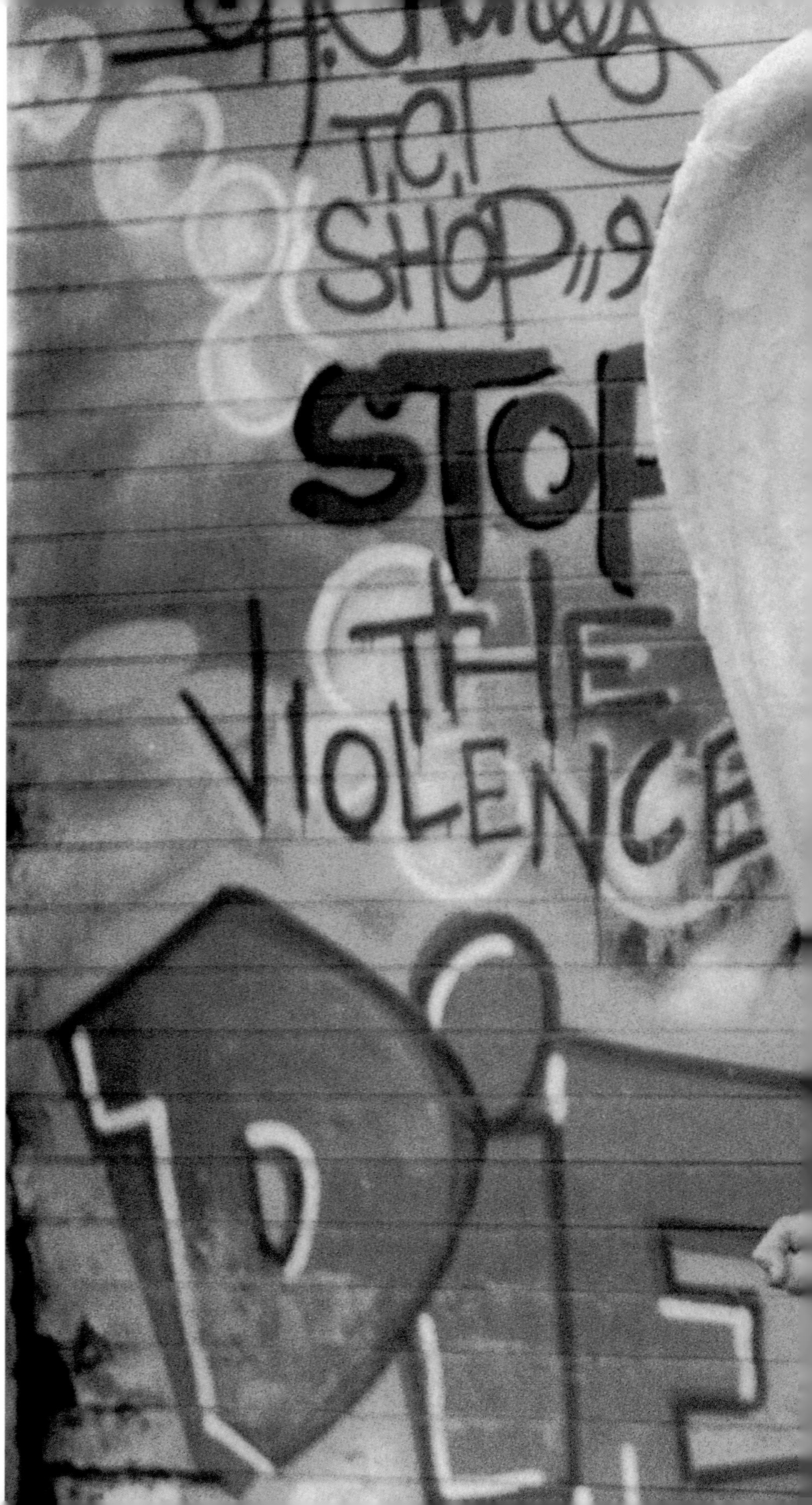

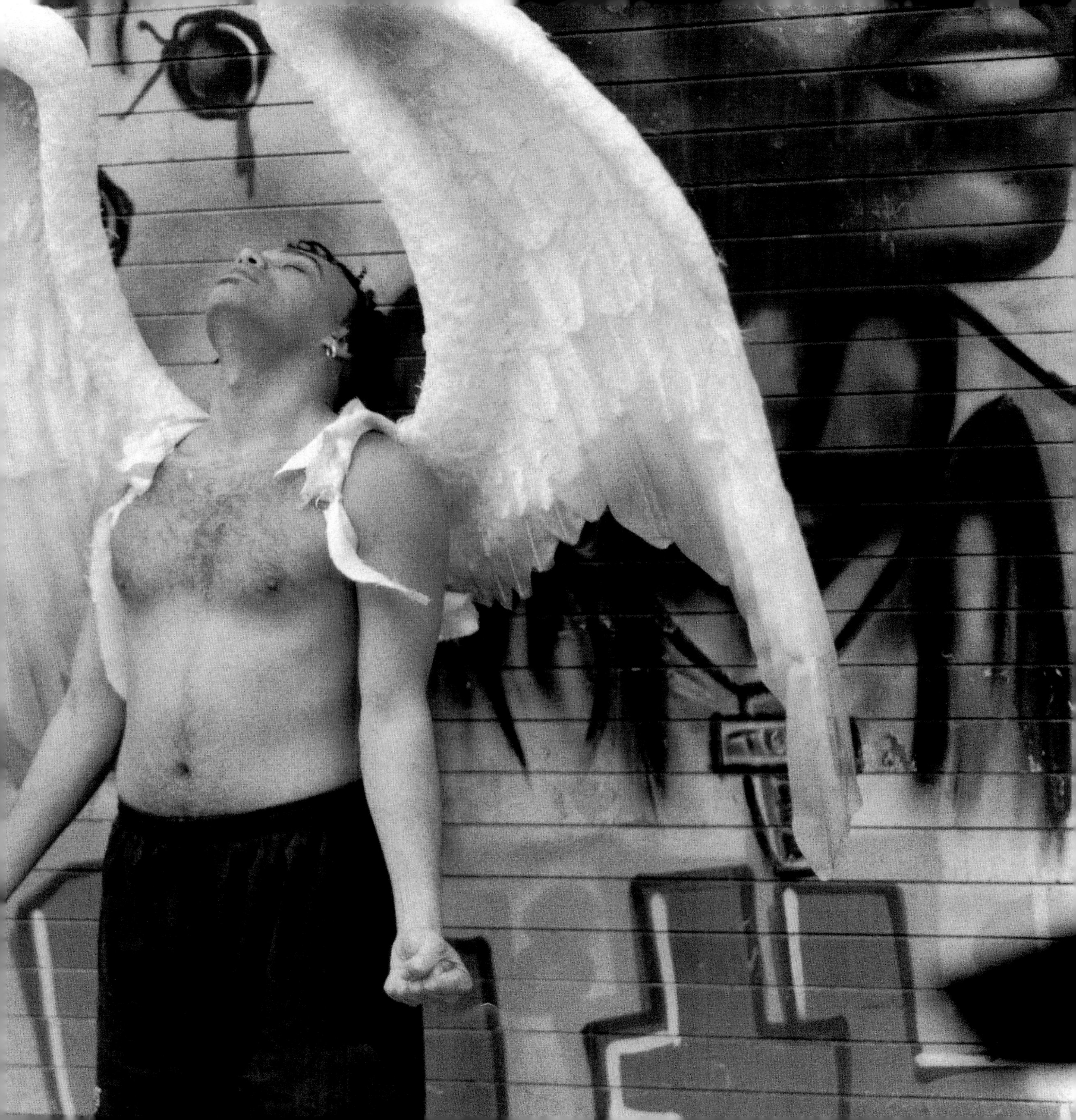

peace to me is
when all tibetans have
their inherent dignity and rights

**tashi**
tibet

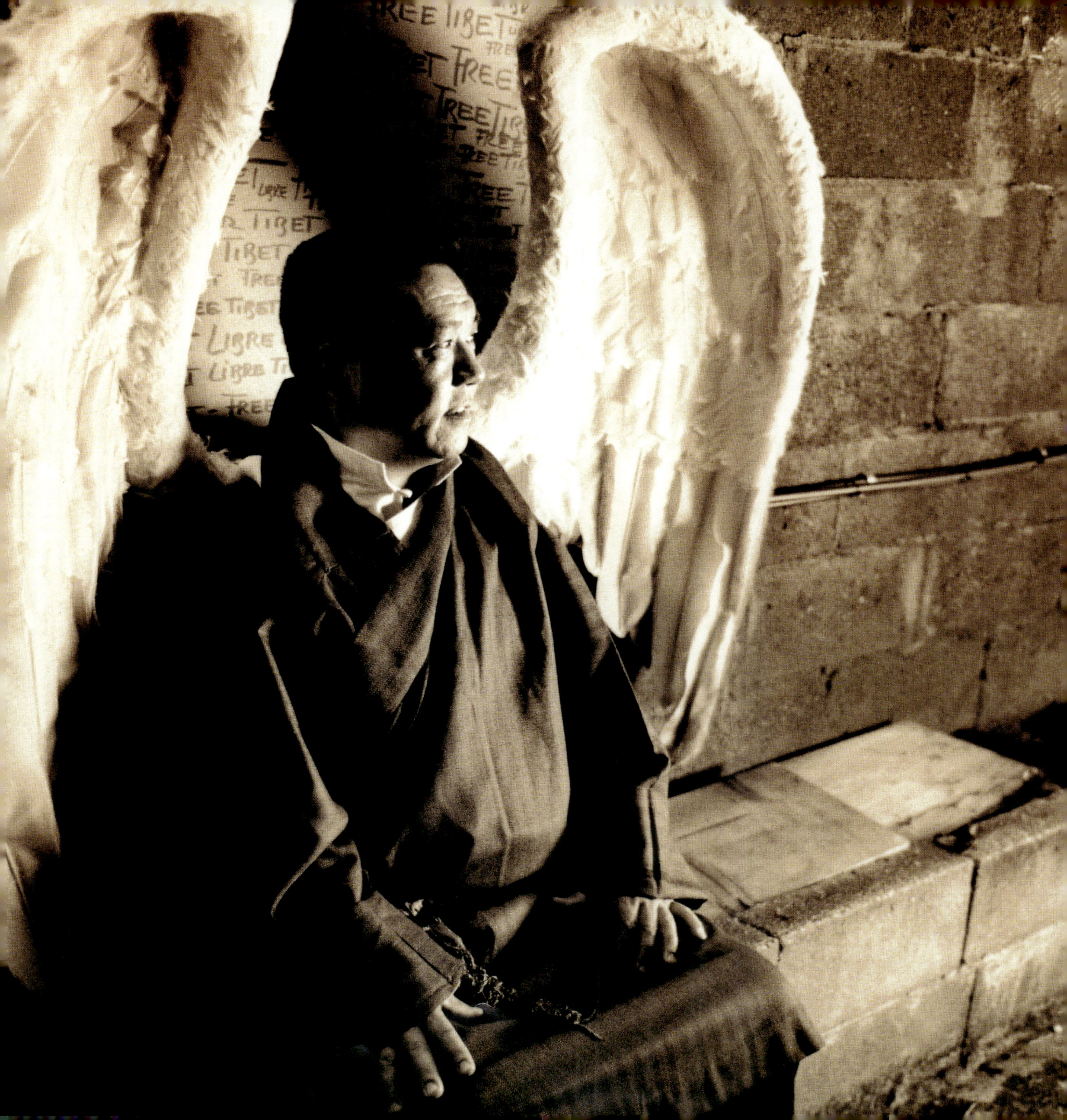
FREE TIBET
LIBRE

peace is for me
love and life
the way of god
true life is peace

**victor**
puerto rico

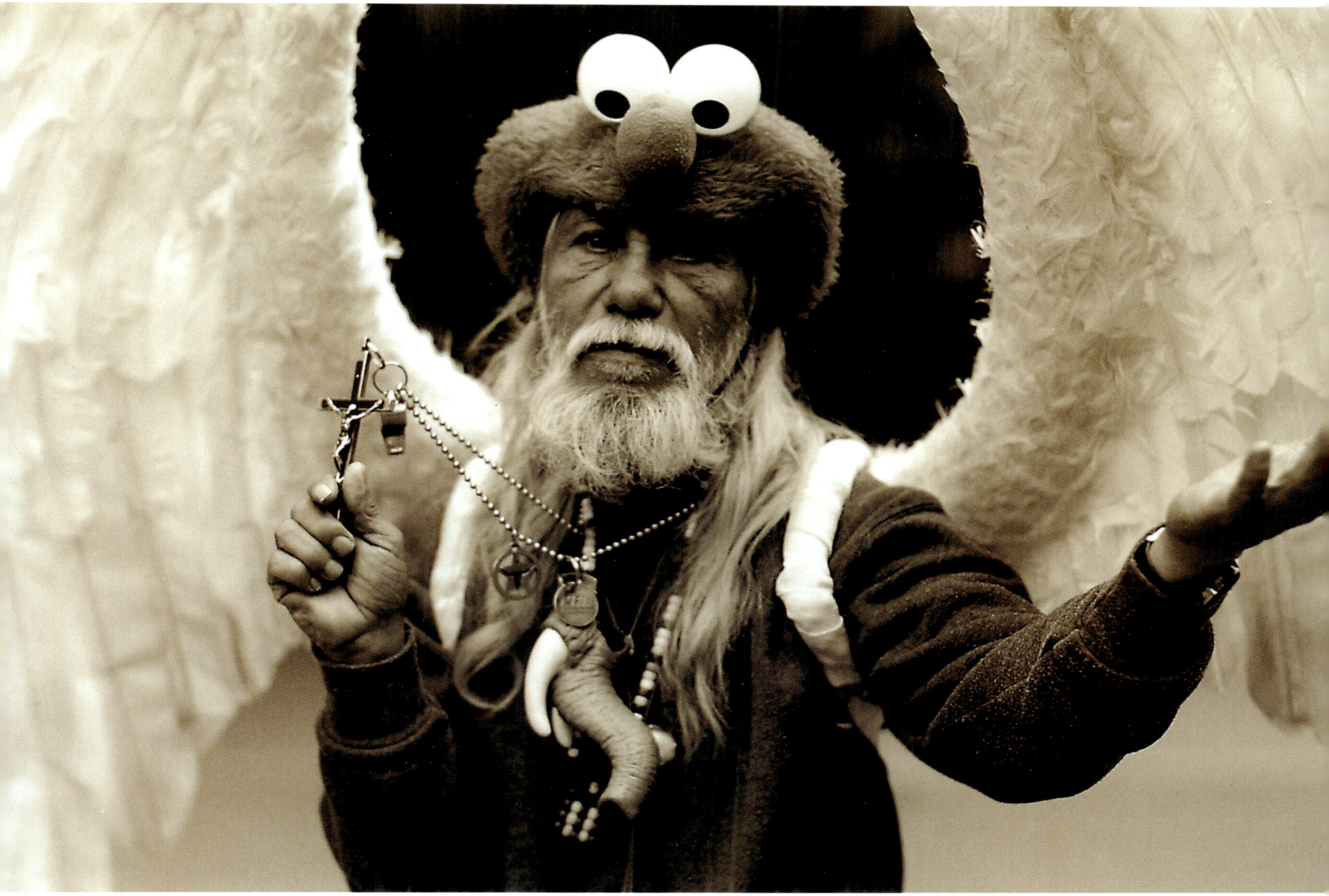

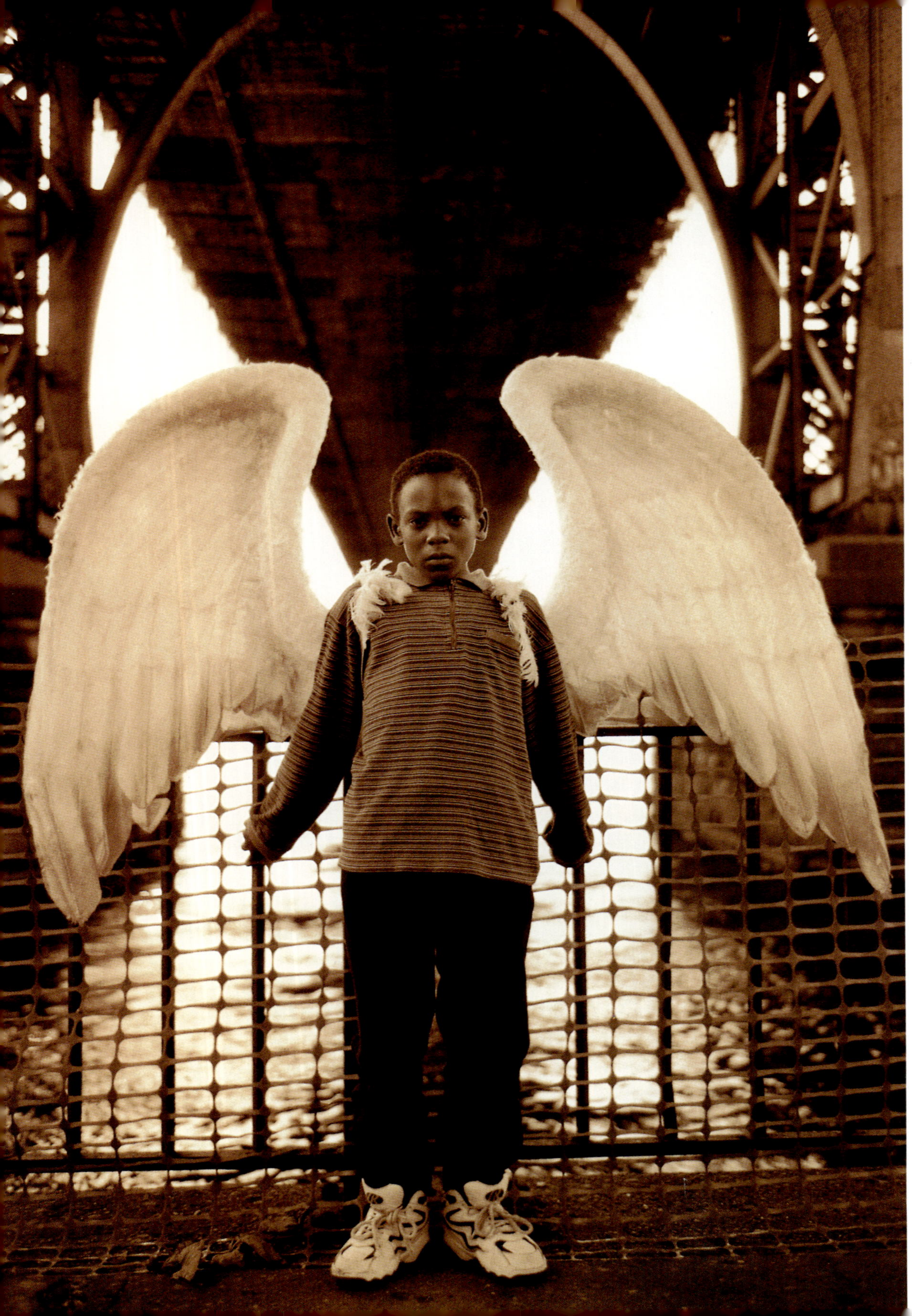

we should stop hating
and start loving
other people

**christopher**
brooklyn

peace
no
i say hotep
our word for peace
i eschew this word peace
coined by hypocrites

**heru ankh-ra semahj**
chief priest in the temple of ptah
nubia

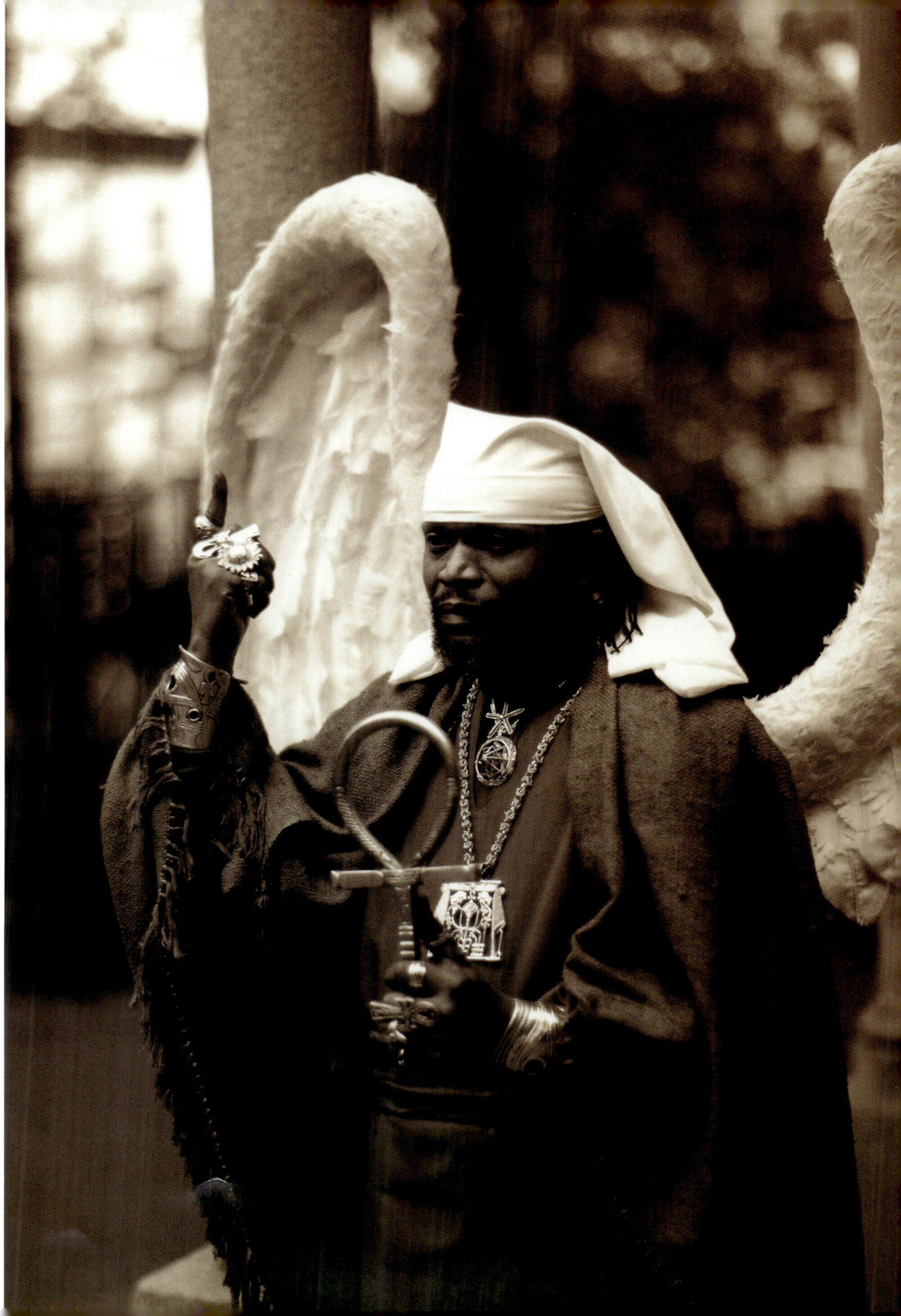

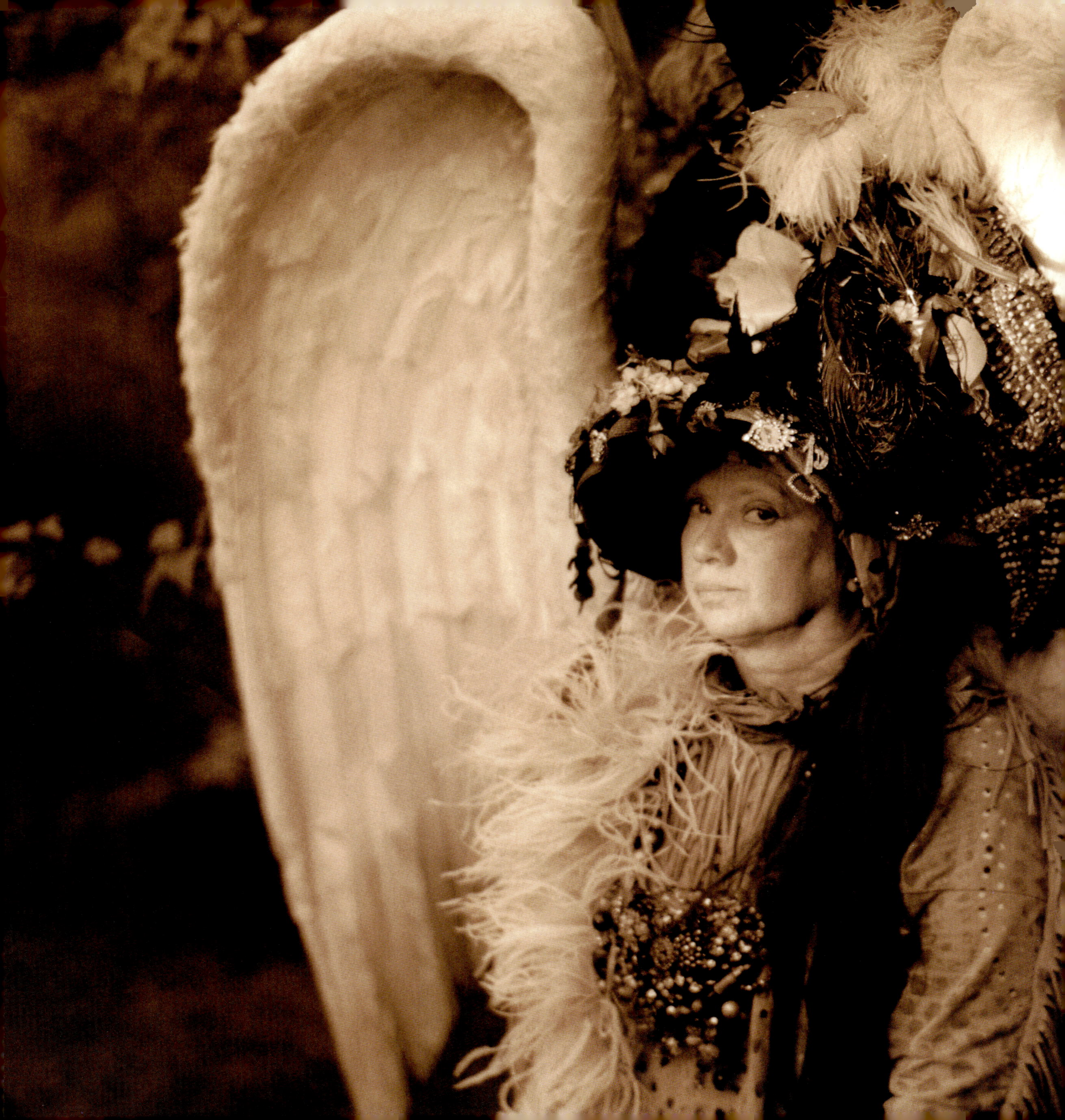

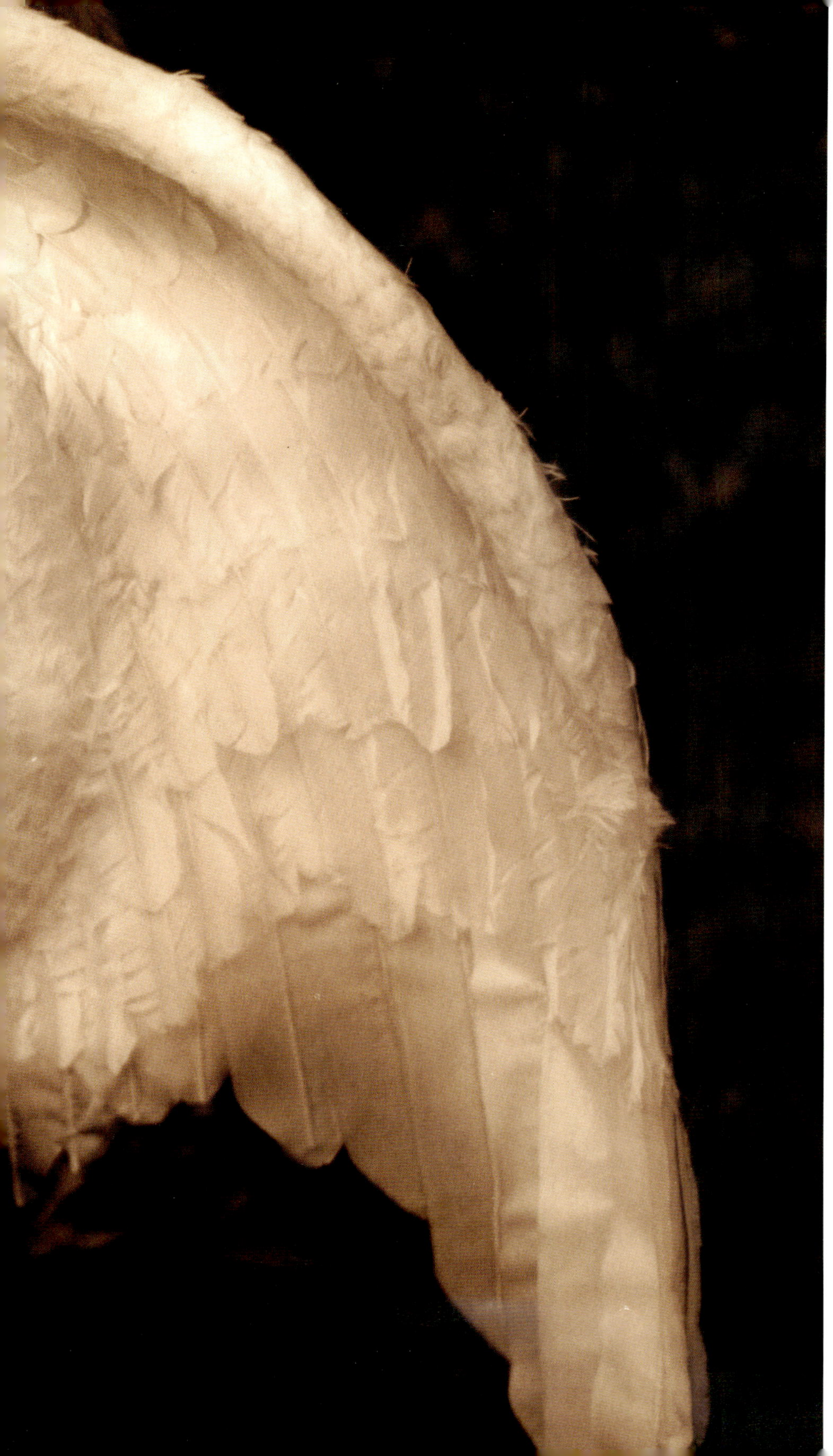

people
can make choices
to live in harmony

**beverly**
norway

when everybody
finds peace within themselves
we will be
at peace with the universe

**elsie**
haiti

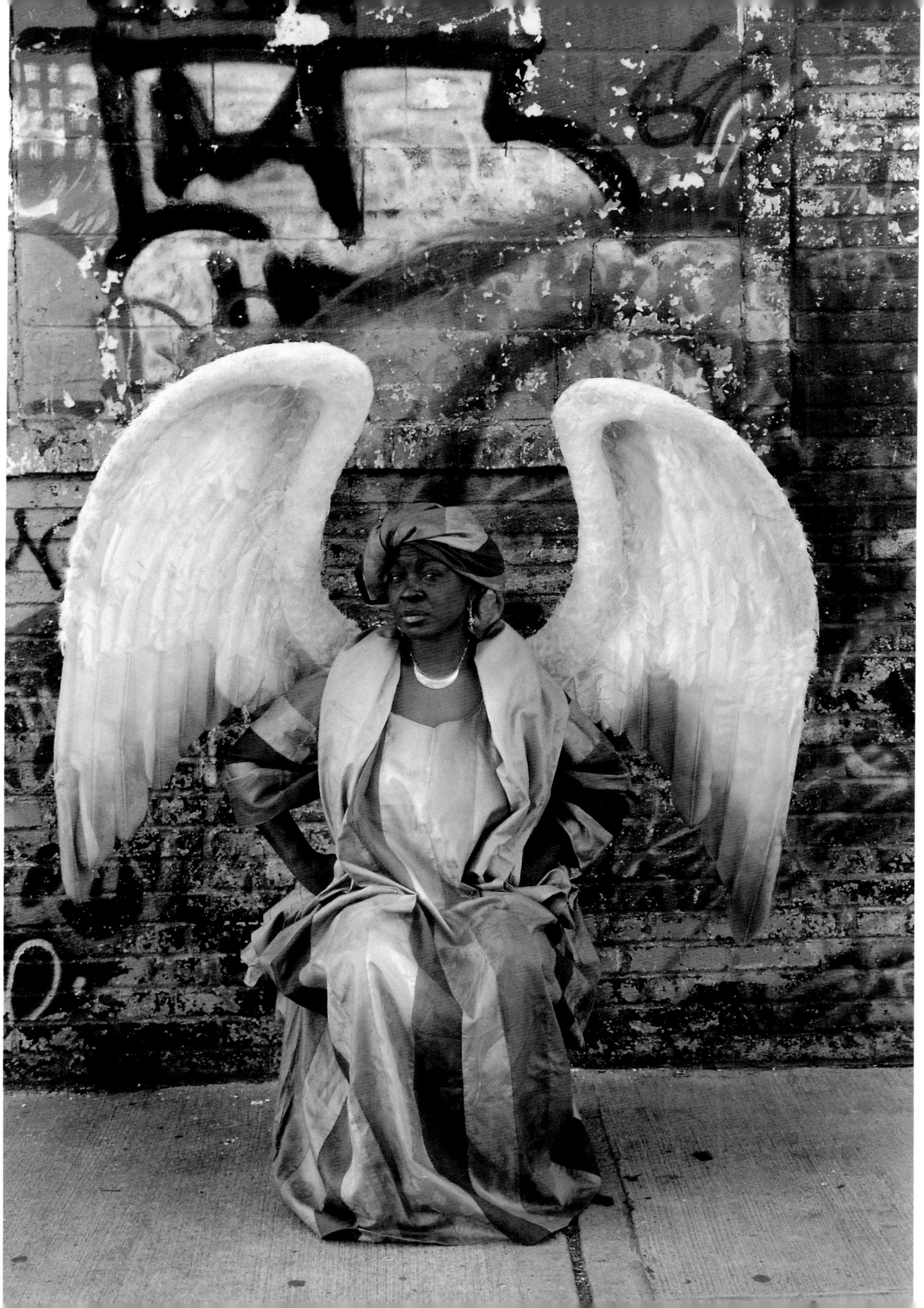

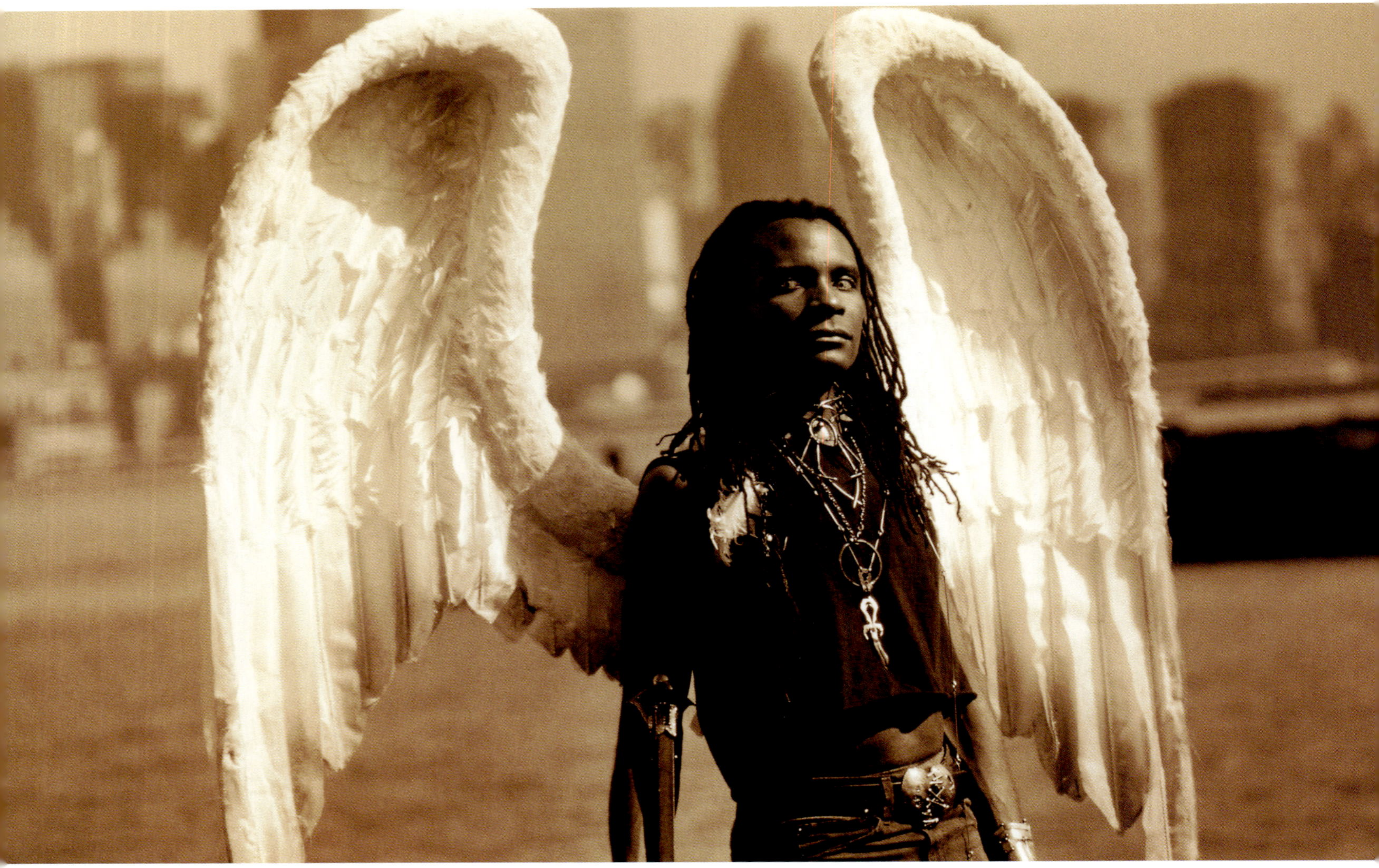

**d-**
new york city

peace is the feeling of
a heavy burden
being lifted from
my shoulders
peace is deep
within oneself
a safe place
that is untouchable

**didier**
algeria

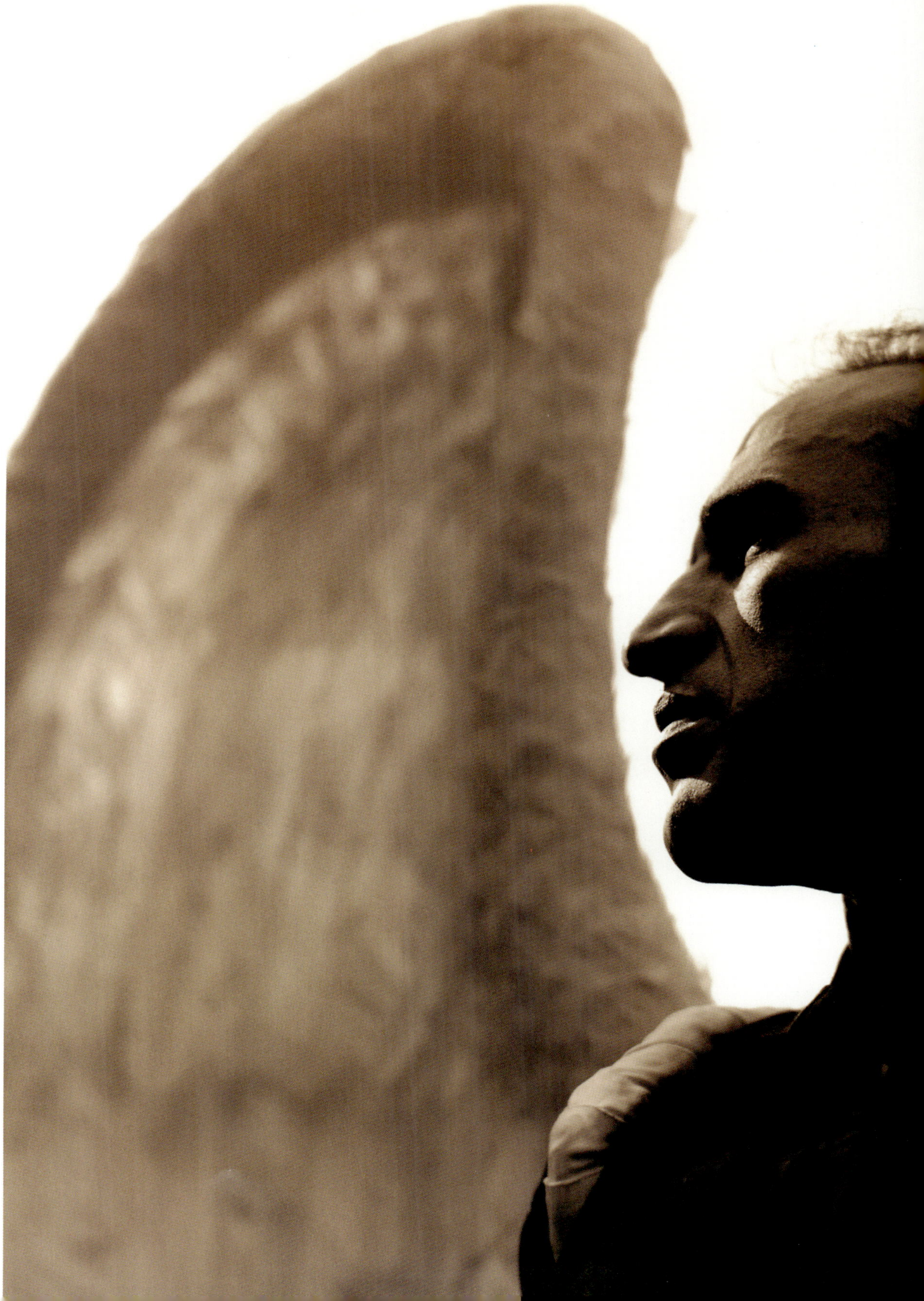

love is the manifesto
on which peace is built

**themba**
south africa

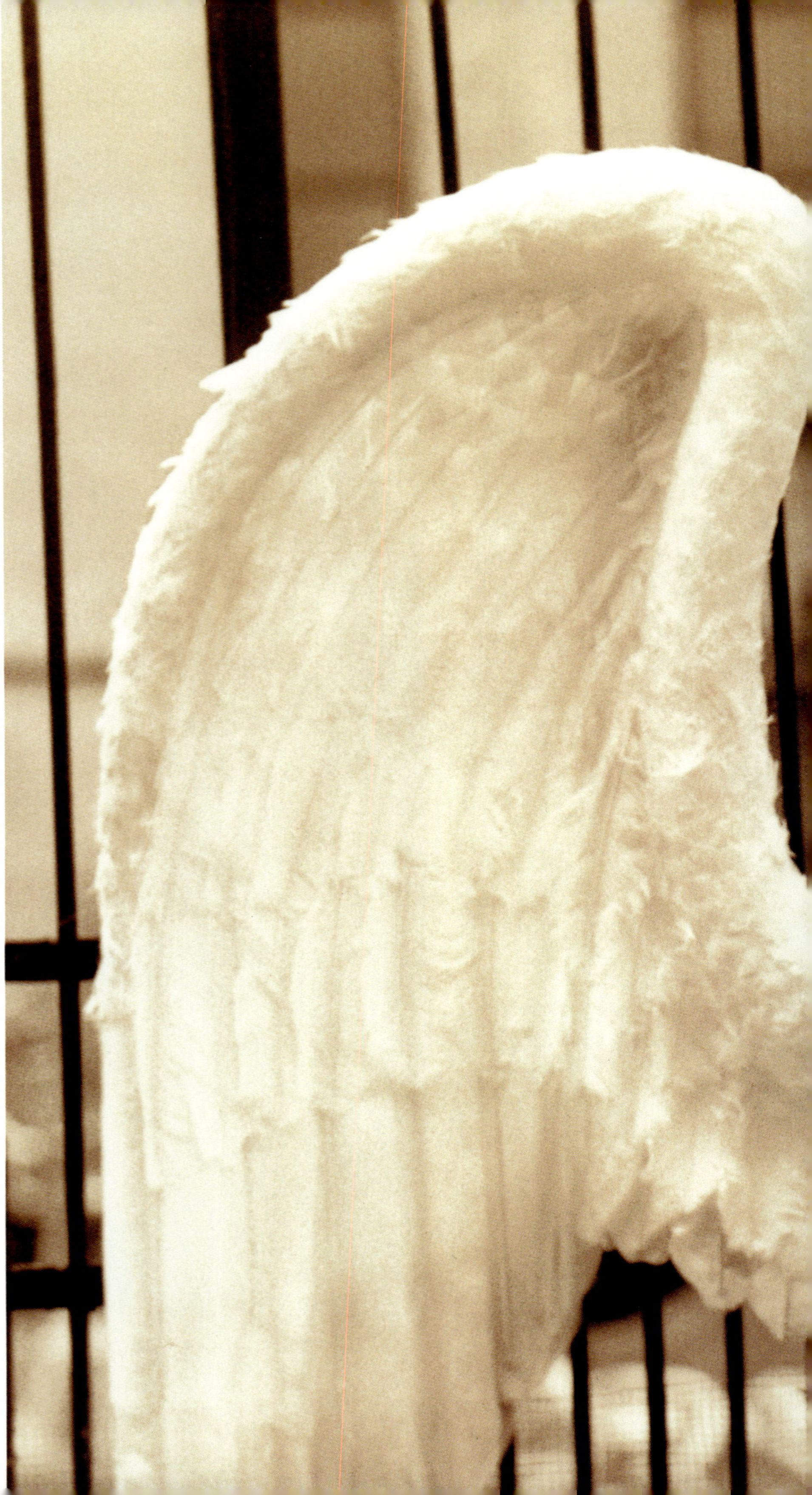

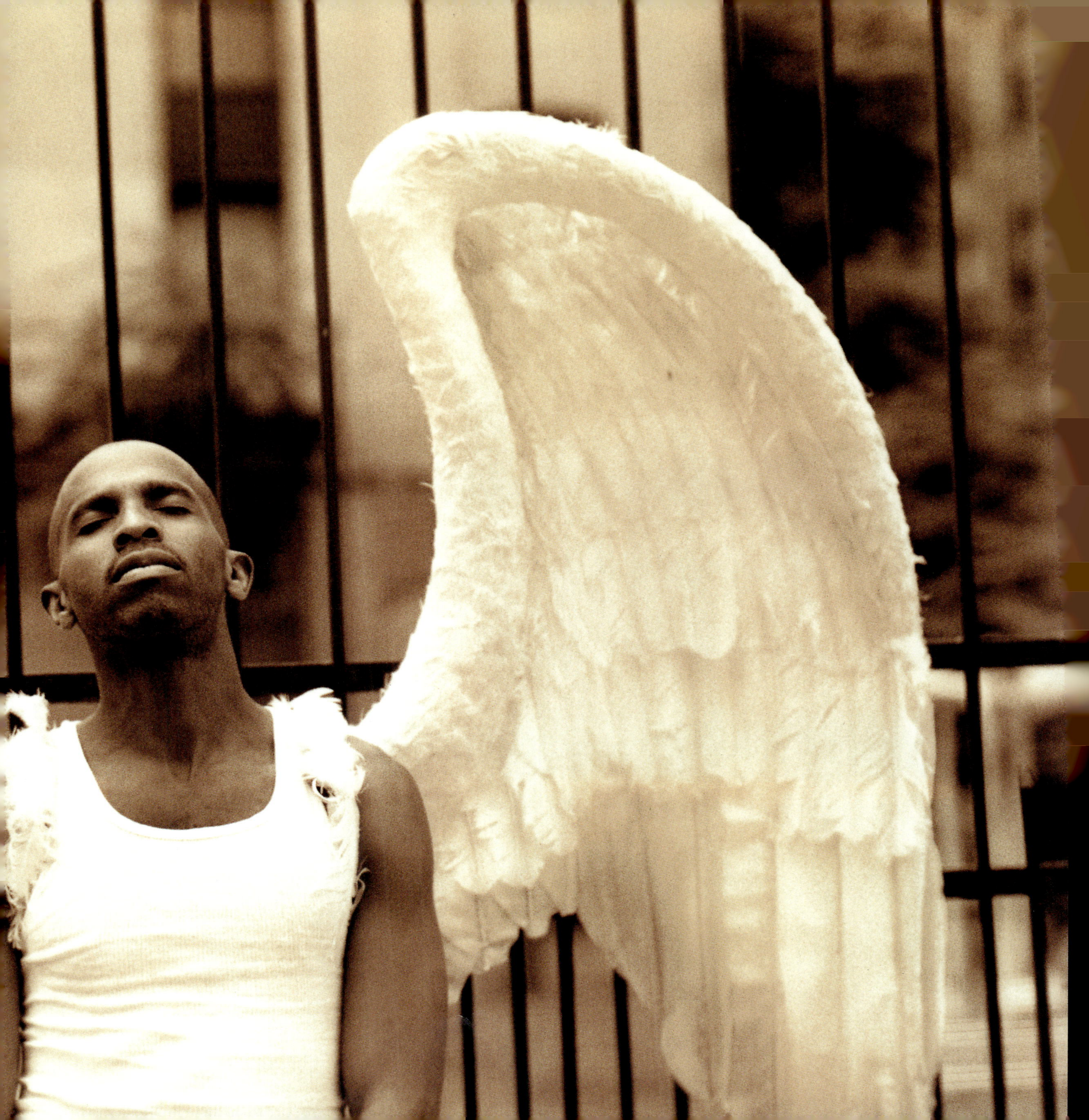

**troy**
ireland

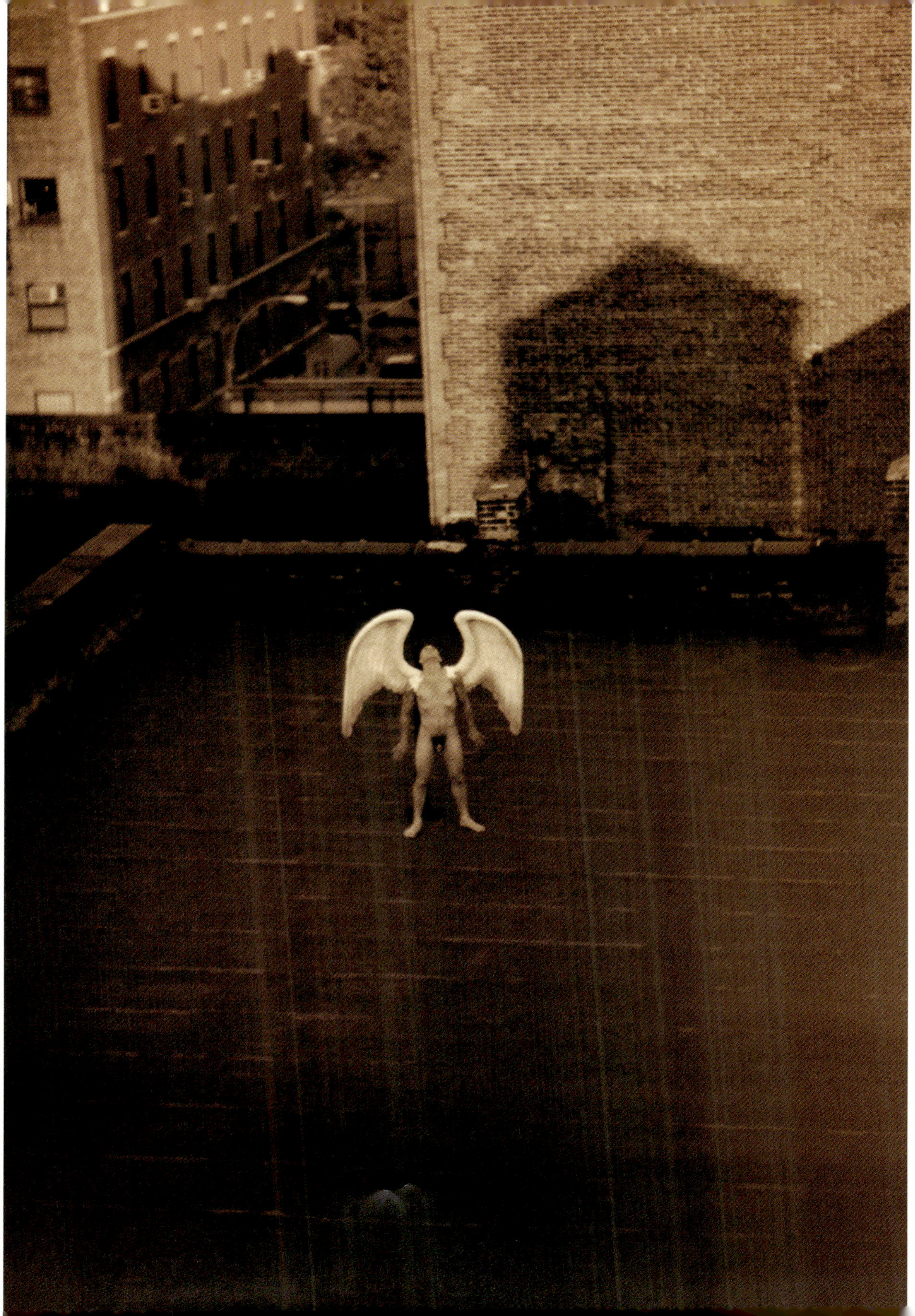

we will sing and dance and live
with the white buffalo
surrounded by the warmth of god
the great spirit

**pony**
new mexico

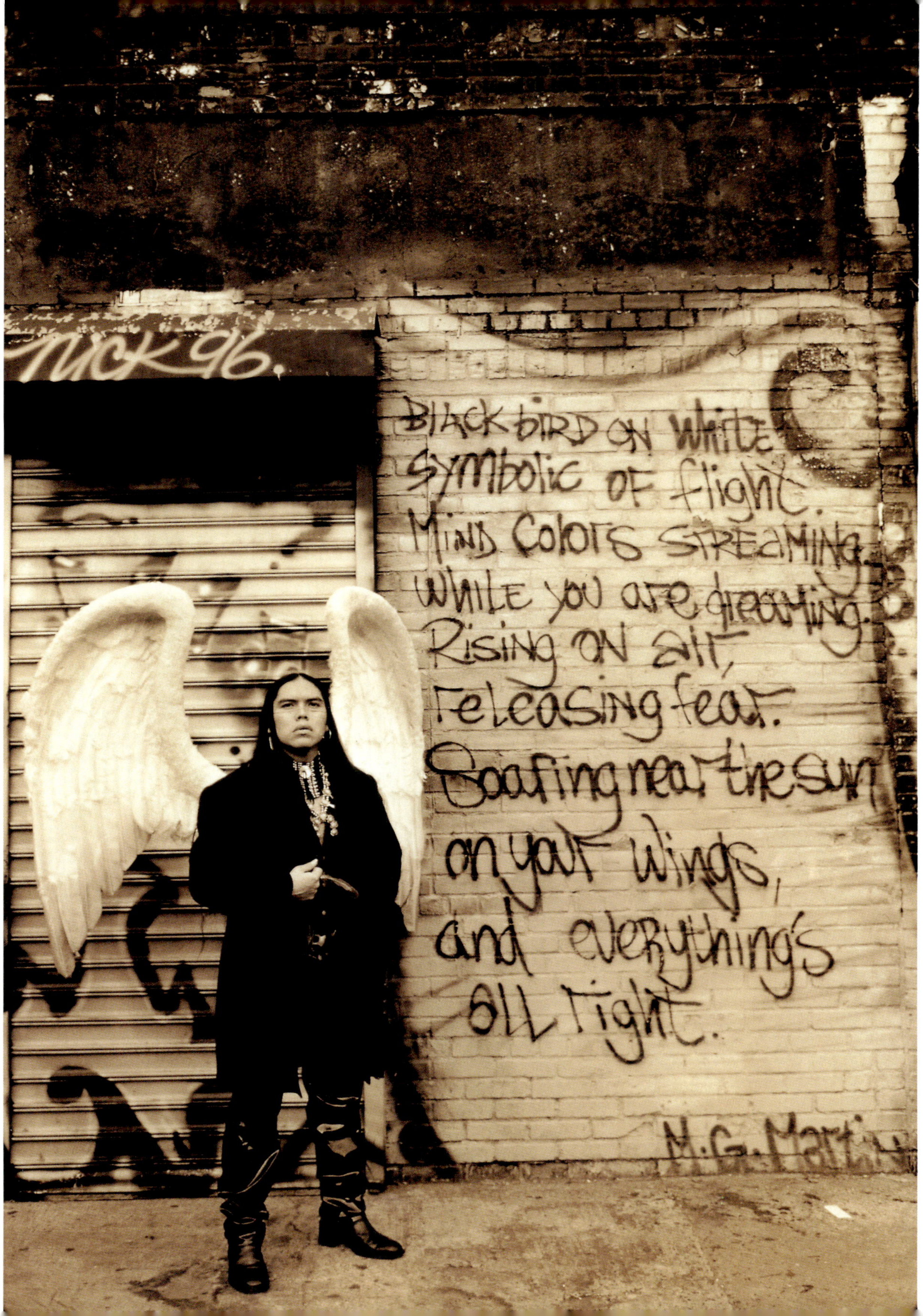
Black bird on white
symbolic of flight.
Mind colors streaming
while you are dreaming.
Rising on air,
releasing fear.
Soaring near the sun
on your wings,
and everything's
all right.
M.G. Martin

peace is knowing
you're in tune
with your mind

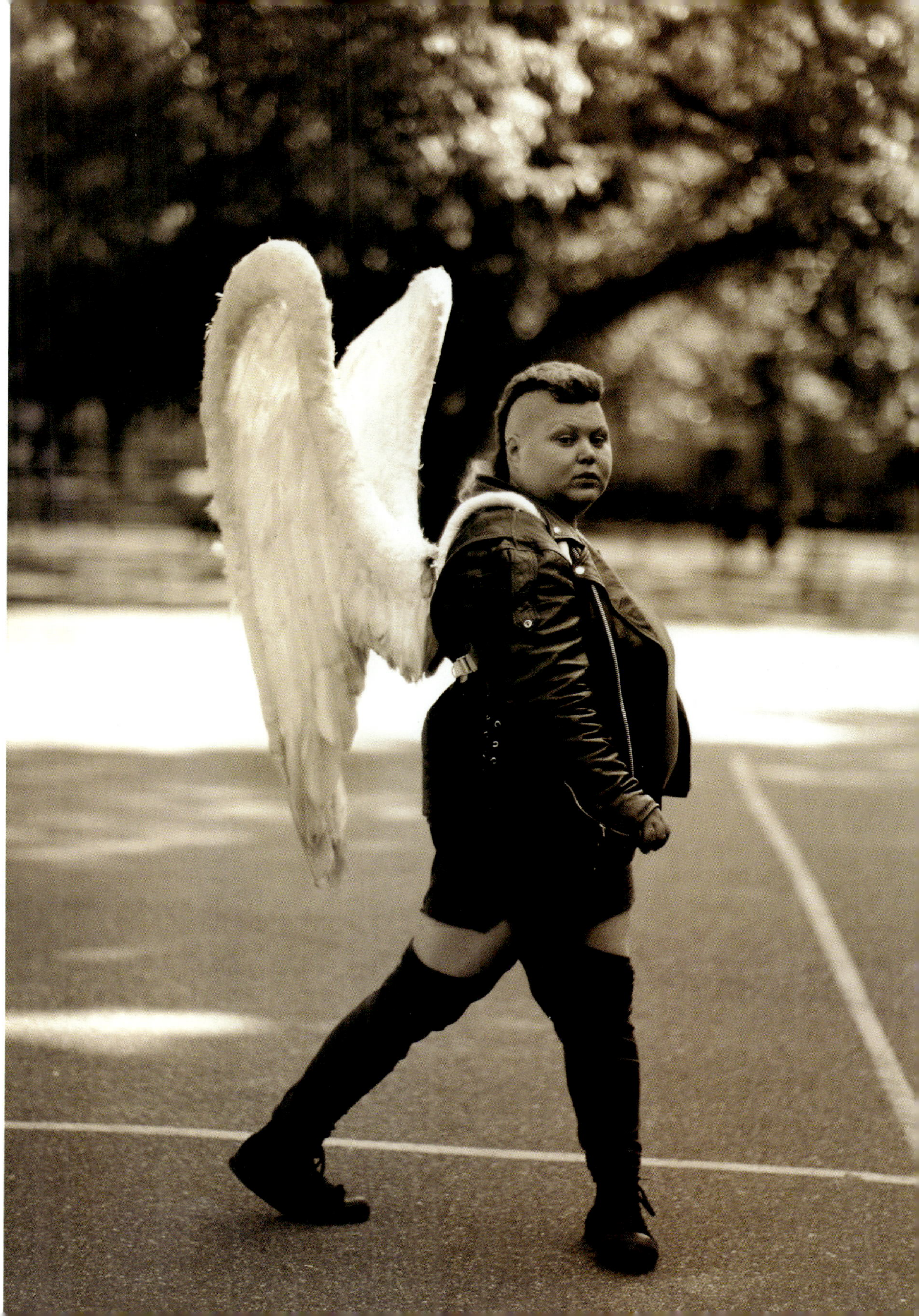

**rebecca**

new york city
lower east side

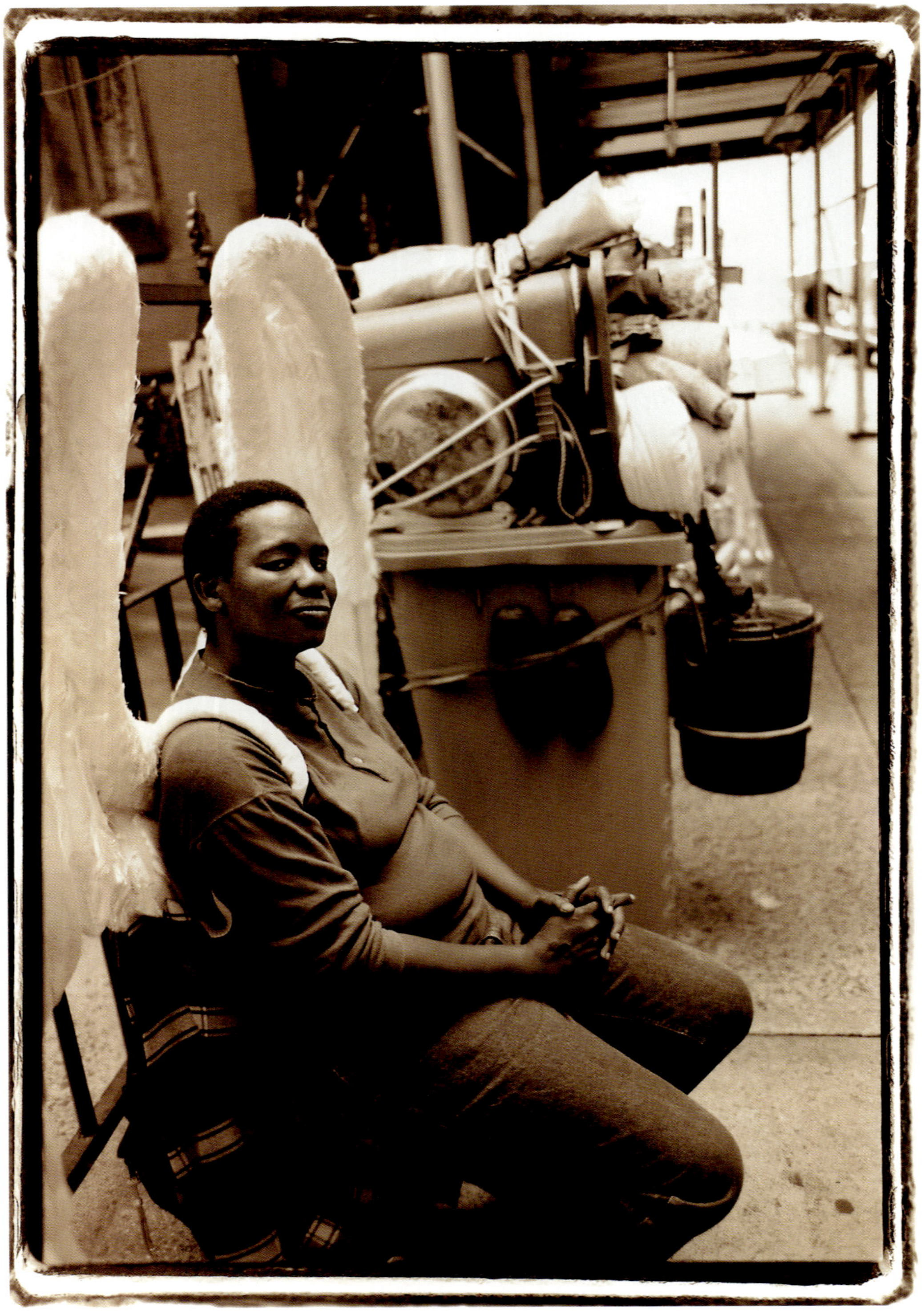

**benita**
dominican republic

only a soldier and a policeman
can really appreciate peace
because they have
the most to lose
during times of chaos

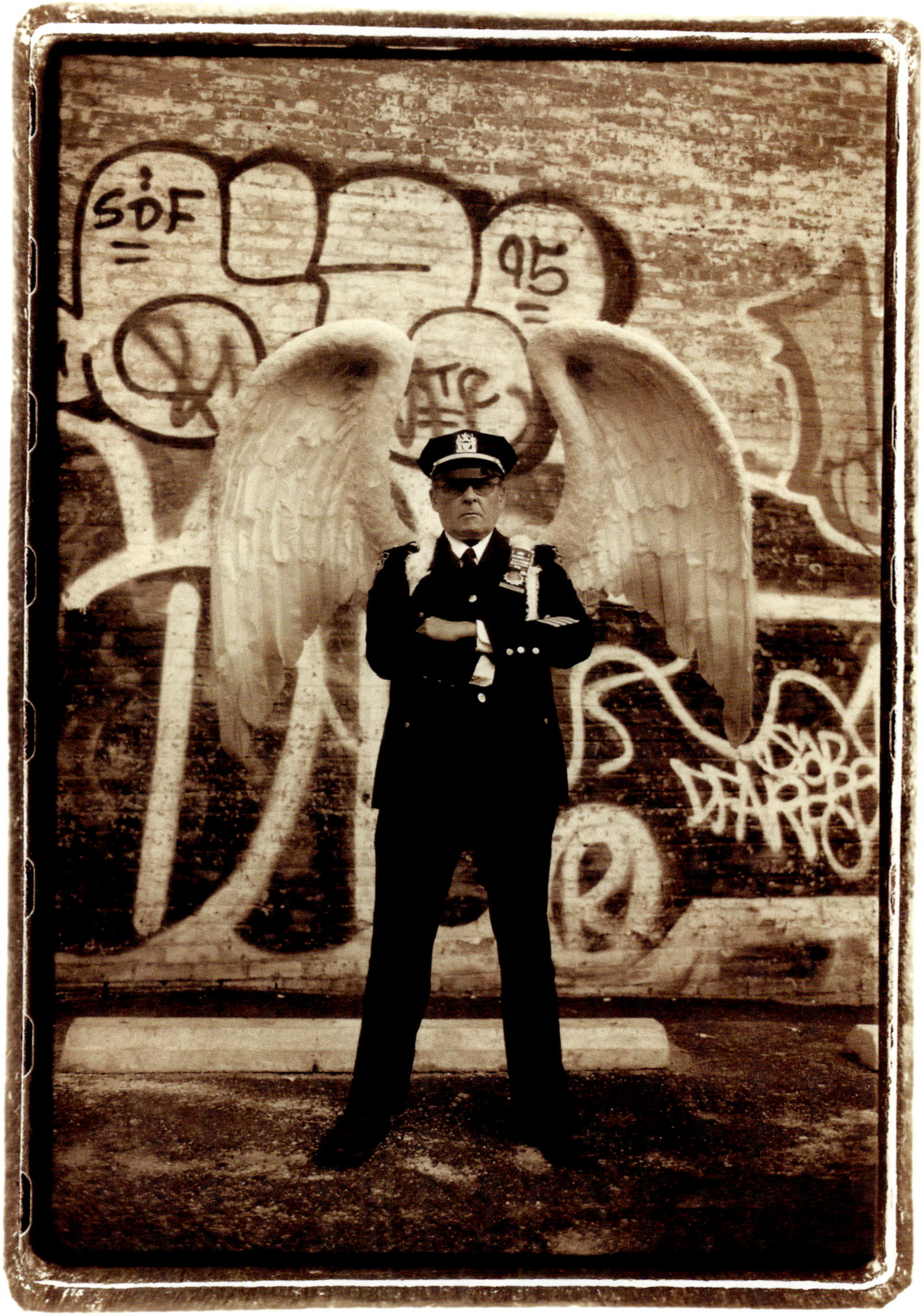


**bob**
germany

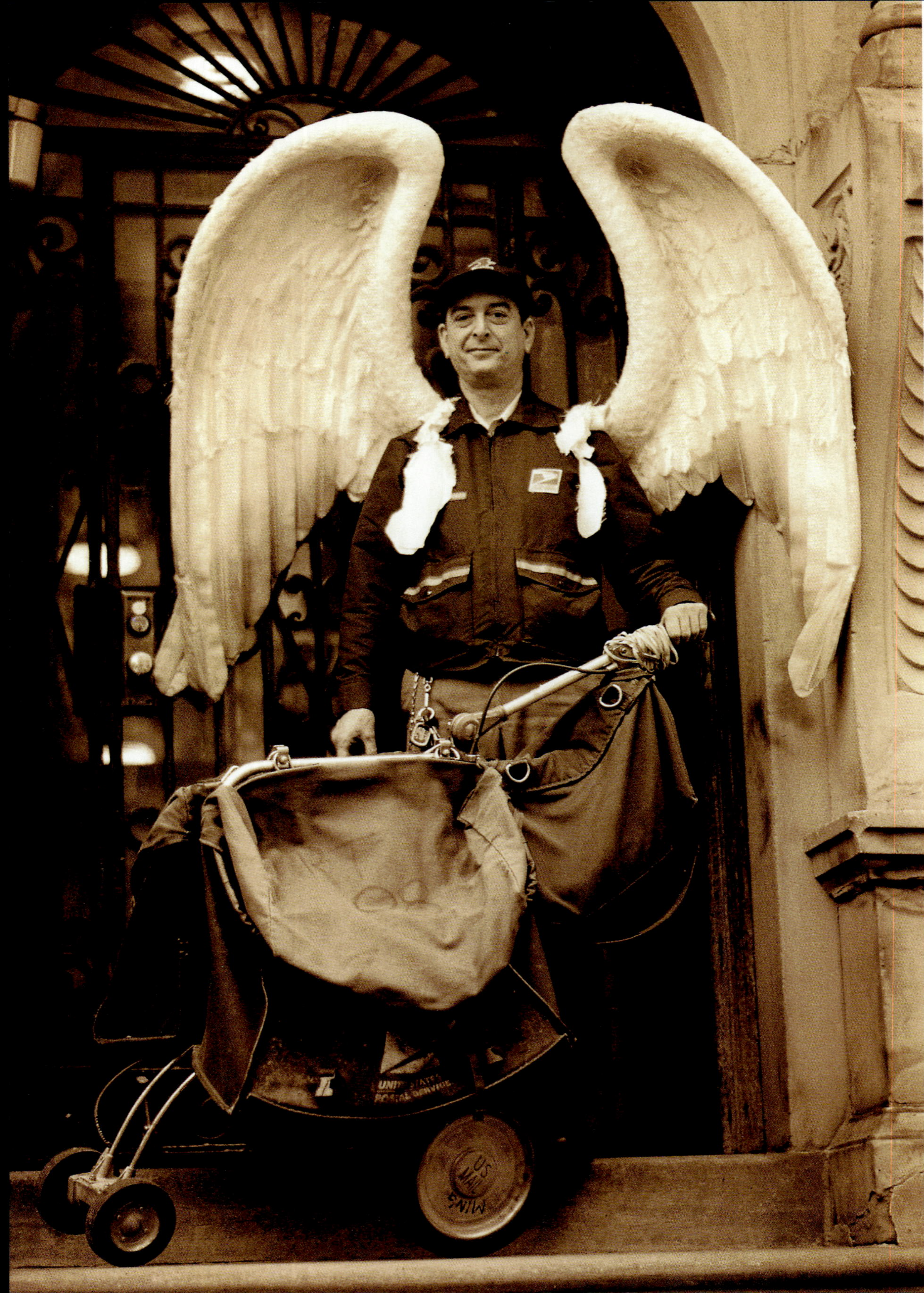


peace is a feeling
of warmth
that fills your soul
it soothes your body
and relaxes the mind

**ira**
turkey

hatred and violence
are abuses
love is peace

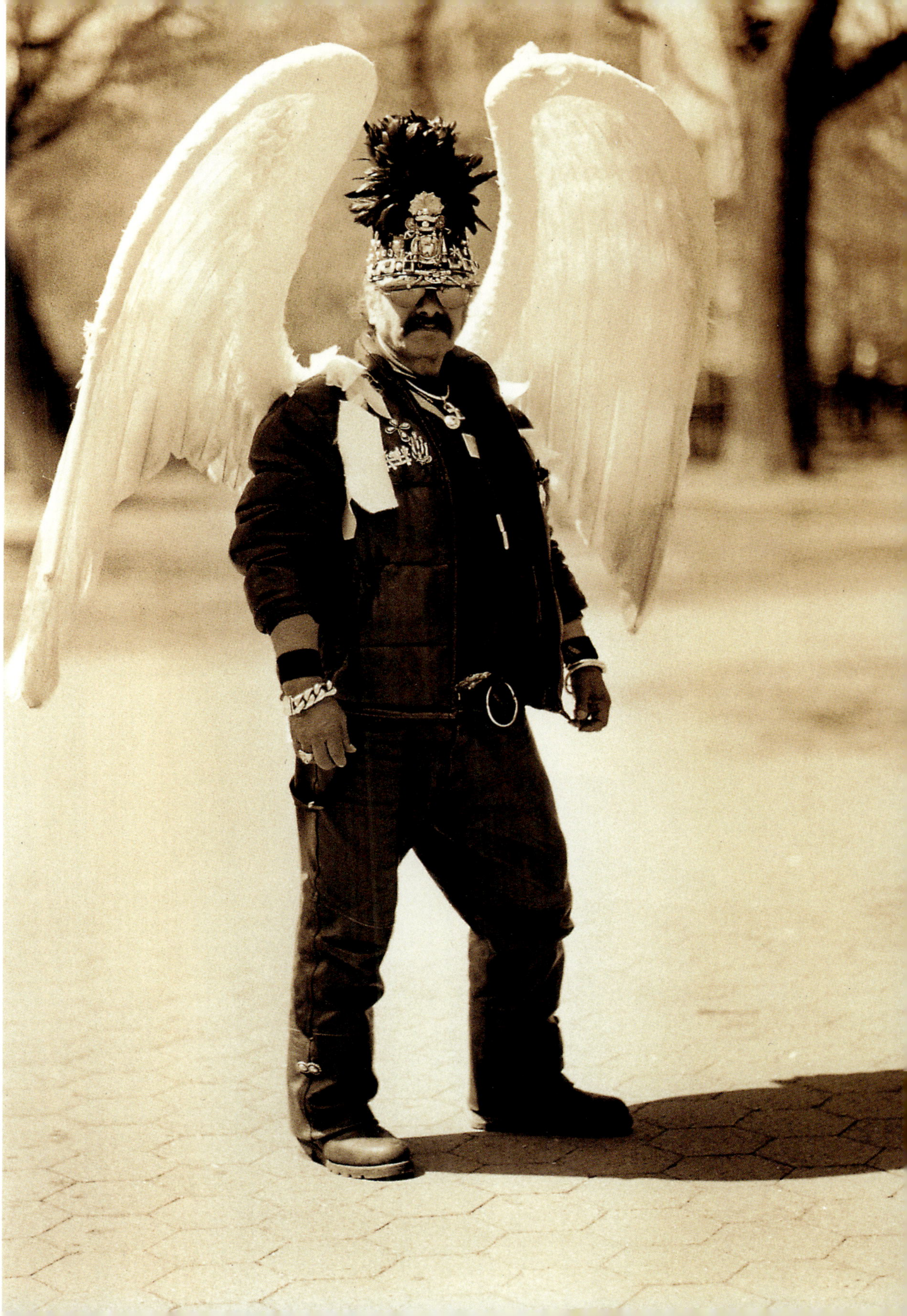

**carlos**
colombia

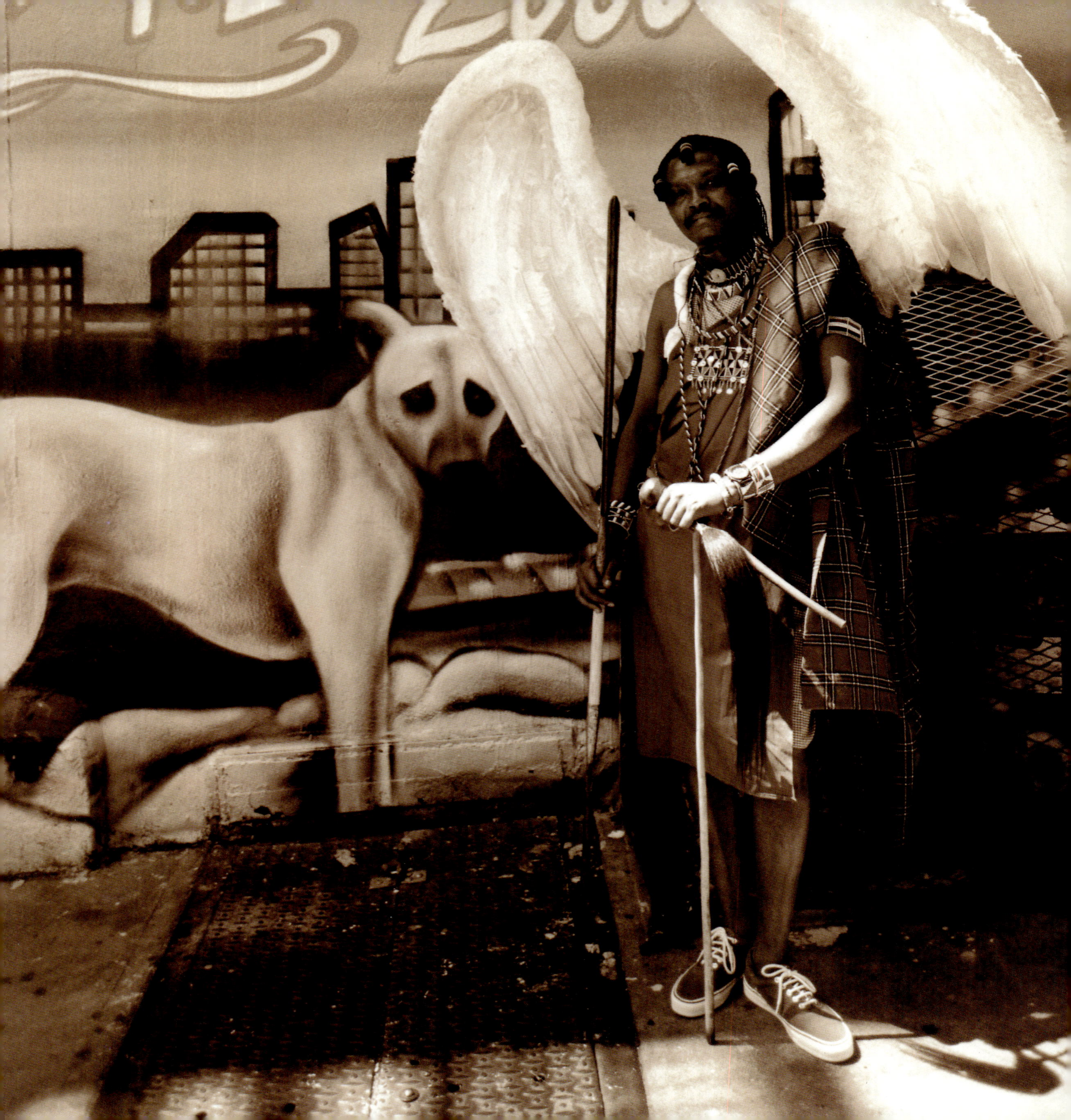

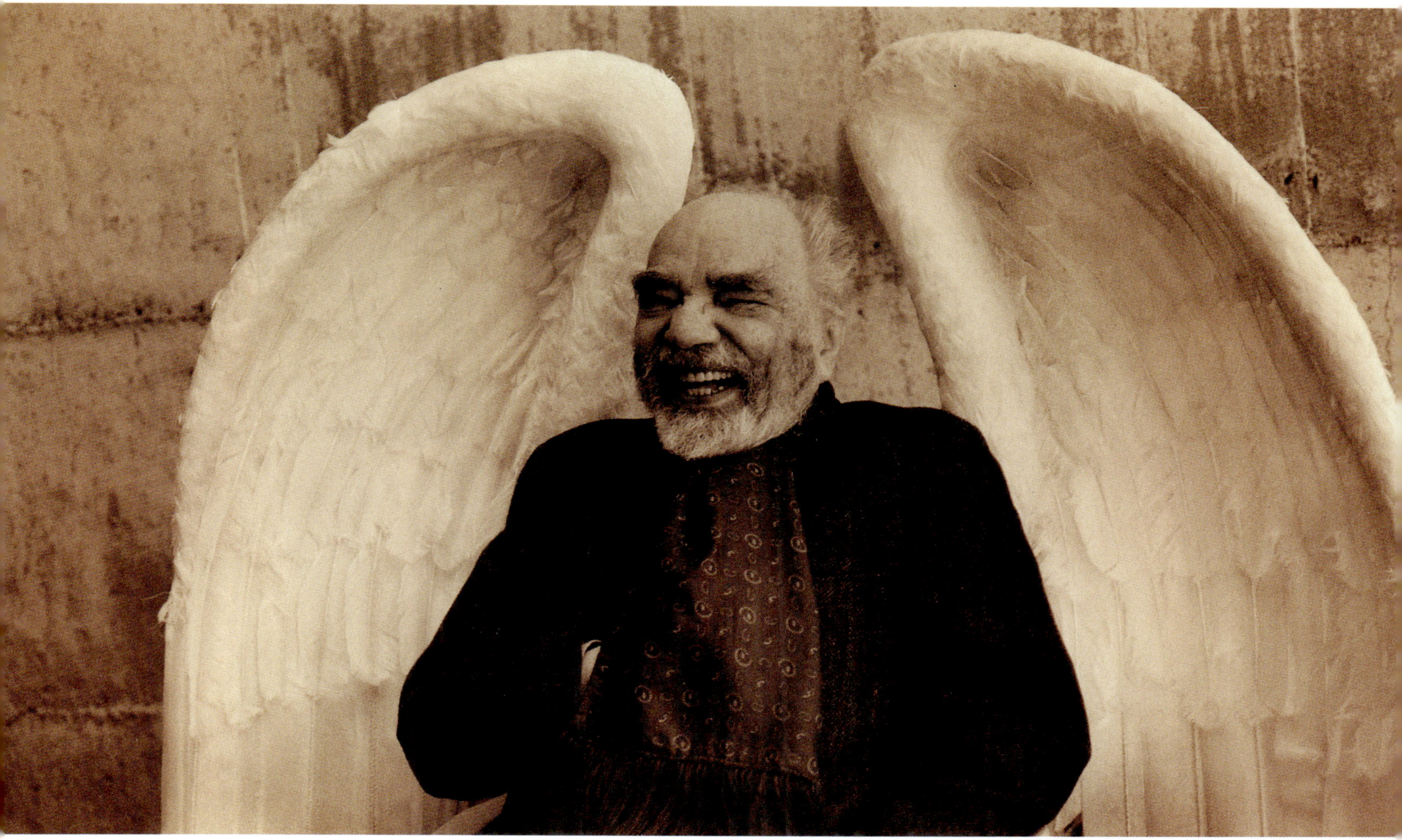

only those at war
are concerned about peace

**peter ledama ole kantai**
massai

**roy schatt**
austria

all of us should be
angels of peace
the sky would then be bluer
the air fresher

**jean**
france

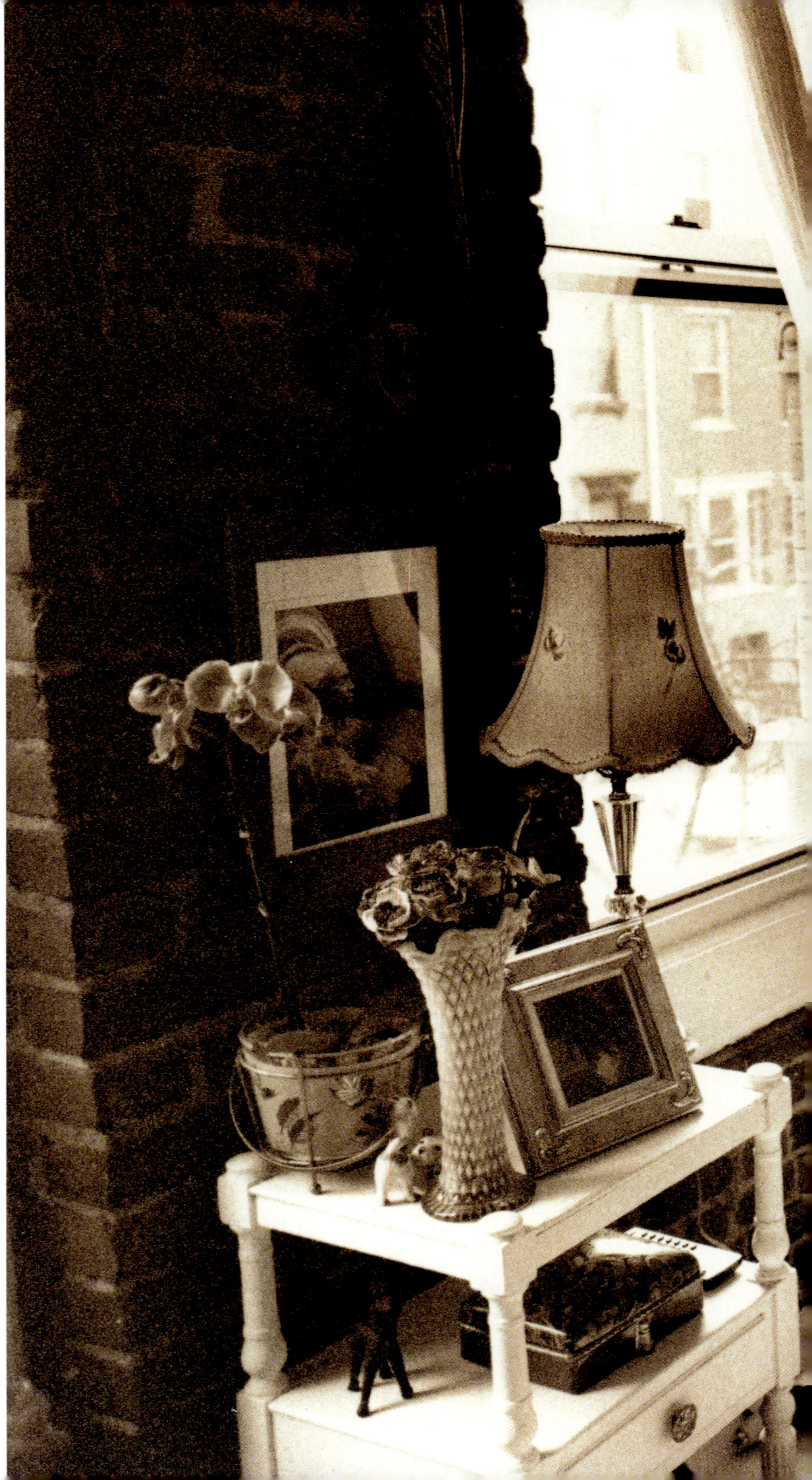

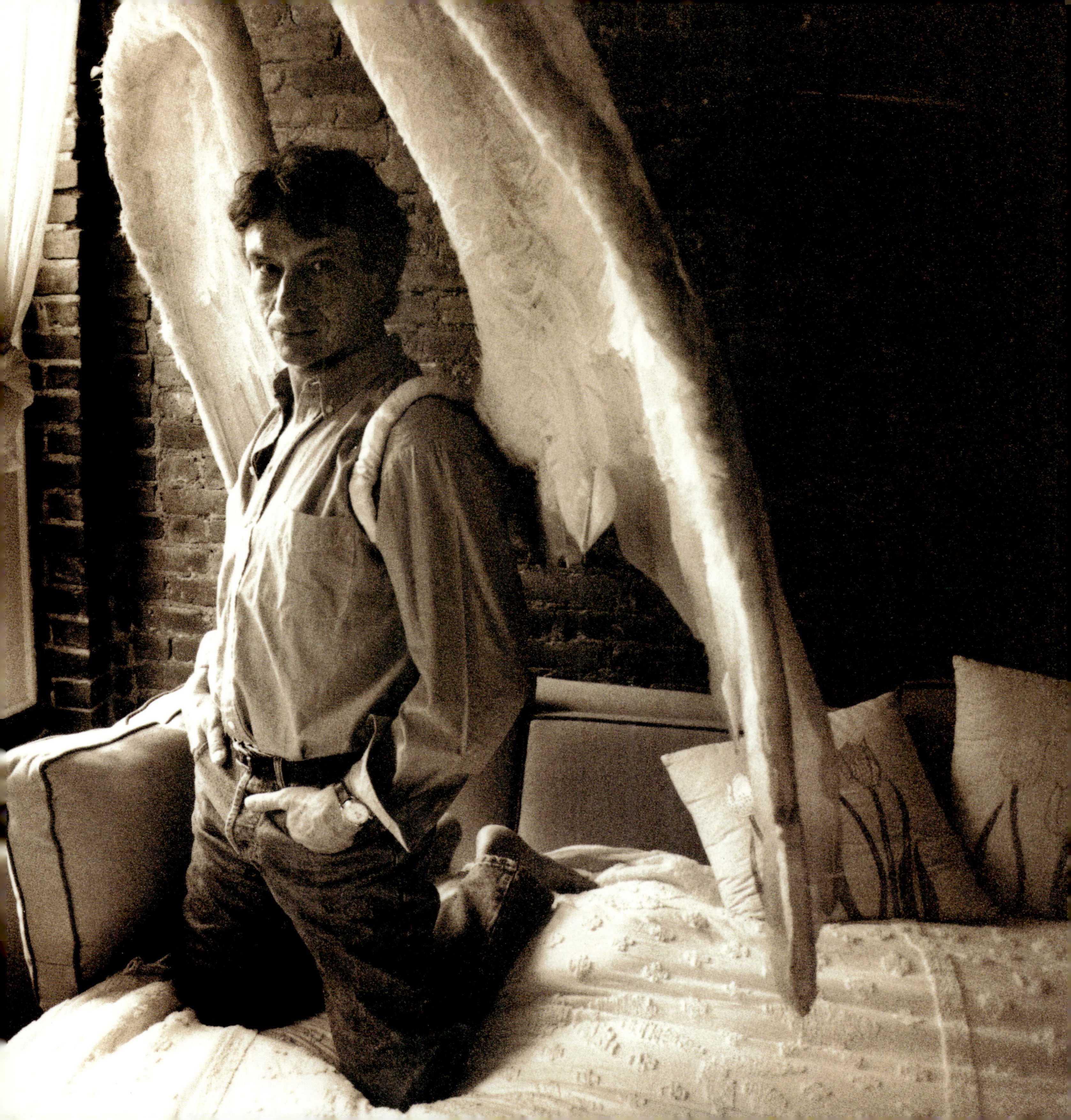

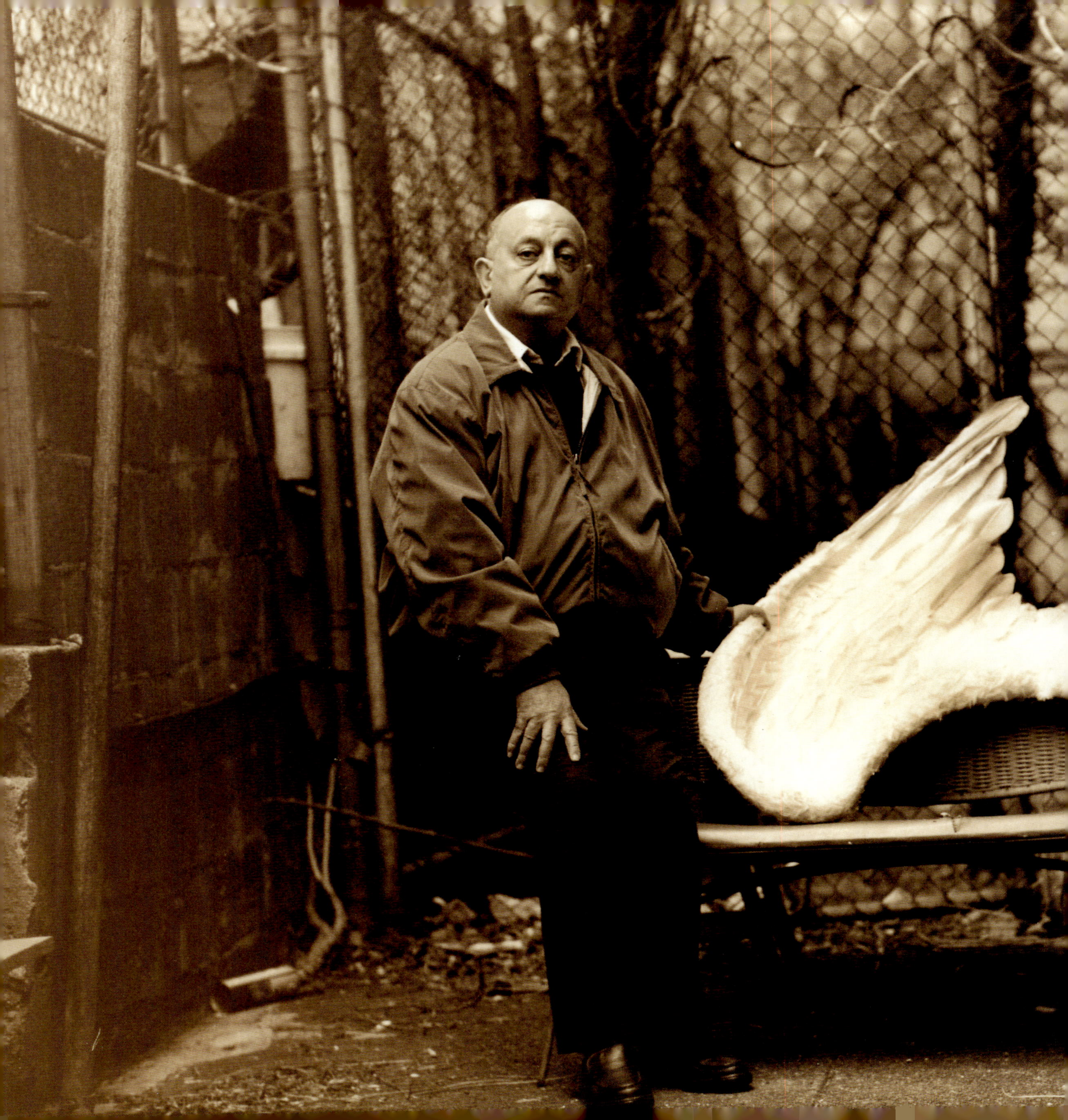

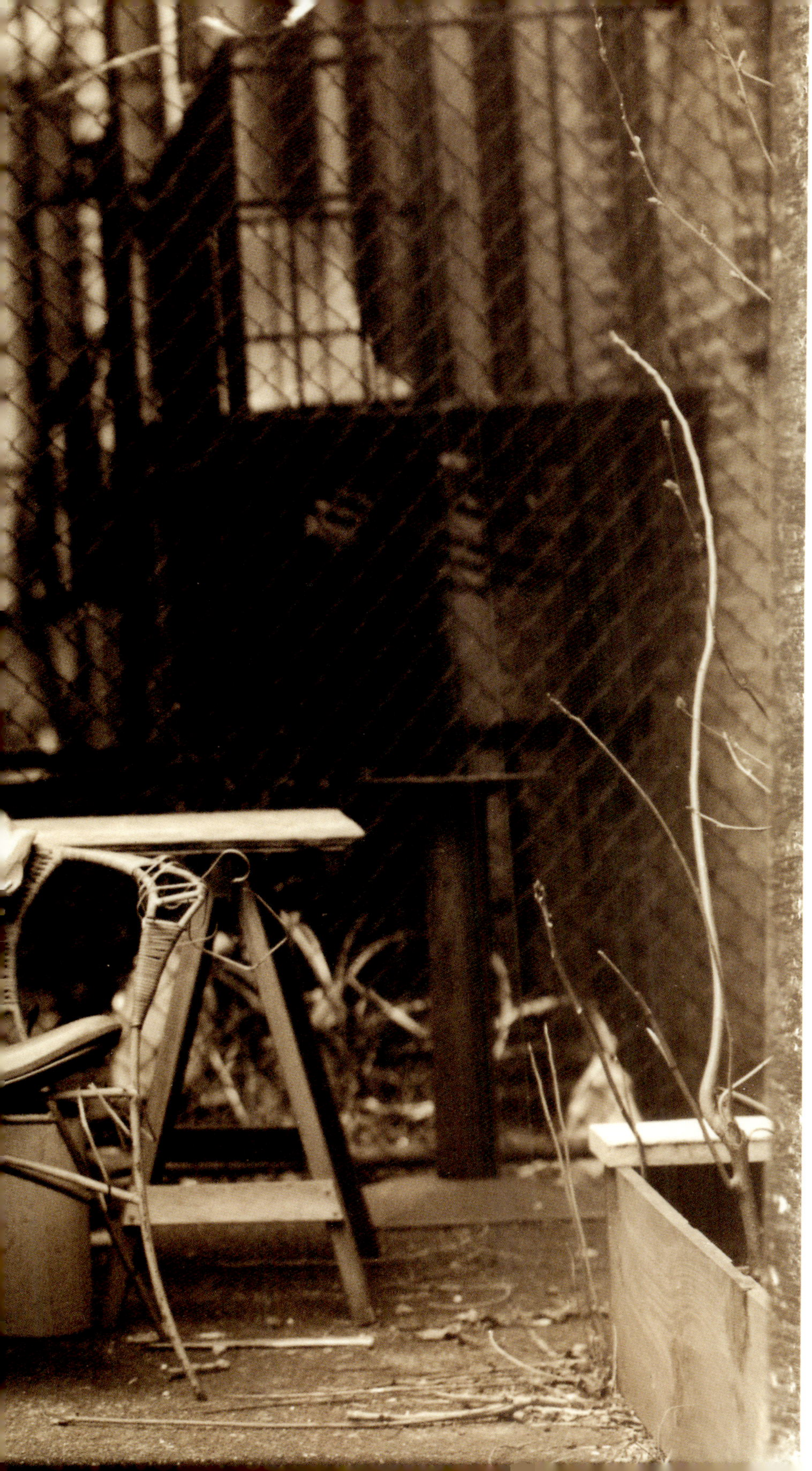

born in iraq
departed to israel
the way of the forefathers
good will and prayers
from where peace shall come

**shaul**
israel

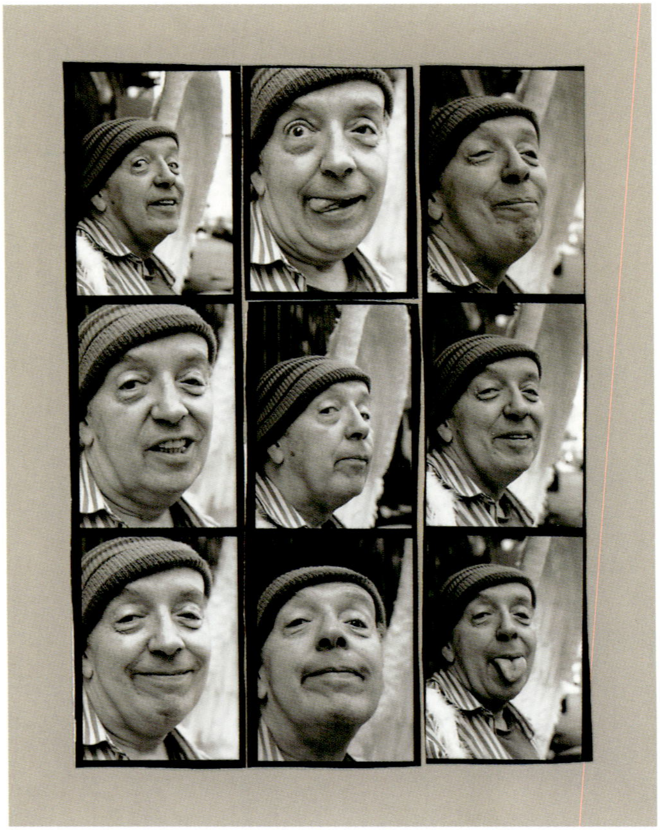

peace is a dove
waiting to fly

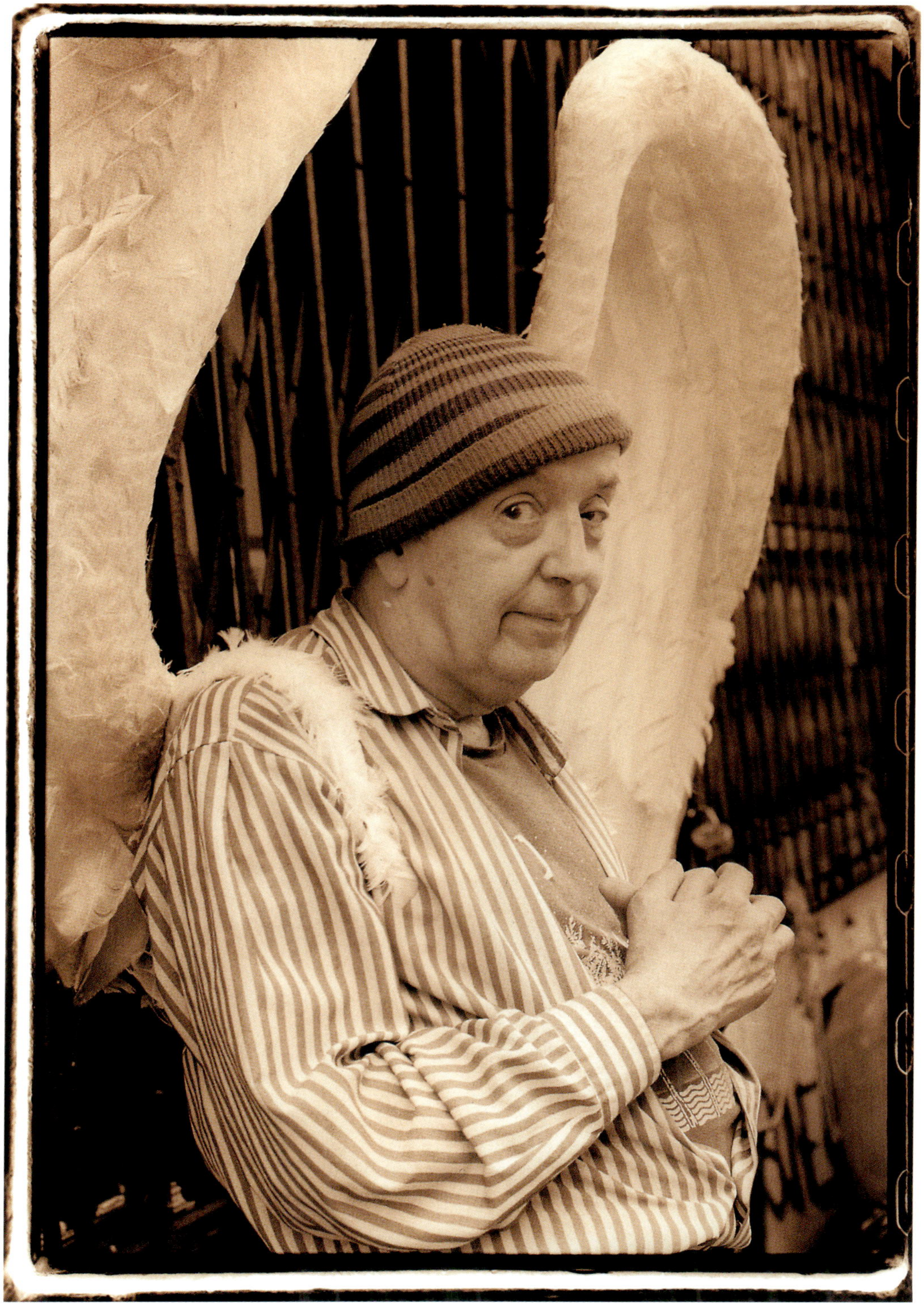

**taylor mead**
great britain

i have grown accustomed
to the shimmering desert heat
the expansive surface
that draws one to the unreachable horizon
where the simple blue prison ends
and the heaven or something else begins

**john**
ukraine

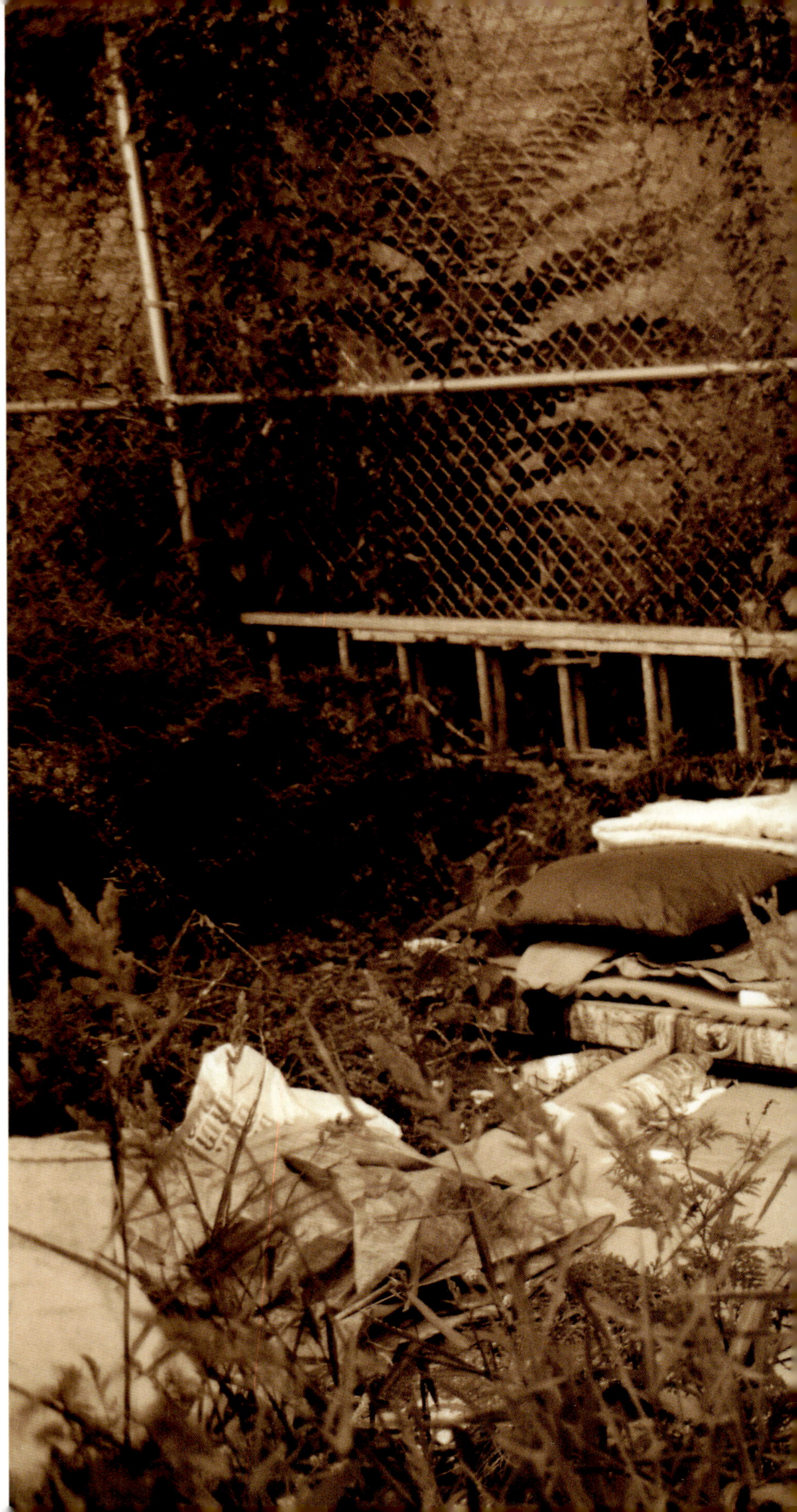

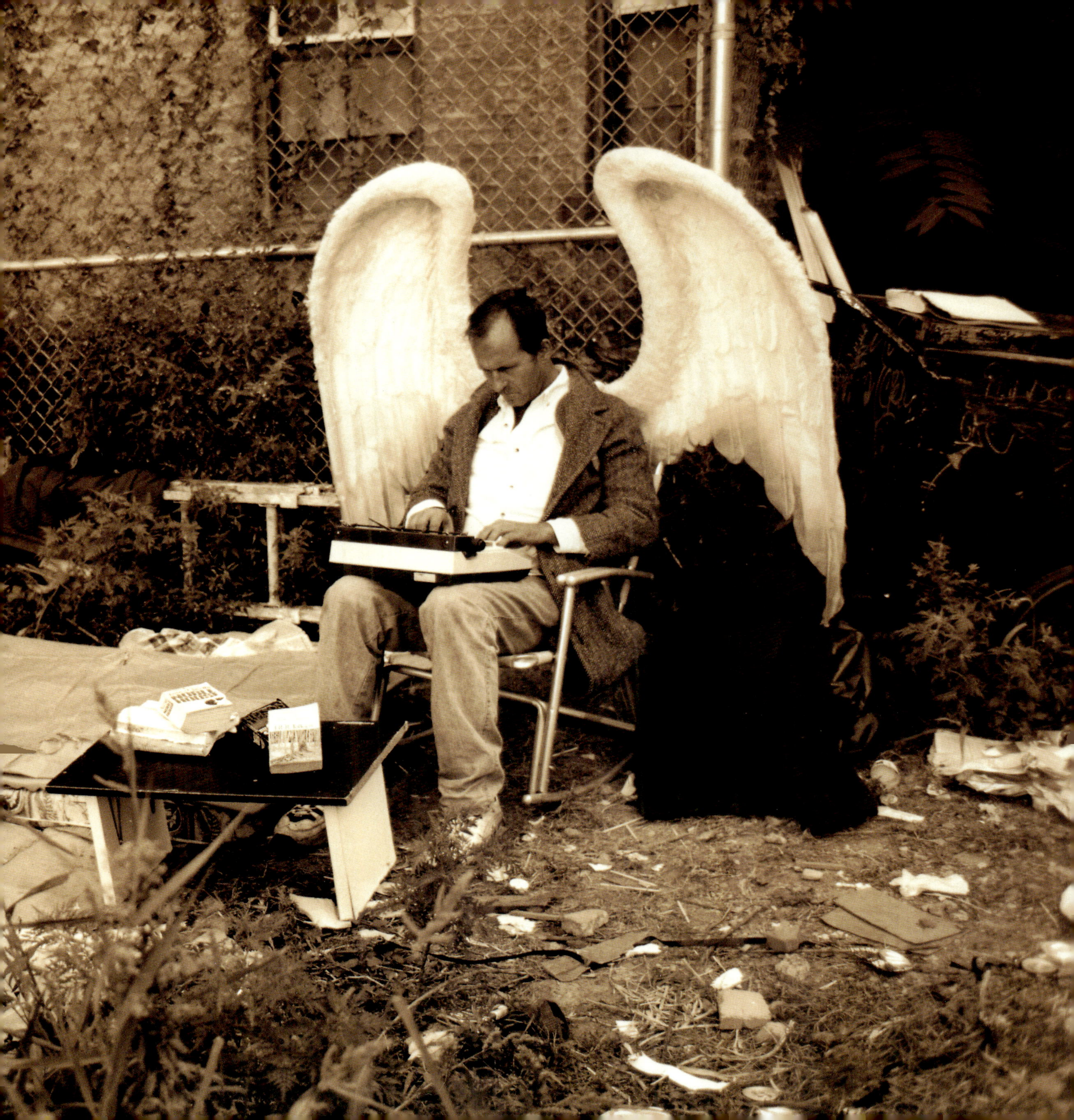

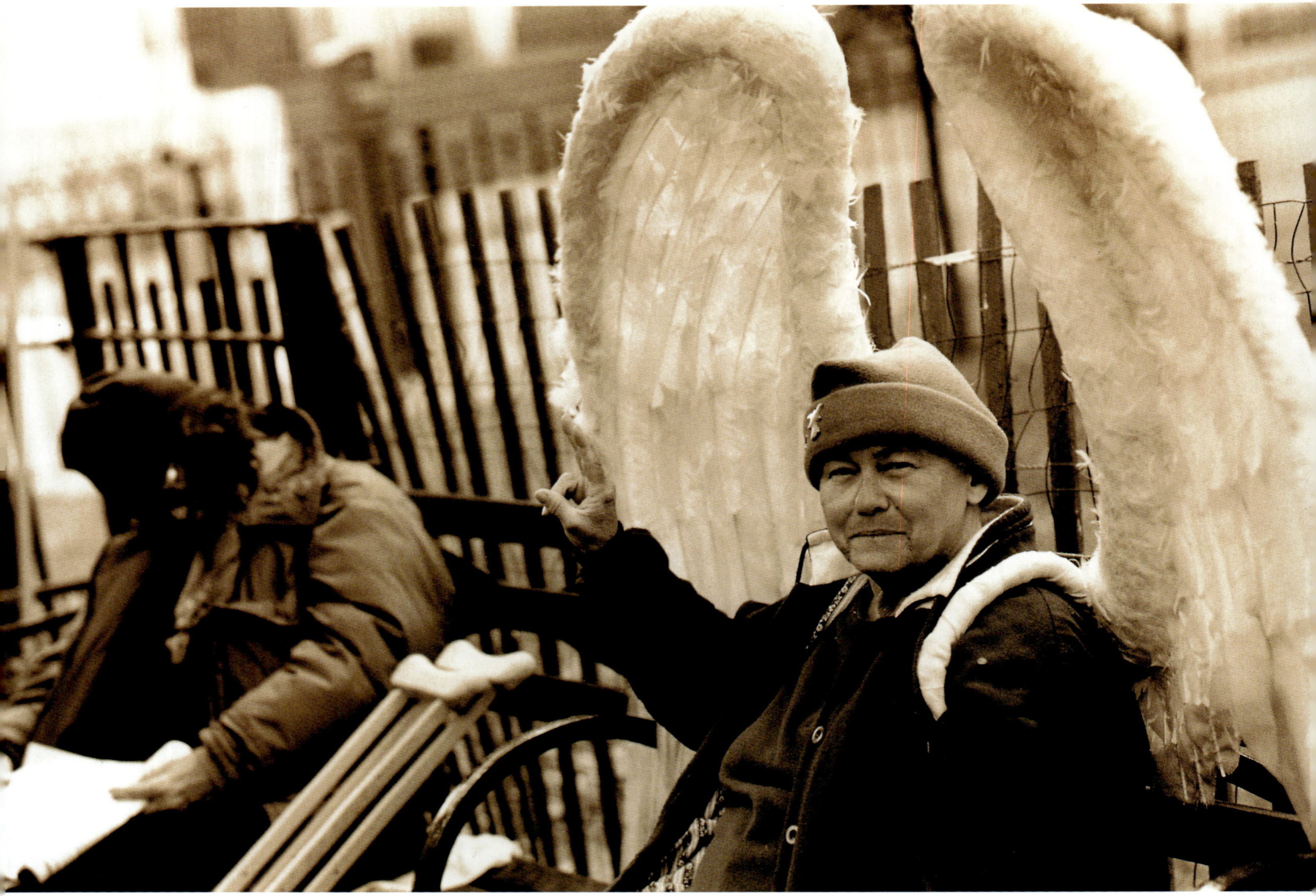

**adele**
netherlands

the angels are beautiful people
i love people
even my enemies

at eve my eyes rest
on the moon's crest
and dream the world awakes
in peace

**cynthia**
lebanon

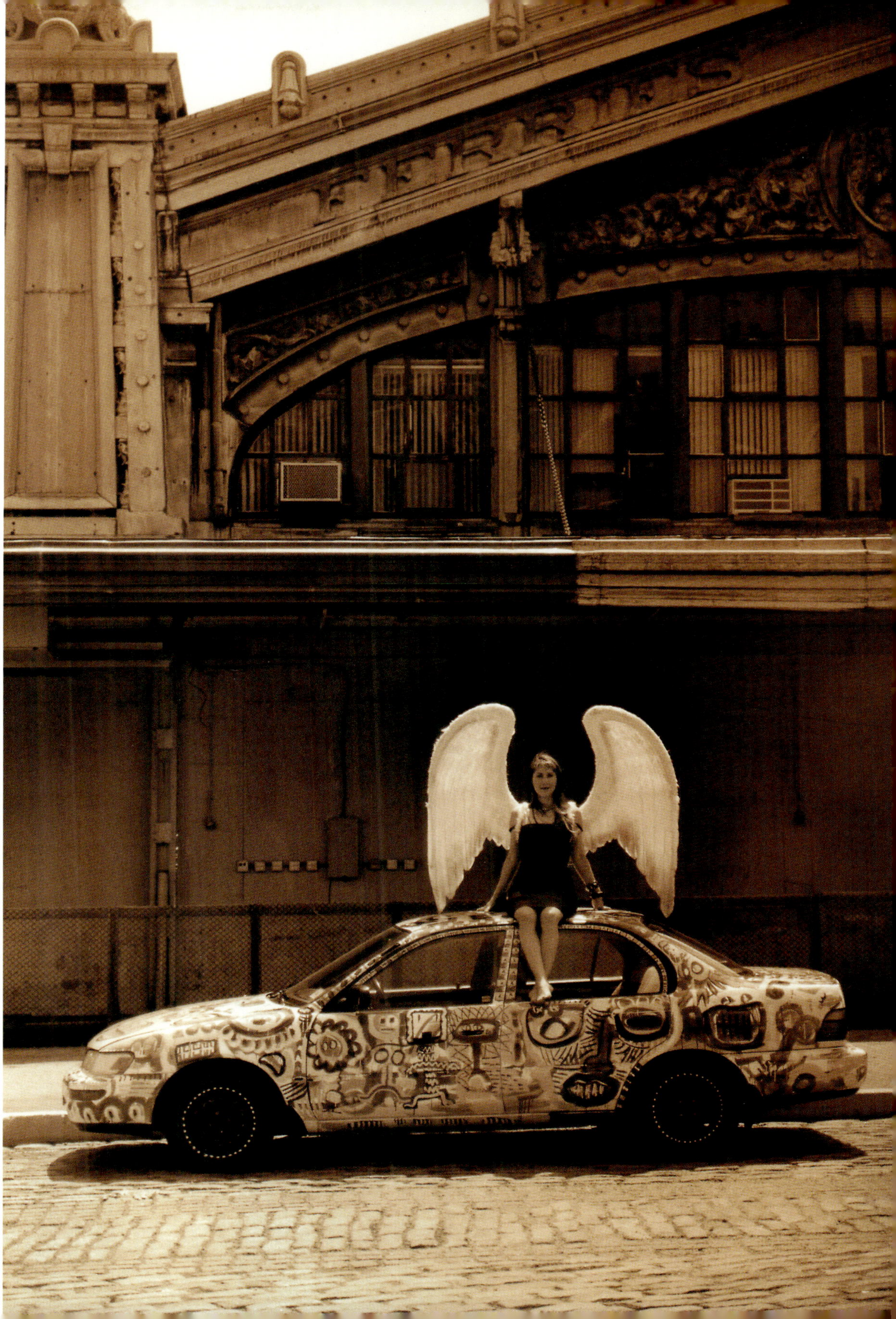

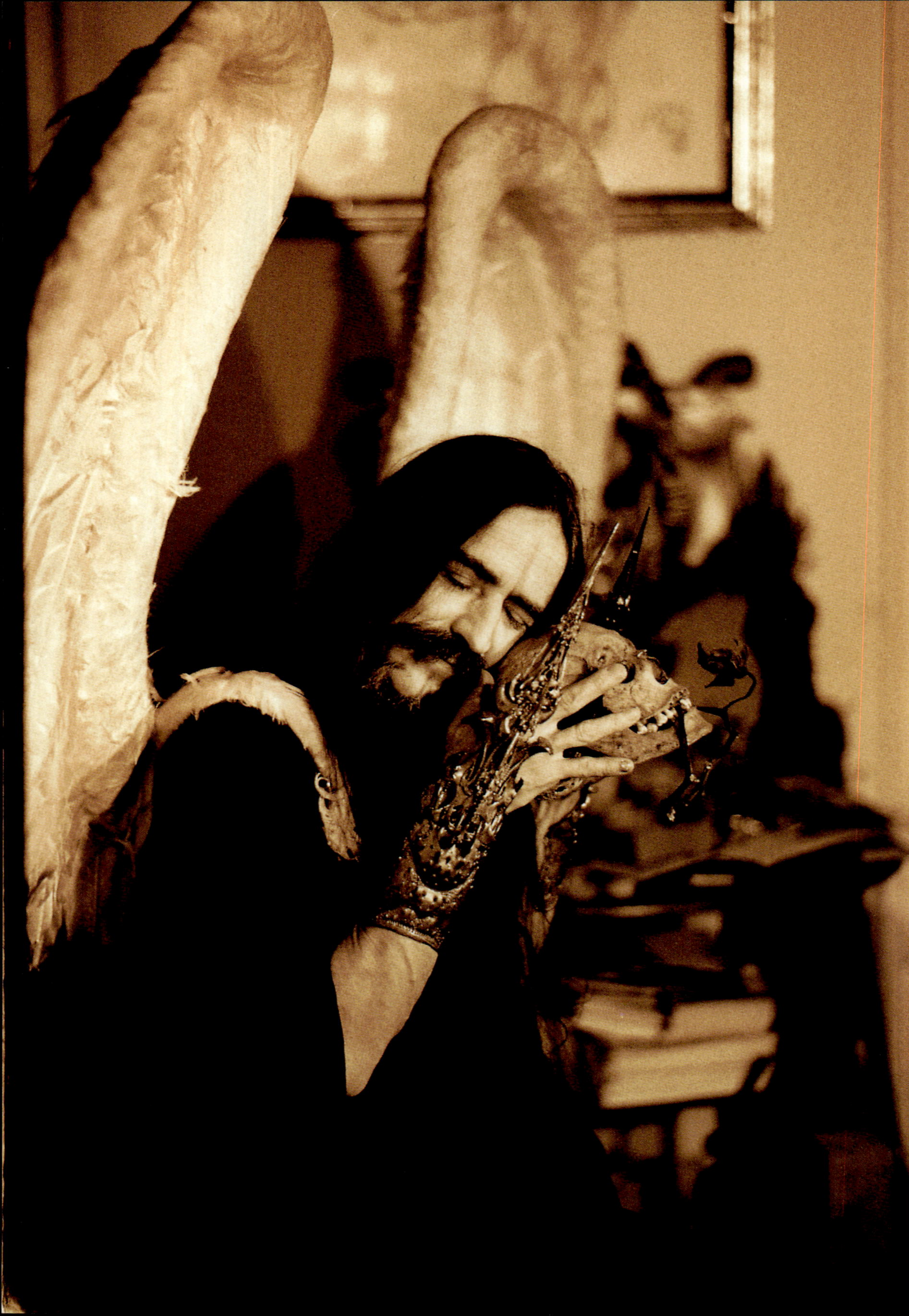

lend me wings
give me flight
let me escape
my shallow loneliness
give me the power
to understand myself
and the knowledge
to use my power
for the perpetuation
of love

**axel**
germany

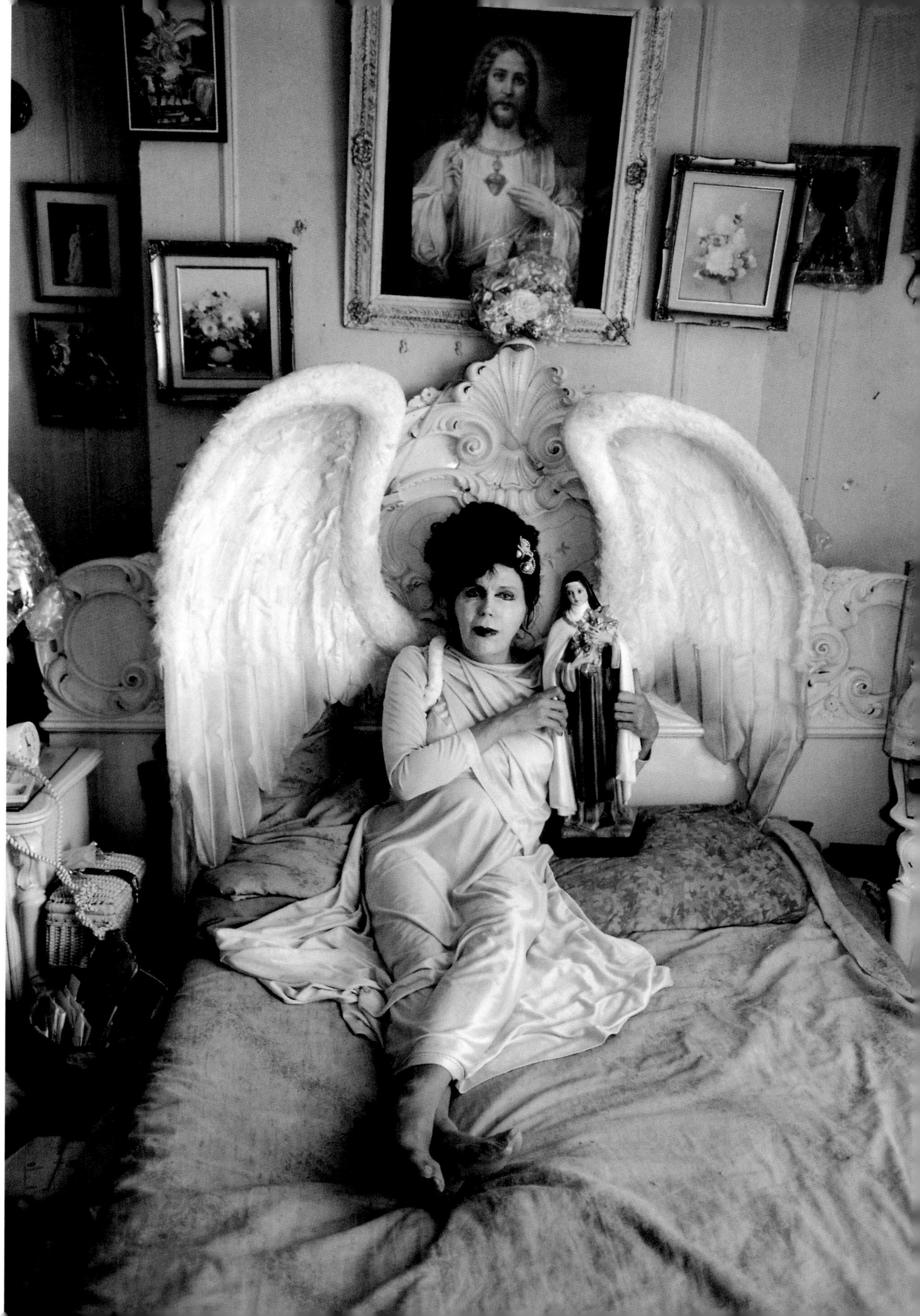

**lucia**
sicily

i believe that peace
comes from within

**mary**
new york city

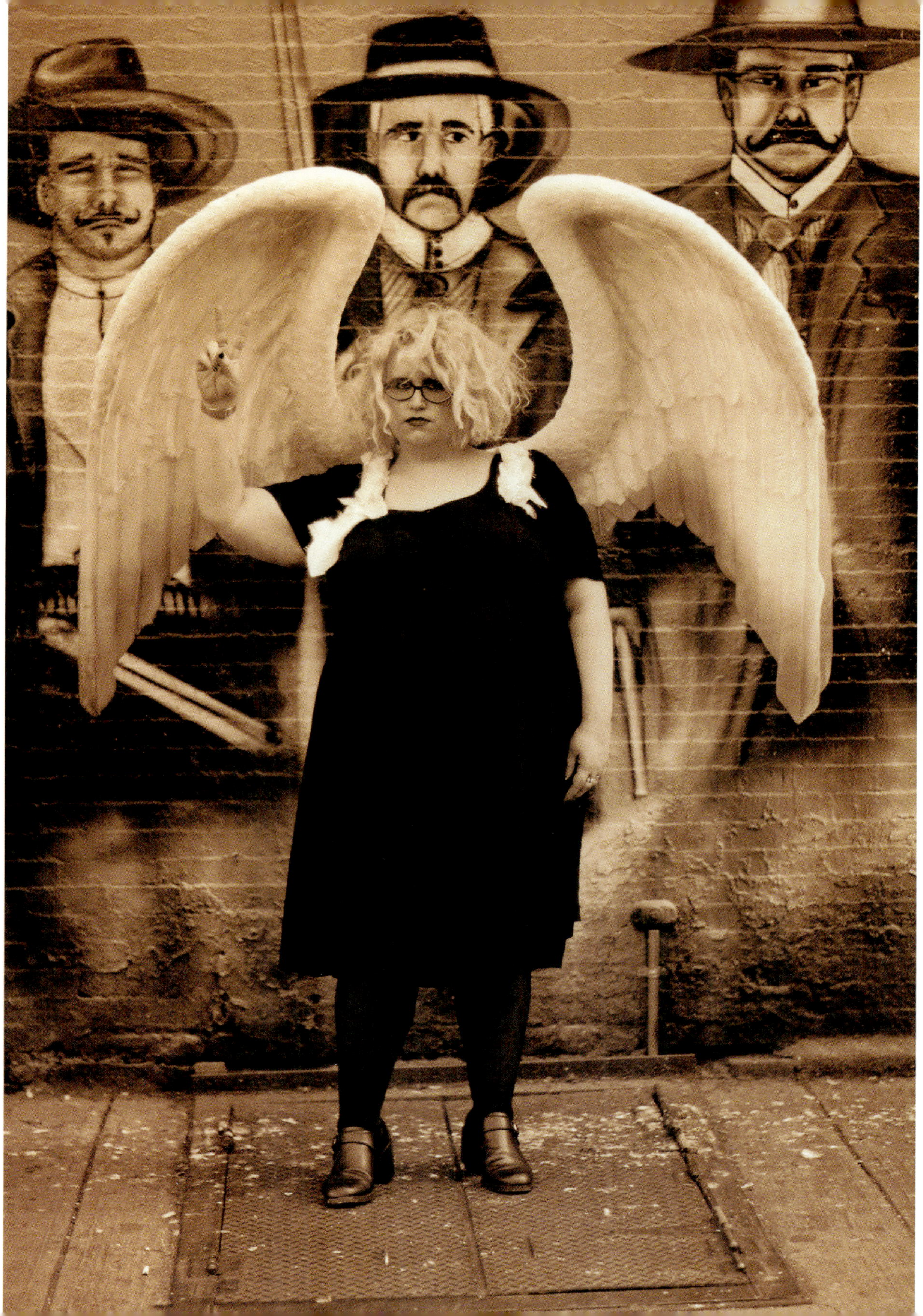

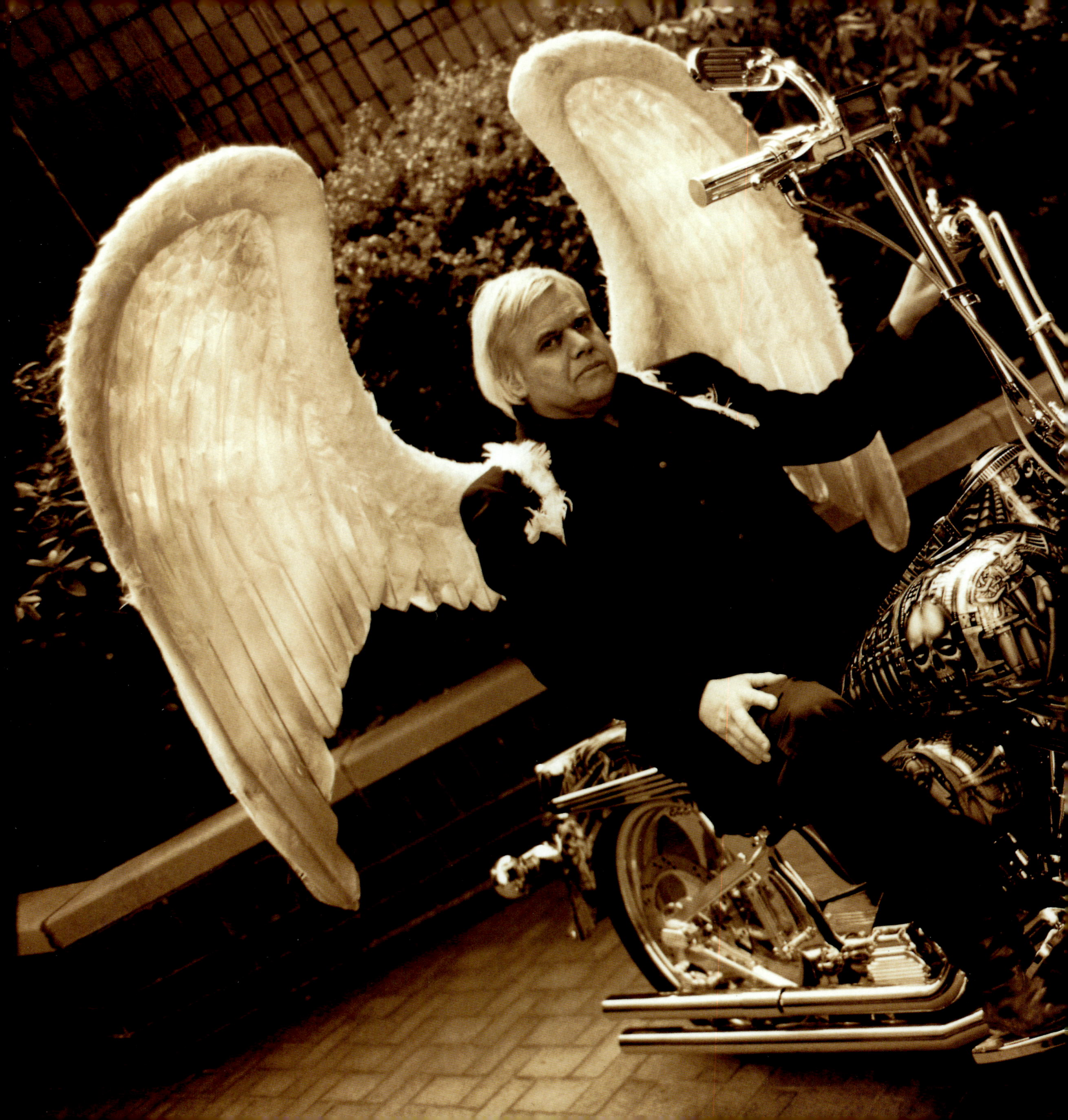

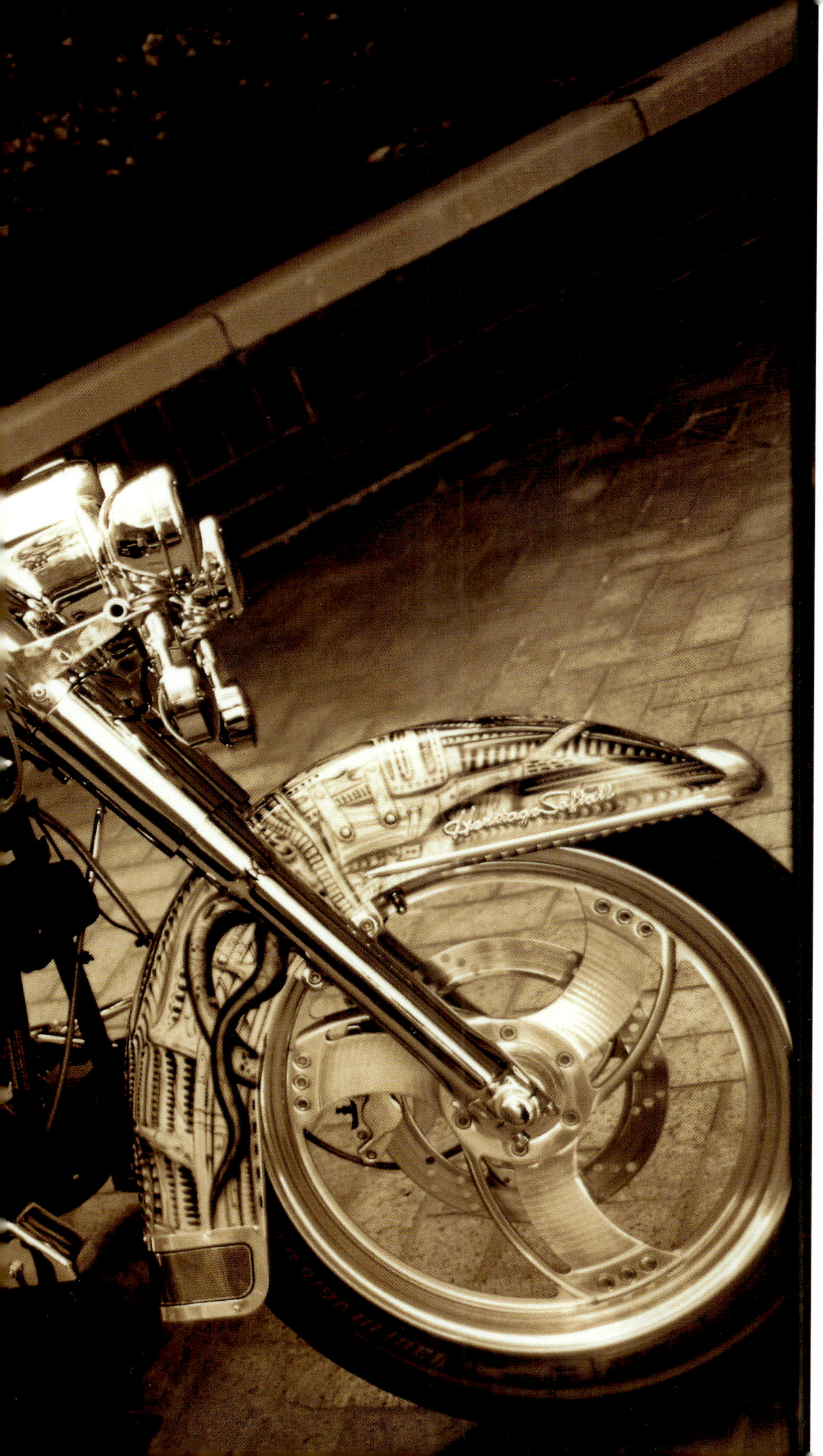

rest in peace
is anyway after life

**h. r. giger**
switzerland

peace is the
natural state of being

**glenn, david & ivy**
france

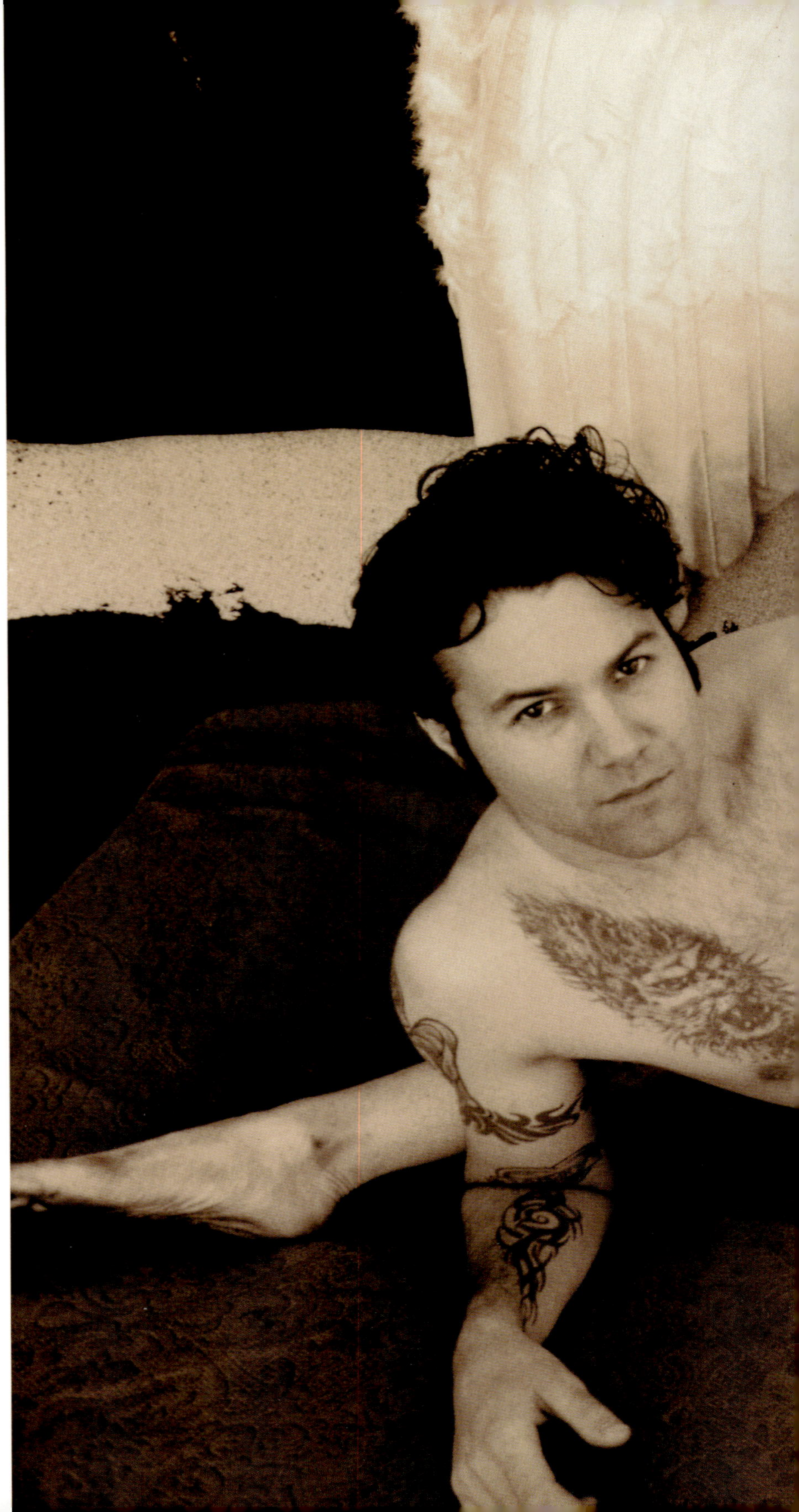

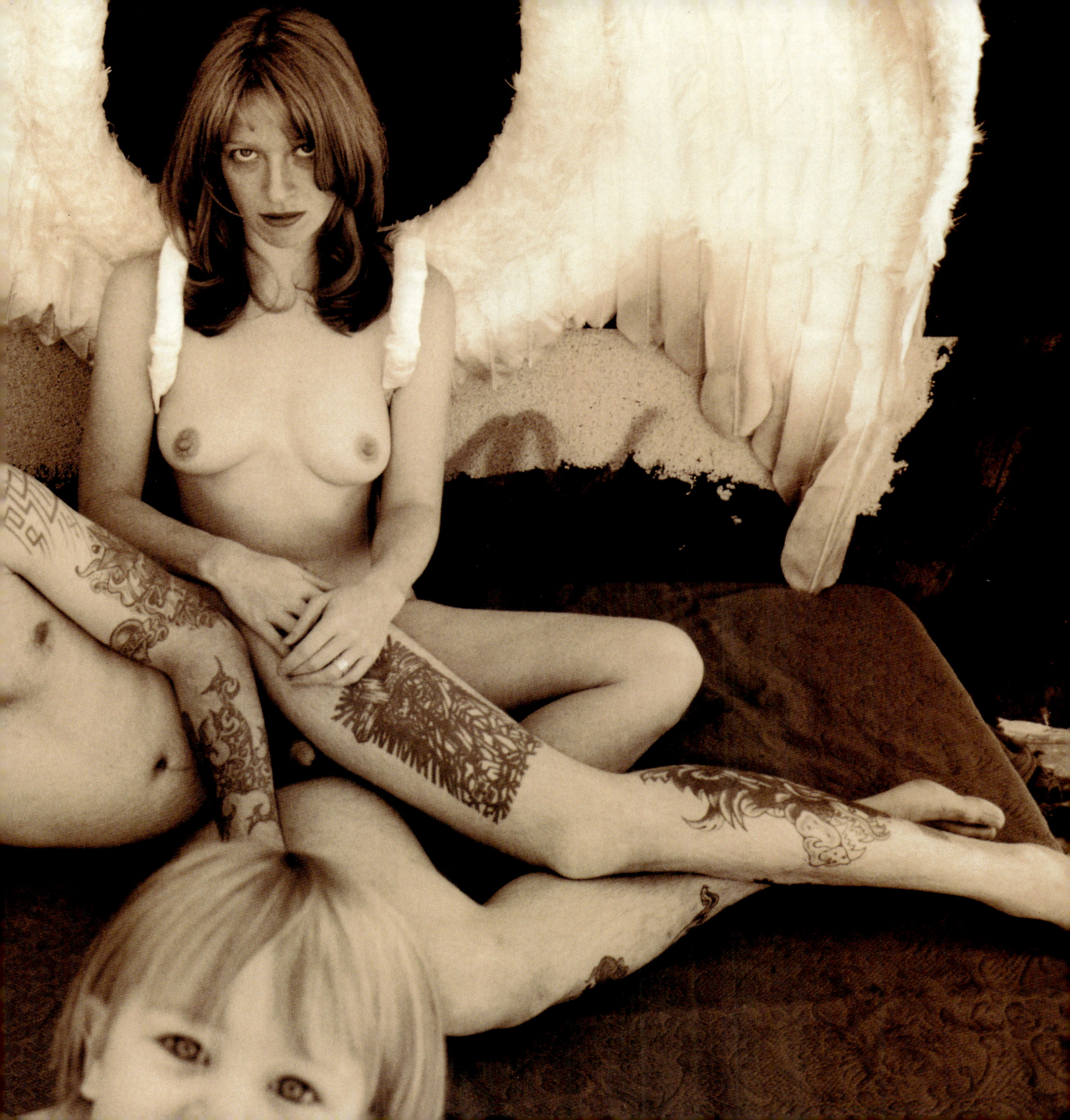

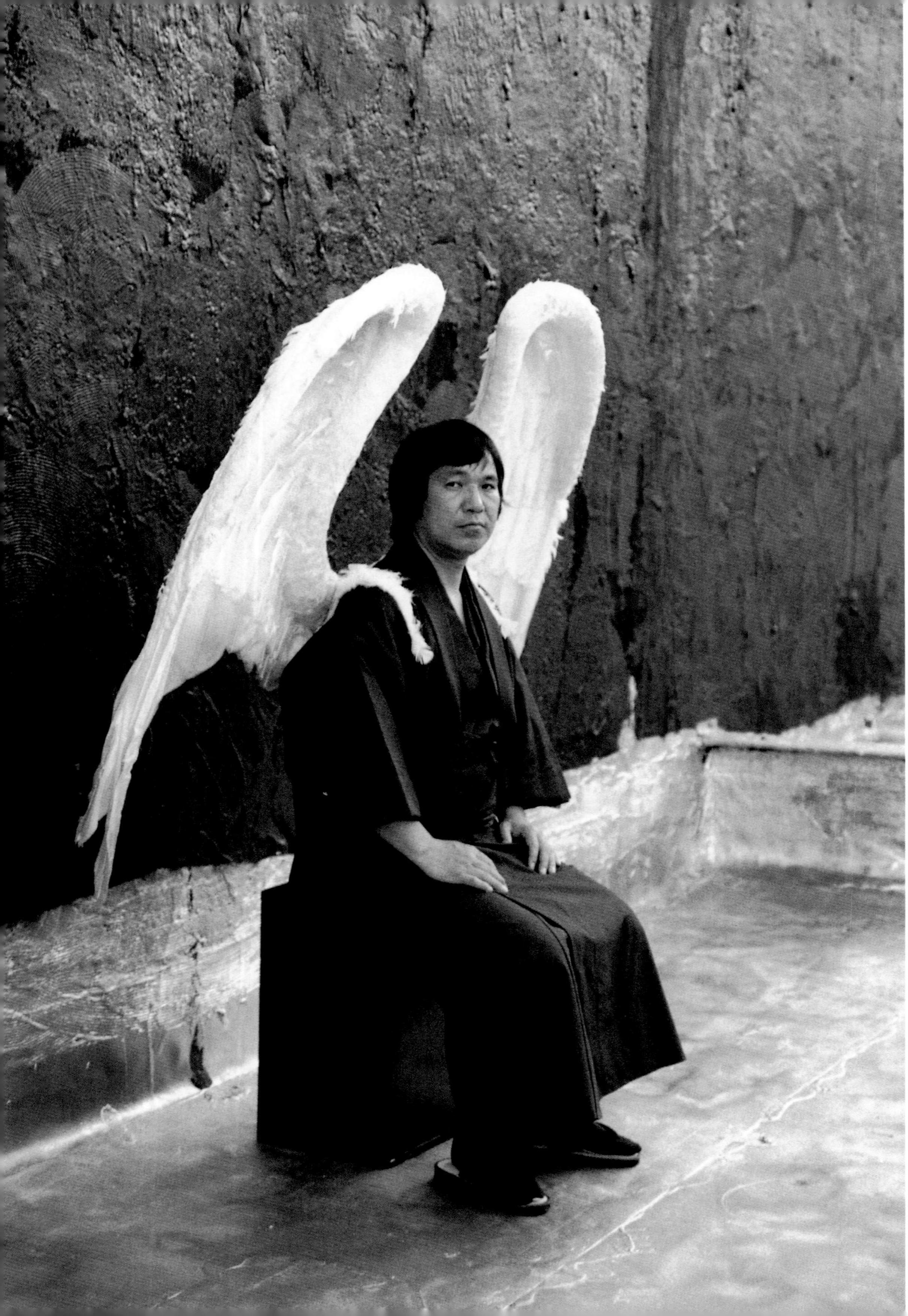

the ultimate peace
is believing in oneself

**susumo sato**
japan

i can do it
you can do it
together we can bring
peace to our lives

**rabbi levy y. shemtow**

new york city
lower east side

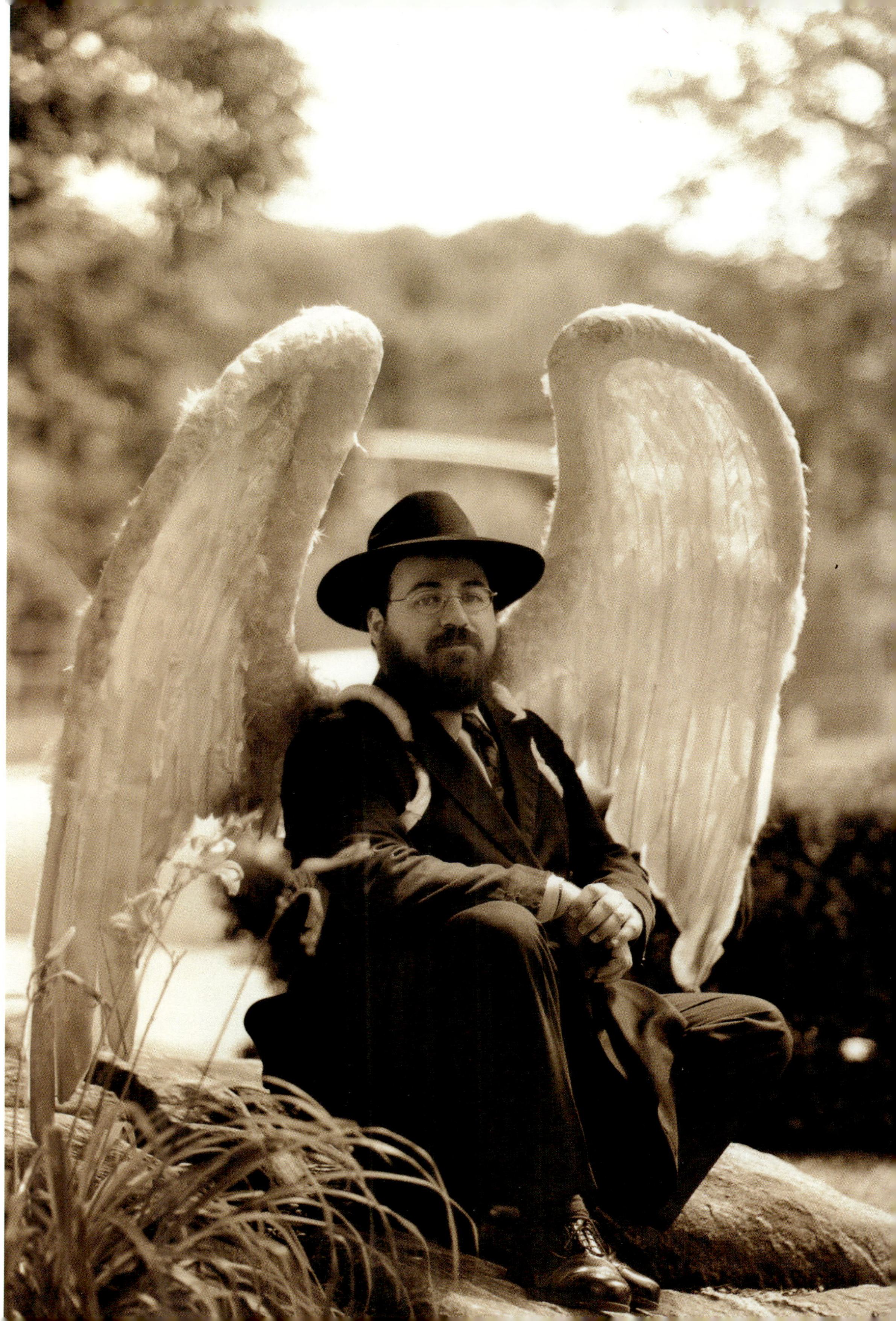

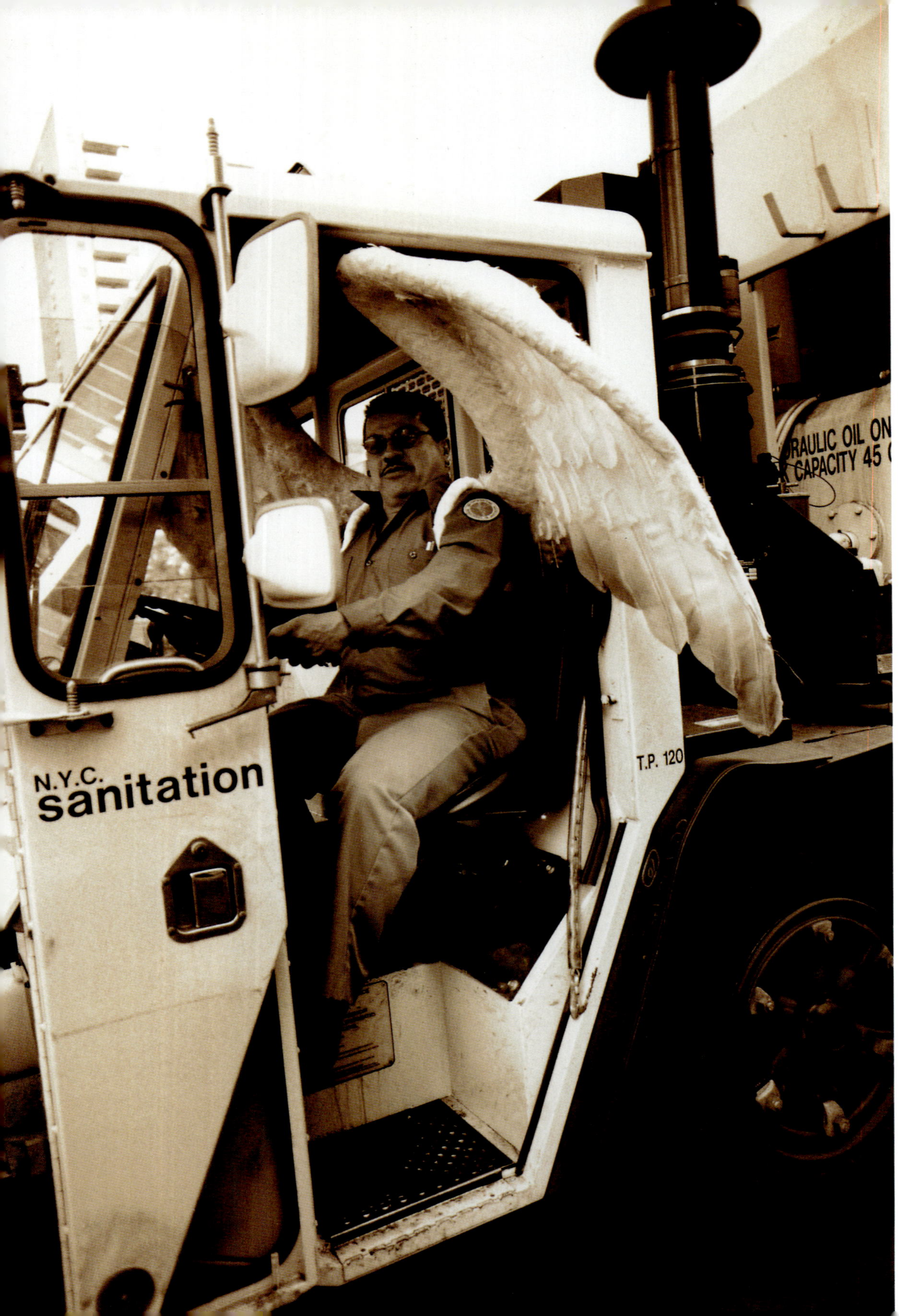


thou shalt not kill

**ismael**
spain

to be with my wife and
the three kids
is peace to me
seeing them smile and
laugh is peace to me

**robert**
italy

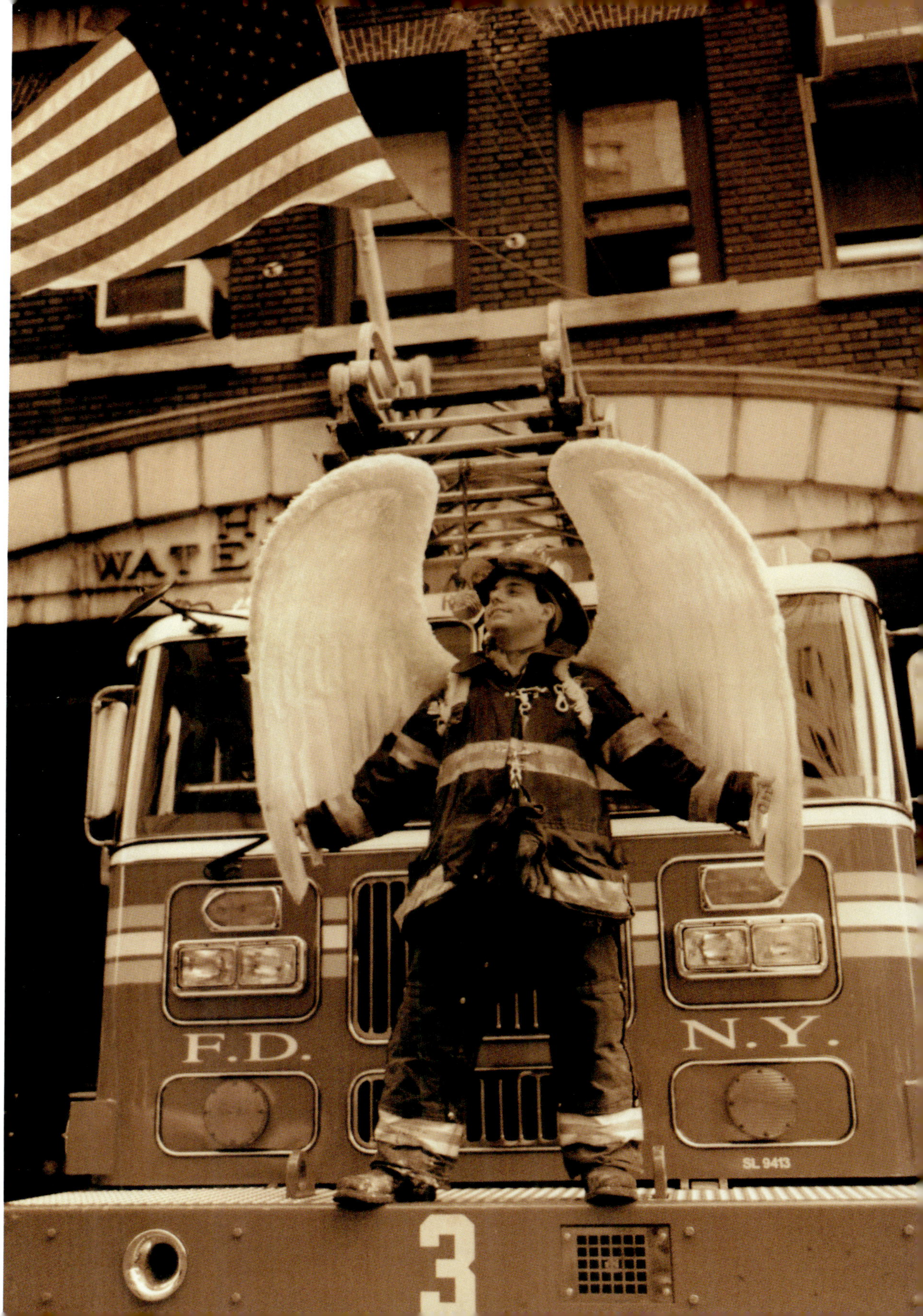

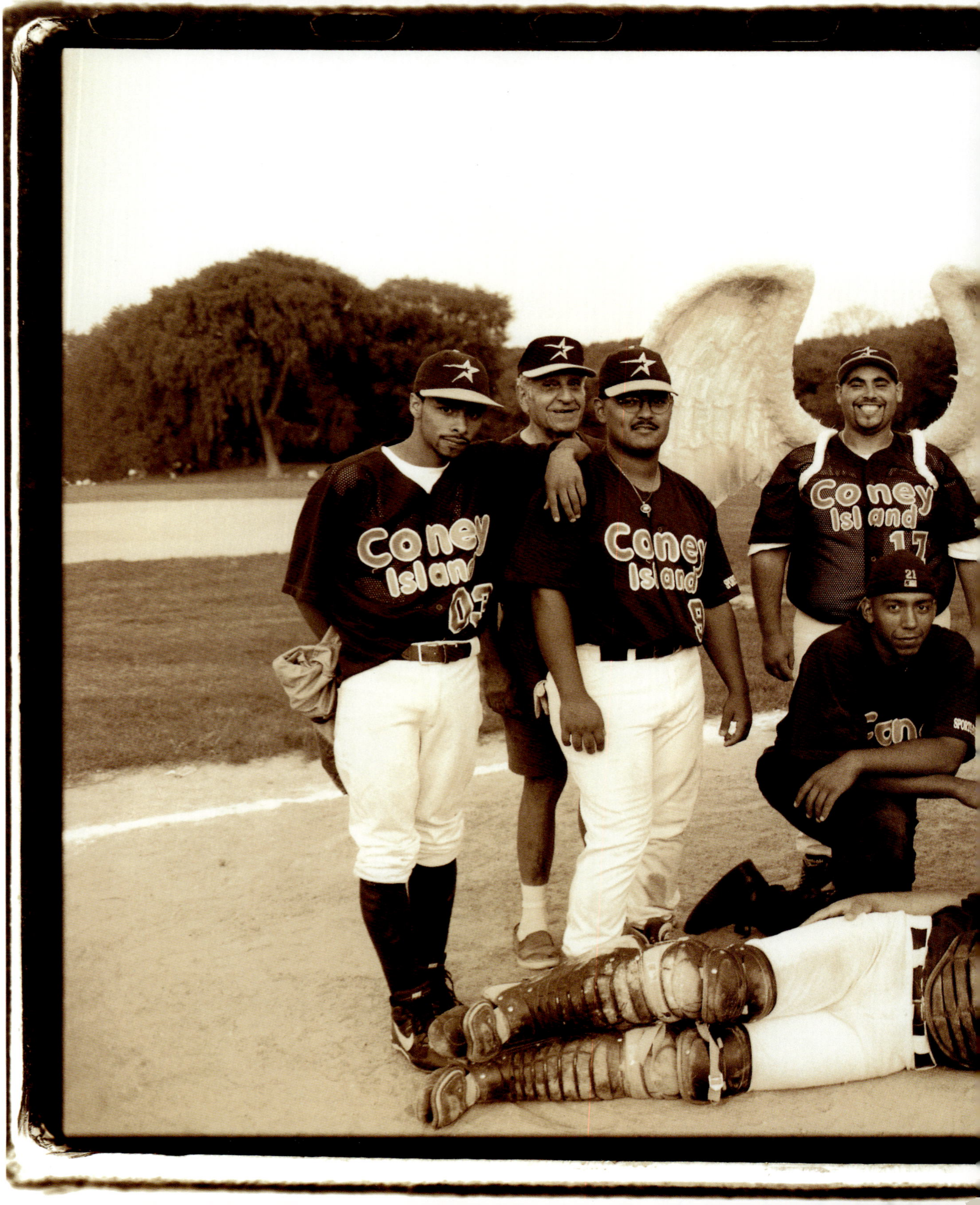
Coney Island
Coney Island
Coney Island

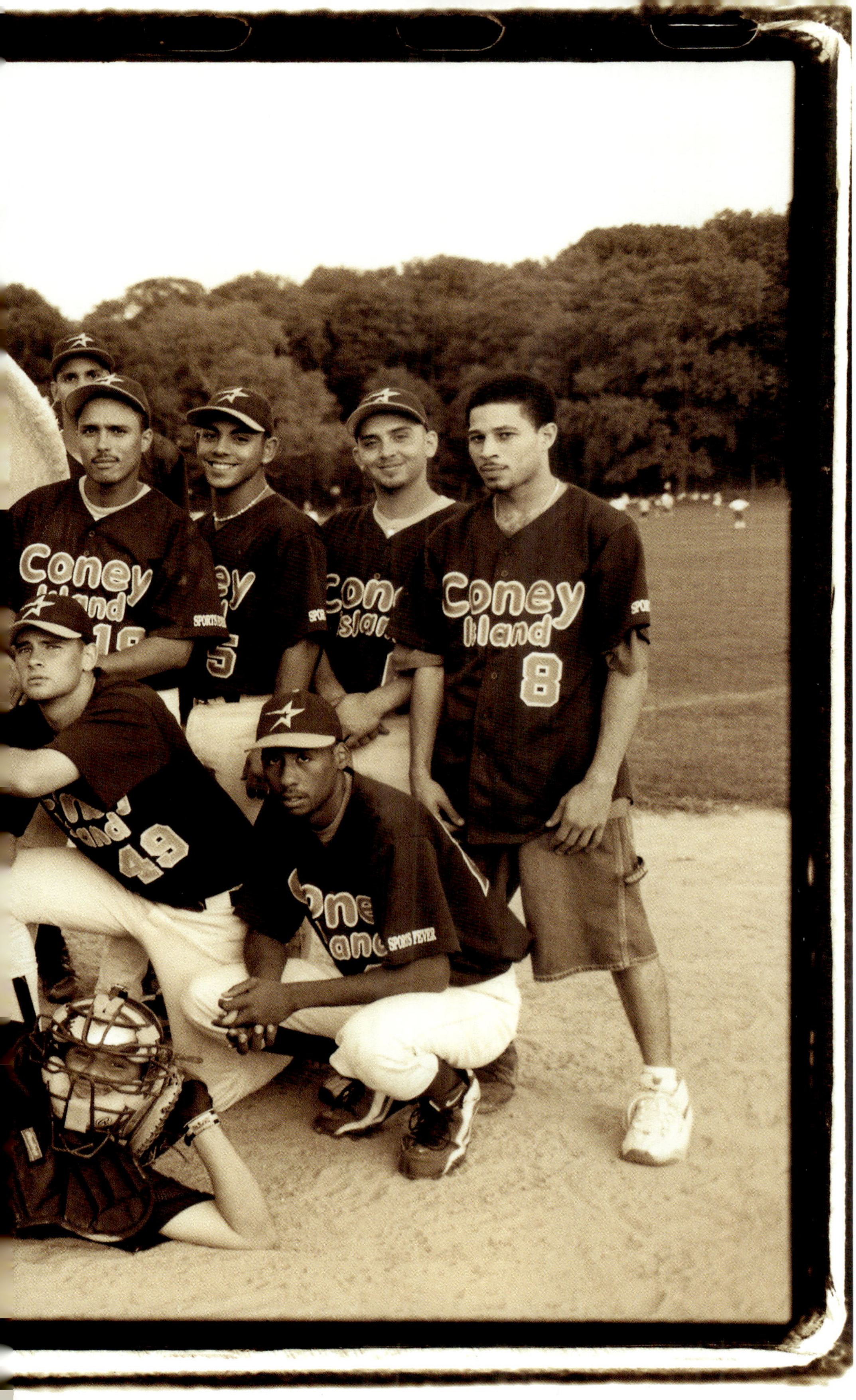


we think of
peace as teamwork

**andrew and his team**
brooklyn

peace is something
that man will always
be searching for

**joe & anna**
ukraine

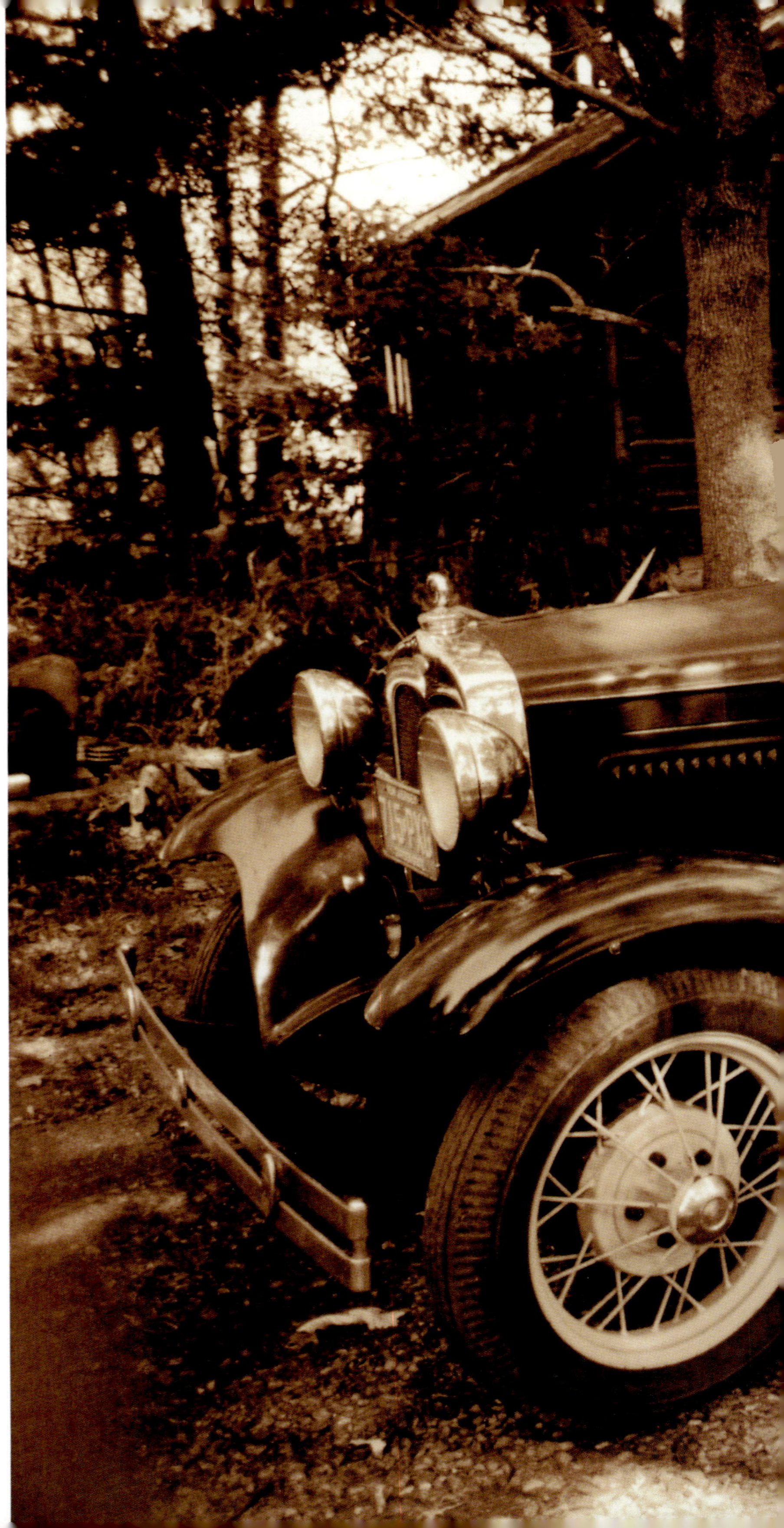

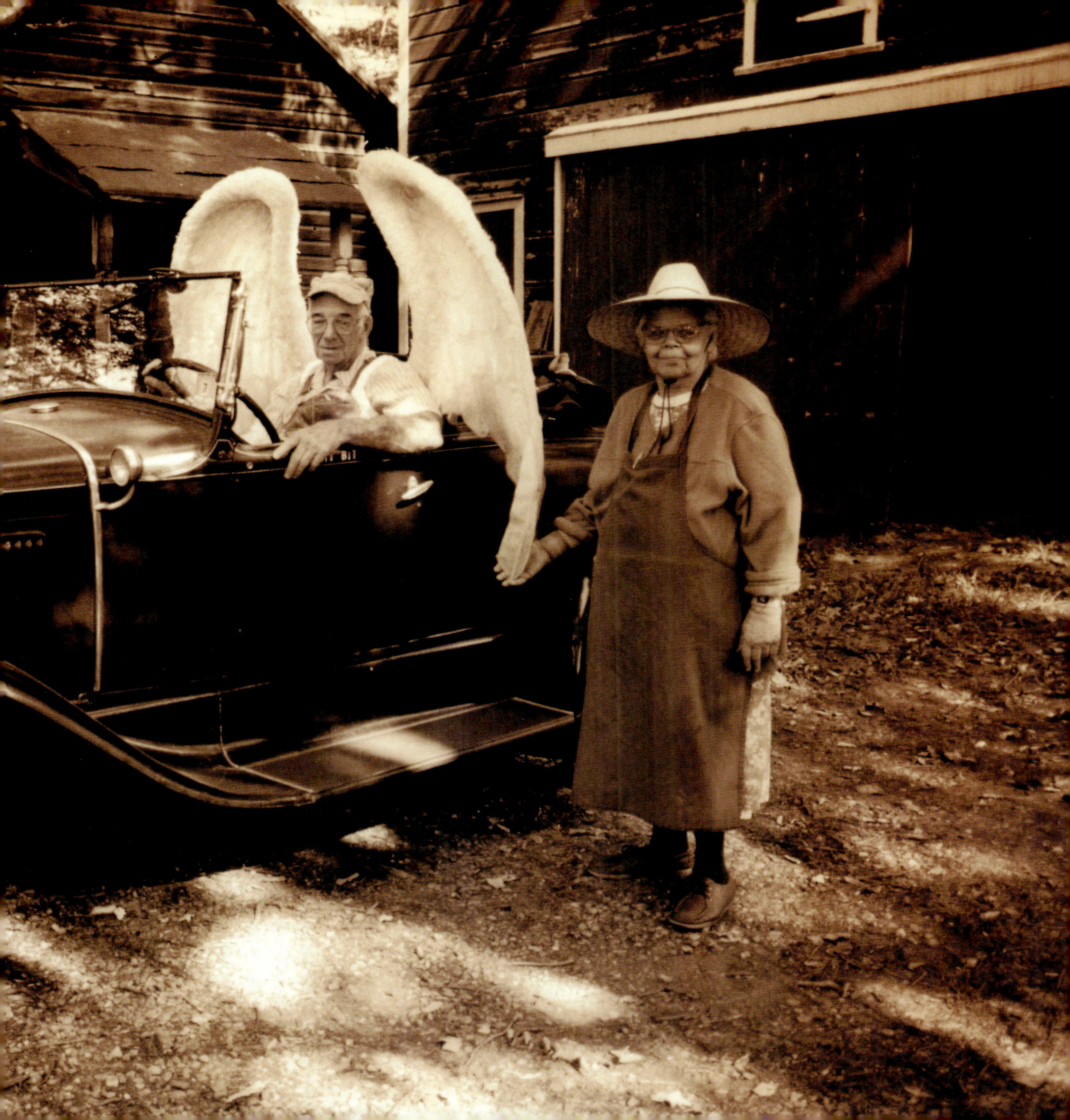

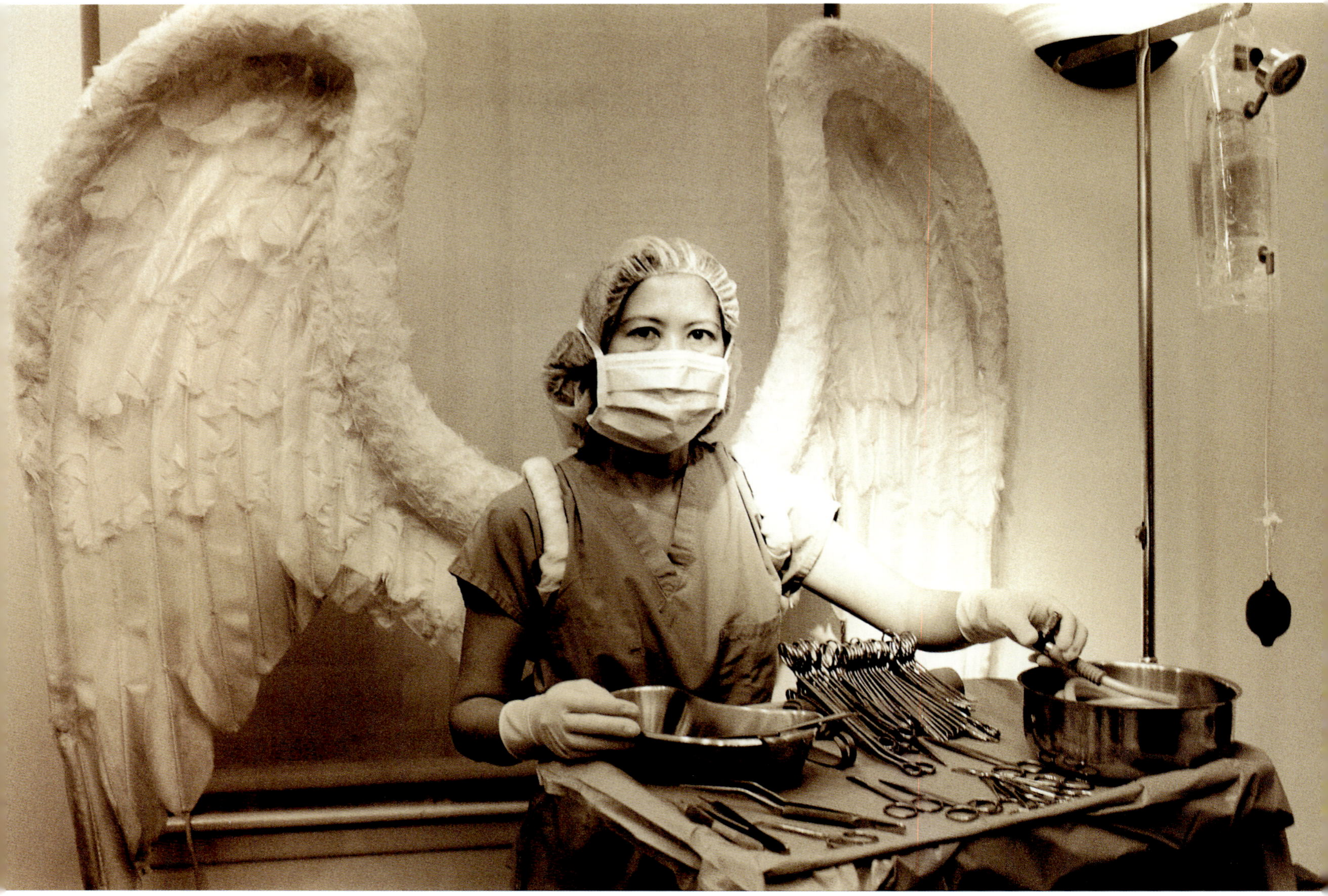

**fatima**
philippines

peace is a family gathering for a meal
smiles and happy faces

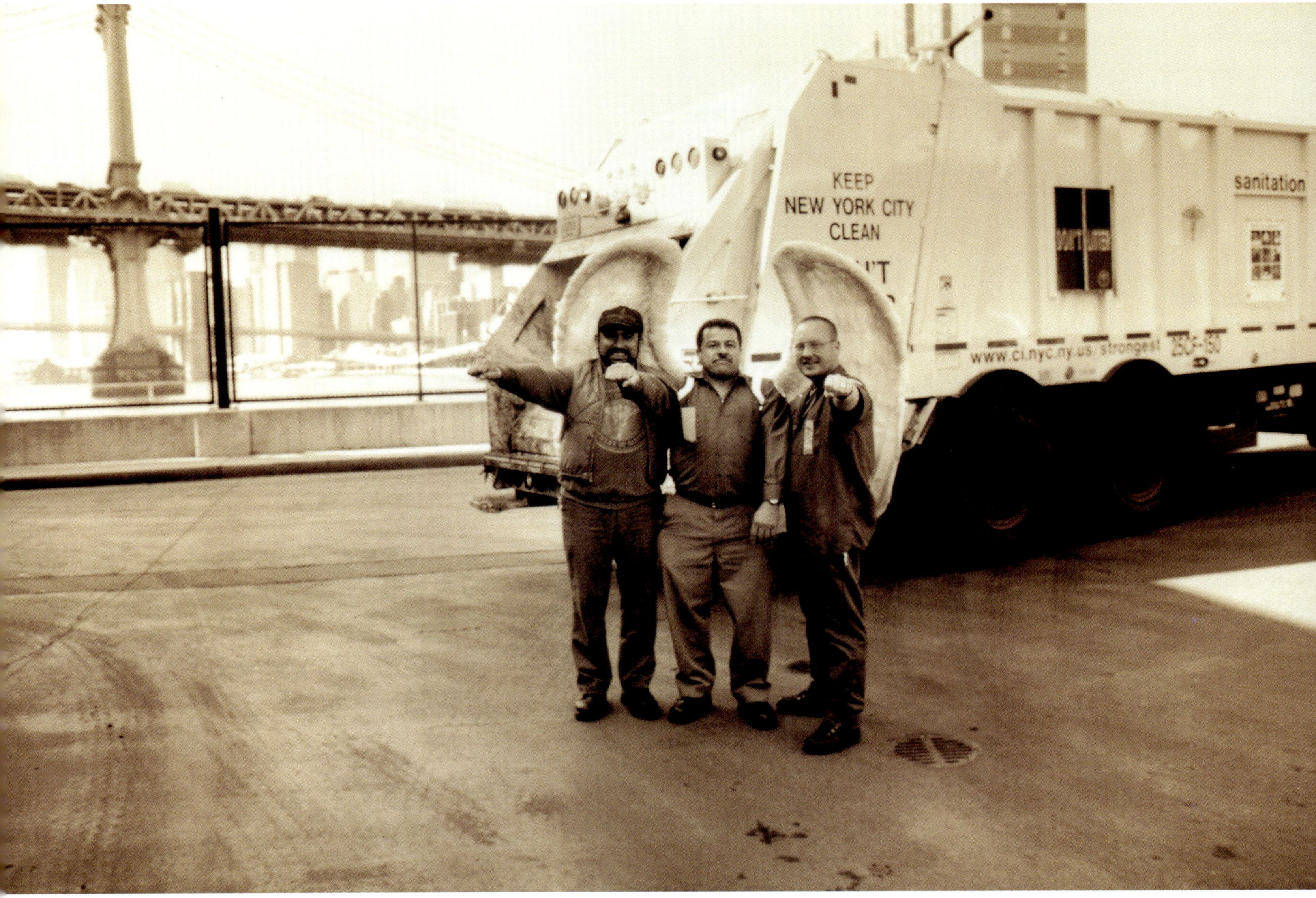


**department of sanitation**
new york city

peace can only be found in the soul today
perhaps one day the people of the world
can share their peace together

**william**
hungary

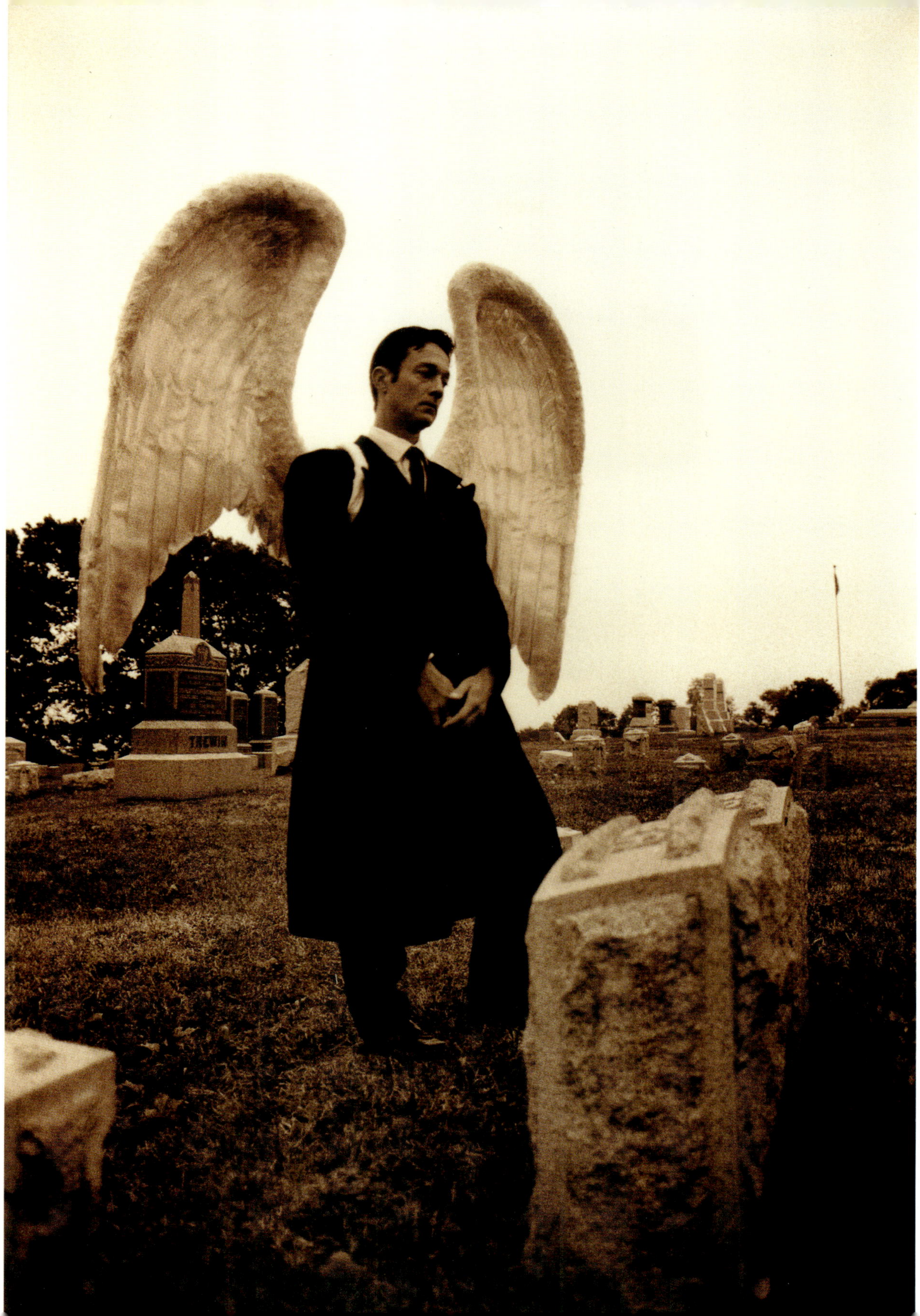
TREWIN

there will never
be peace on earth
until anyone can
go into any deli in the
world and order a
ham sandwich

**roberto**
mexico

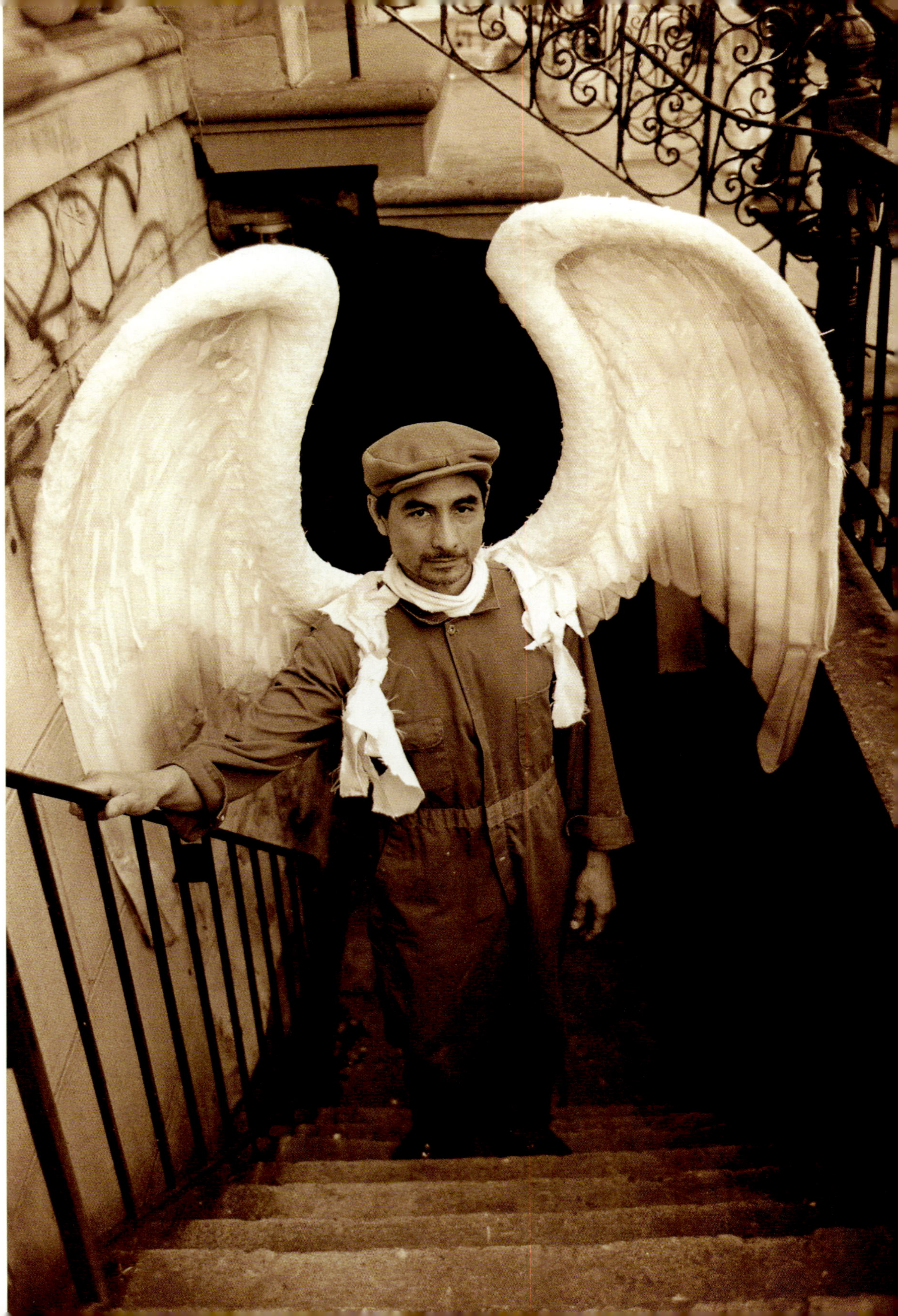

peace is different
to different people

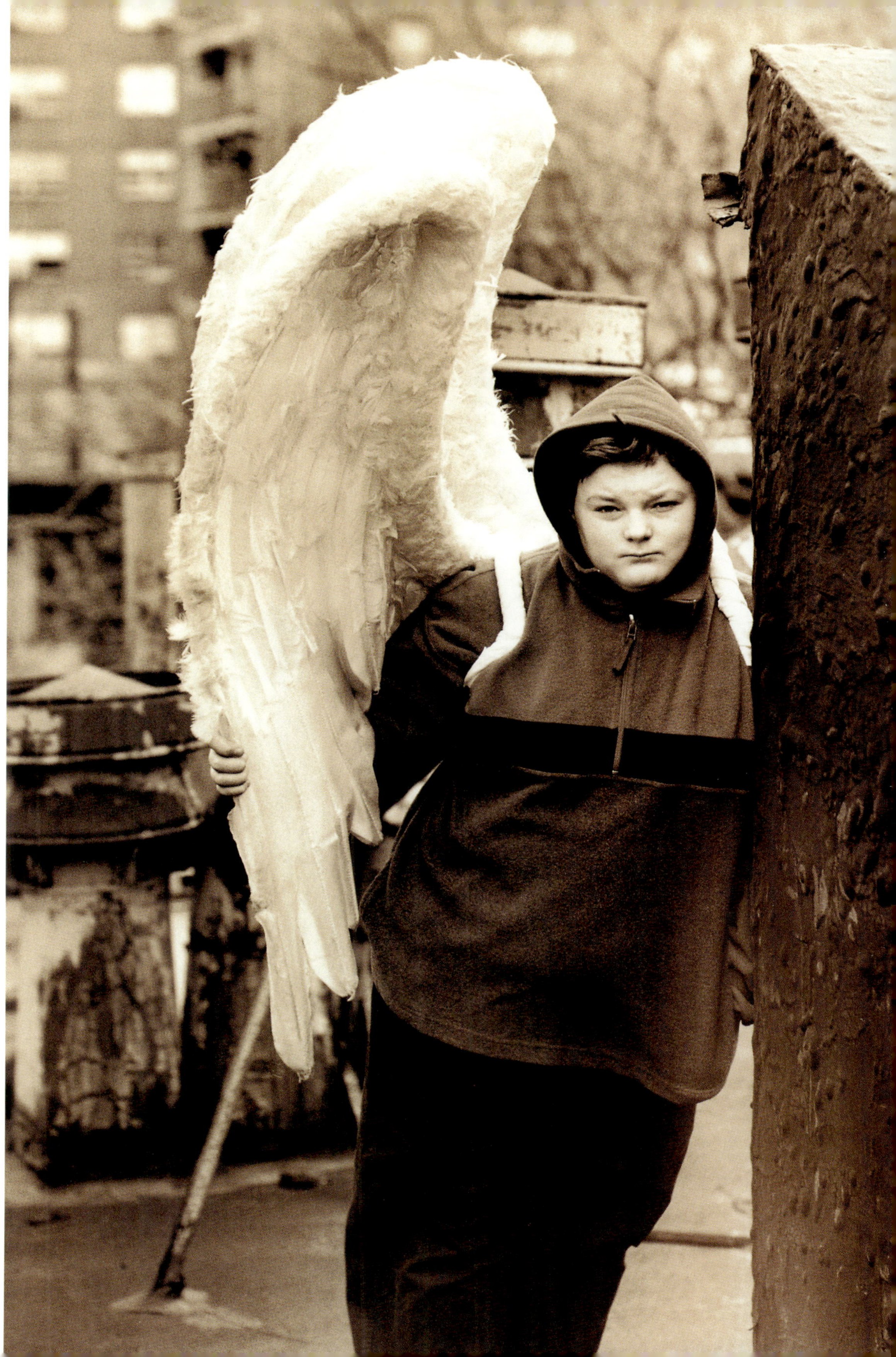

**jordan**
germany

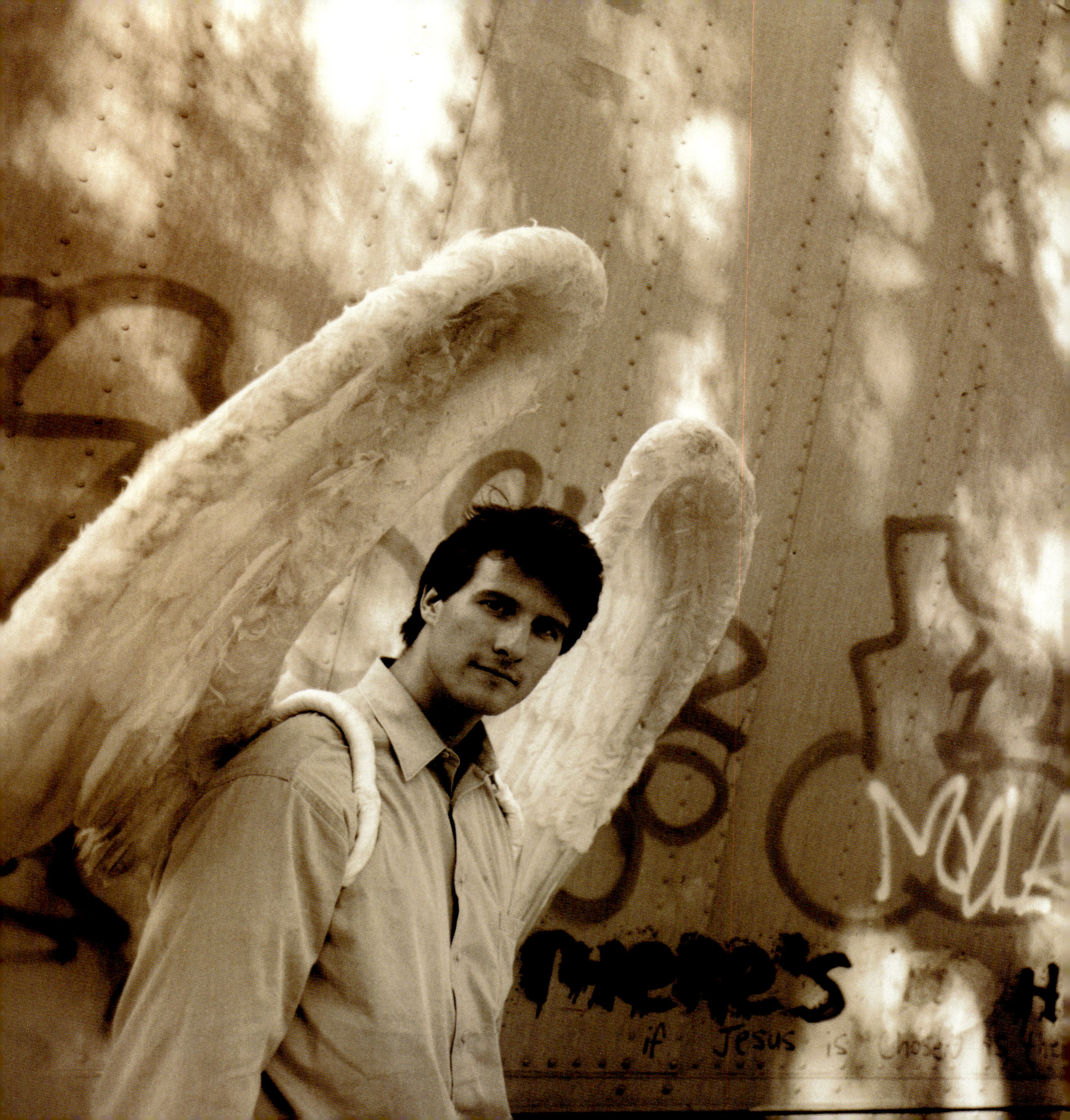
if Jesus is

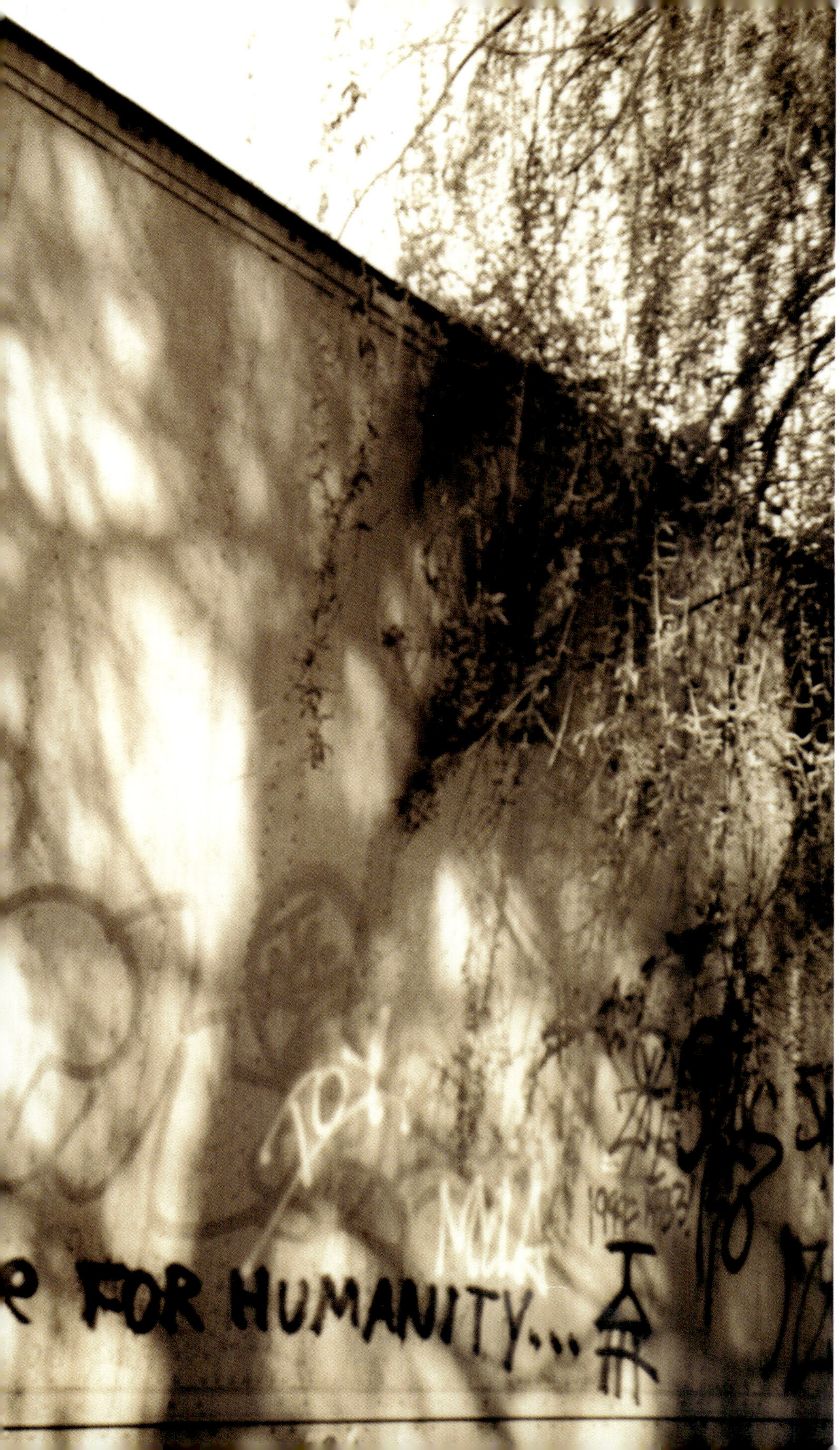


there is hope for humanity
if people continue to be inspired
to smile at a total stranger
passing in the street

**uros**
slovenia

i am
american
native
african
human

**stephanie**
blackfoot
new york city

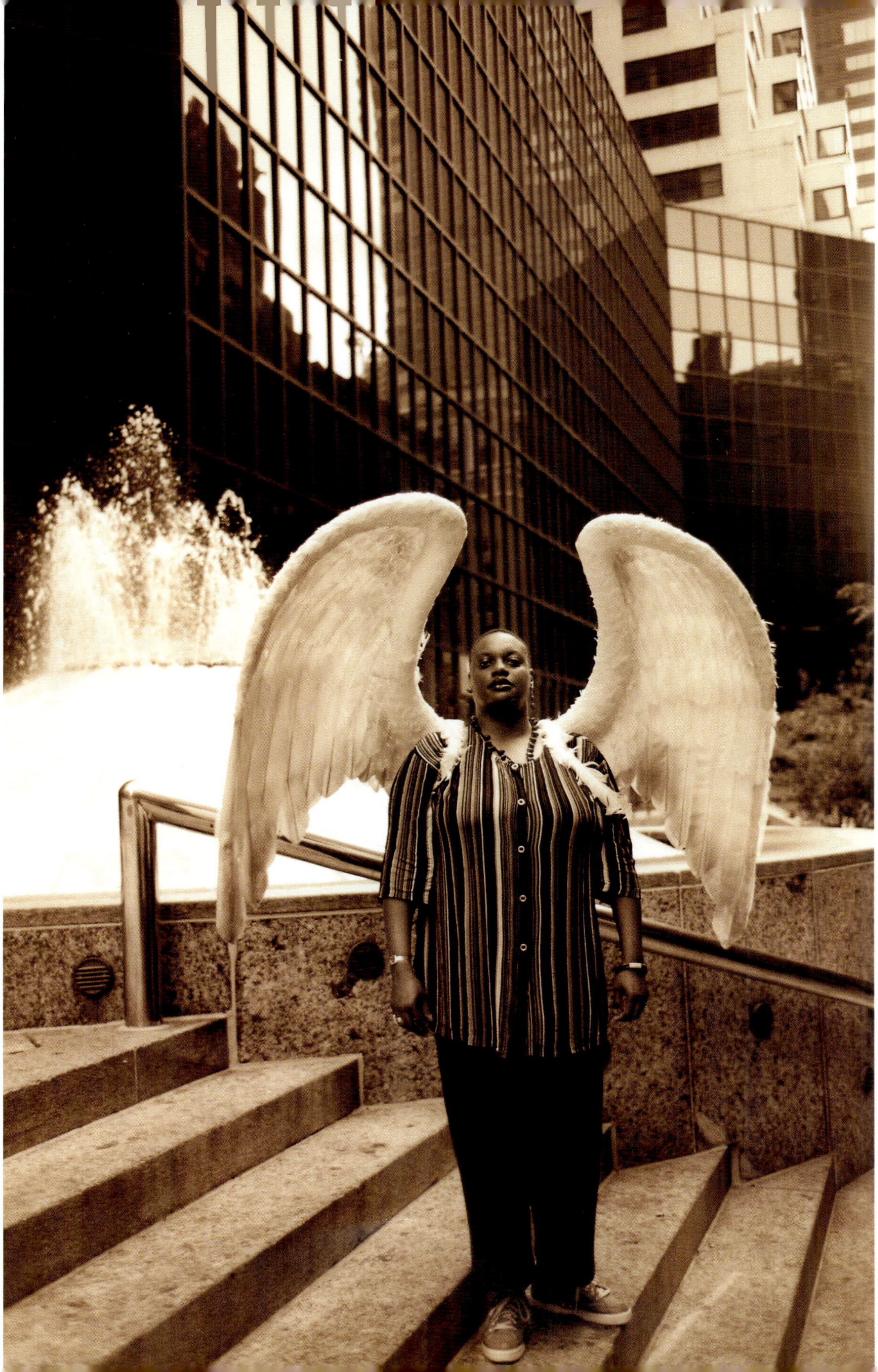

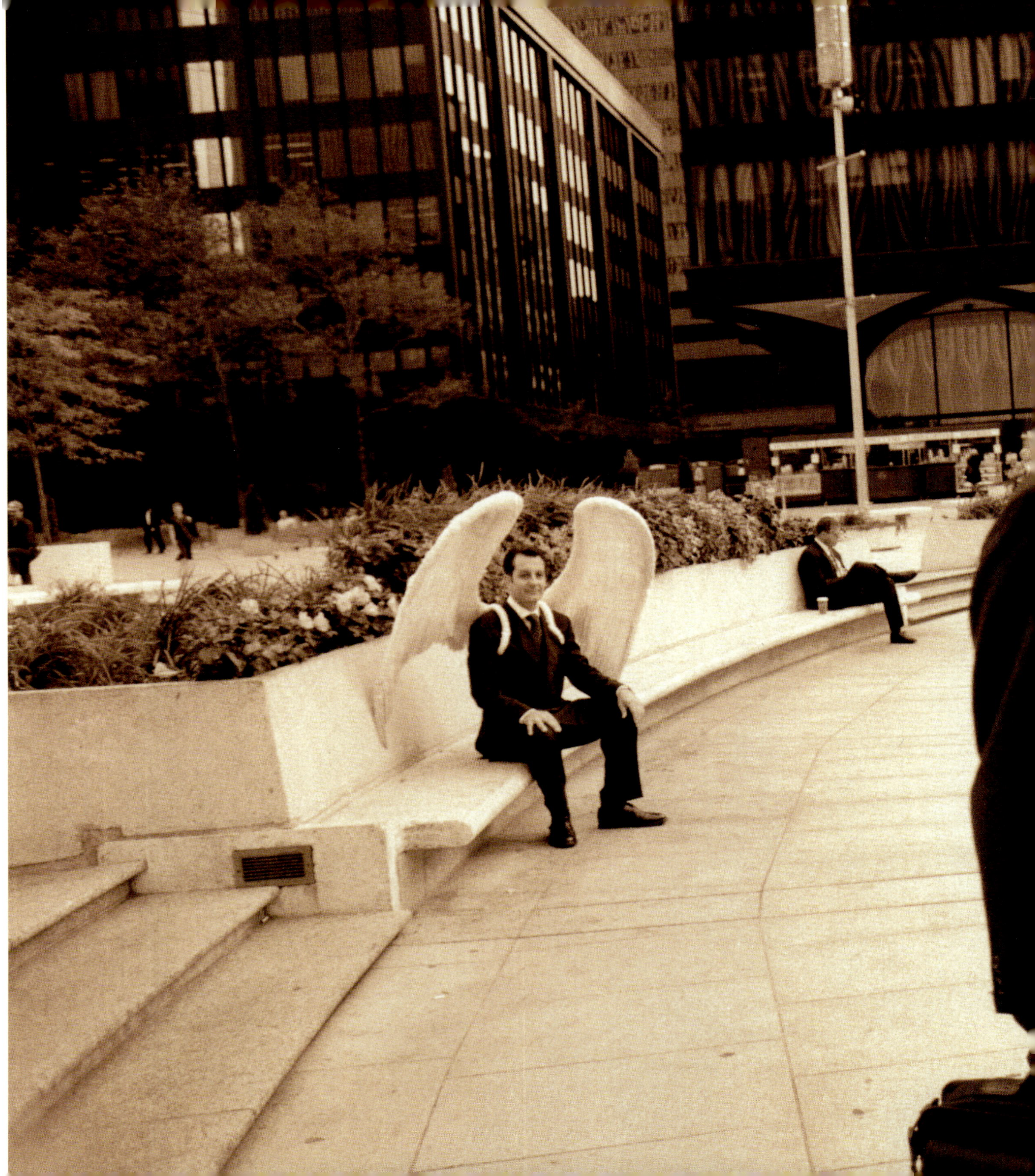

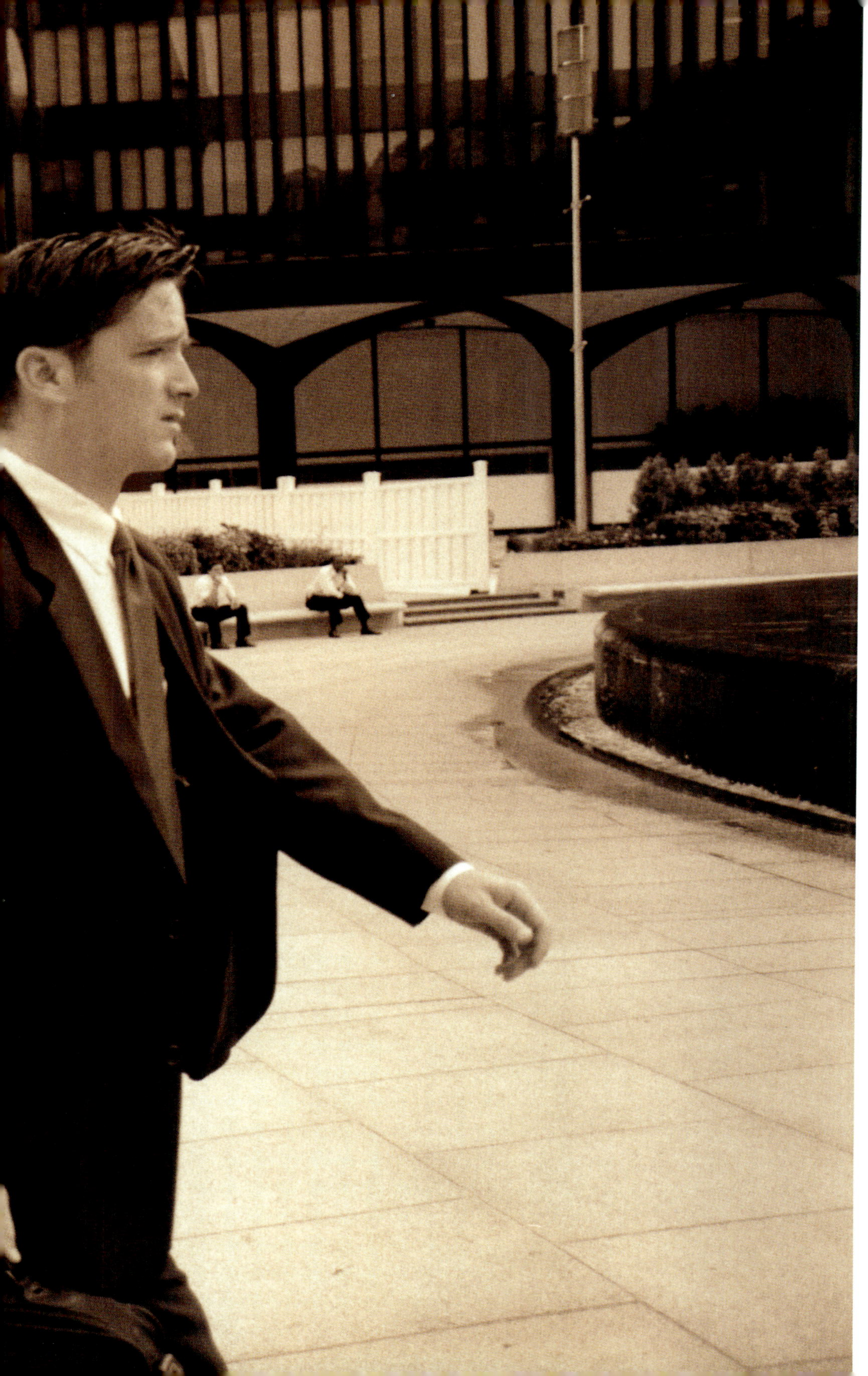

nationalism
human greed
and the hatred towards the
ones who are different from us
are the nemeses
of peace

**juan josé**
argentine

peace is
a fairy tale

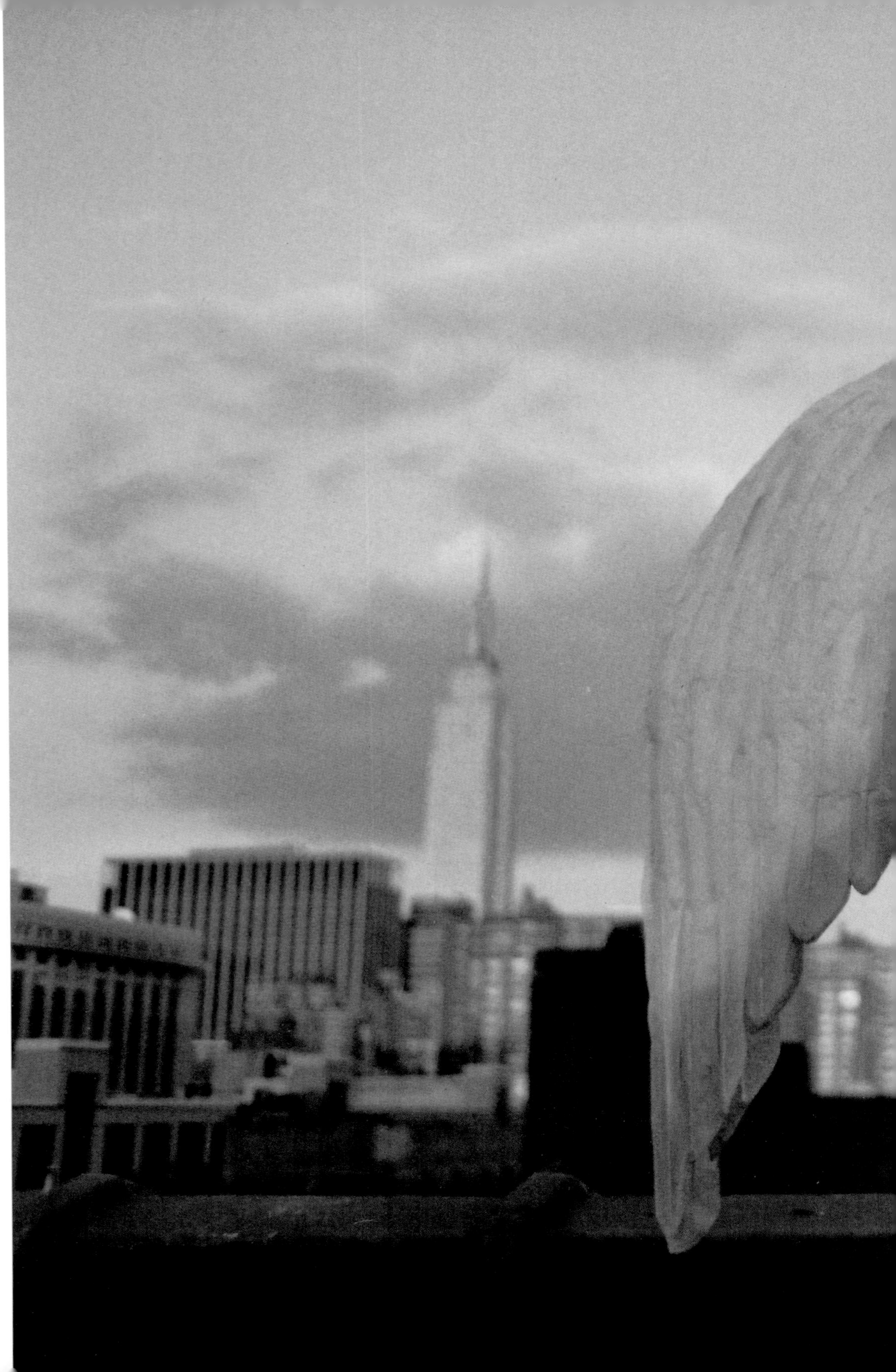

**troy**
ireland

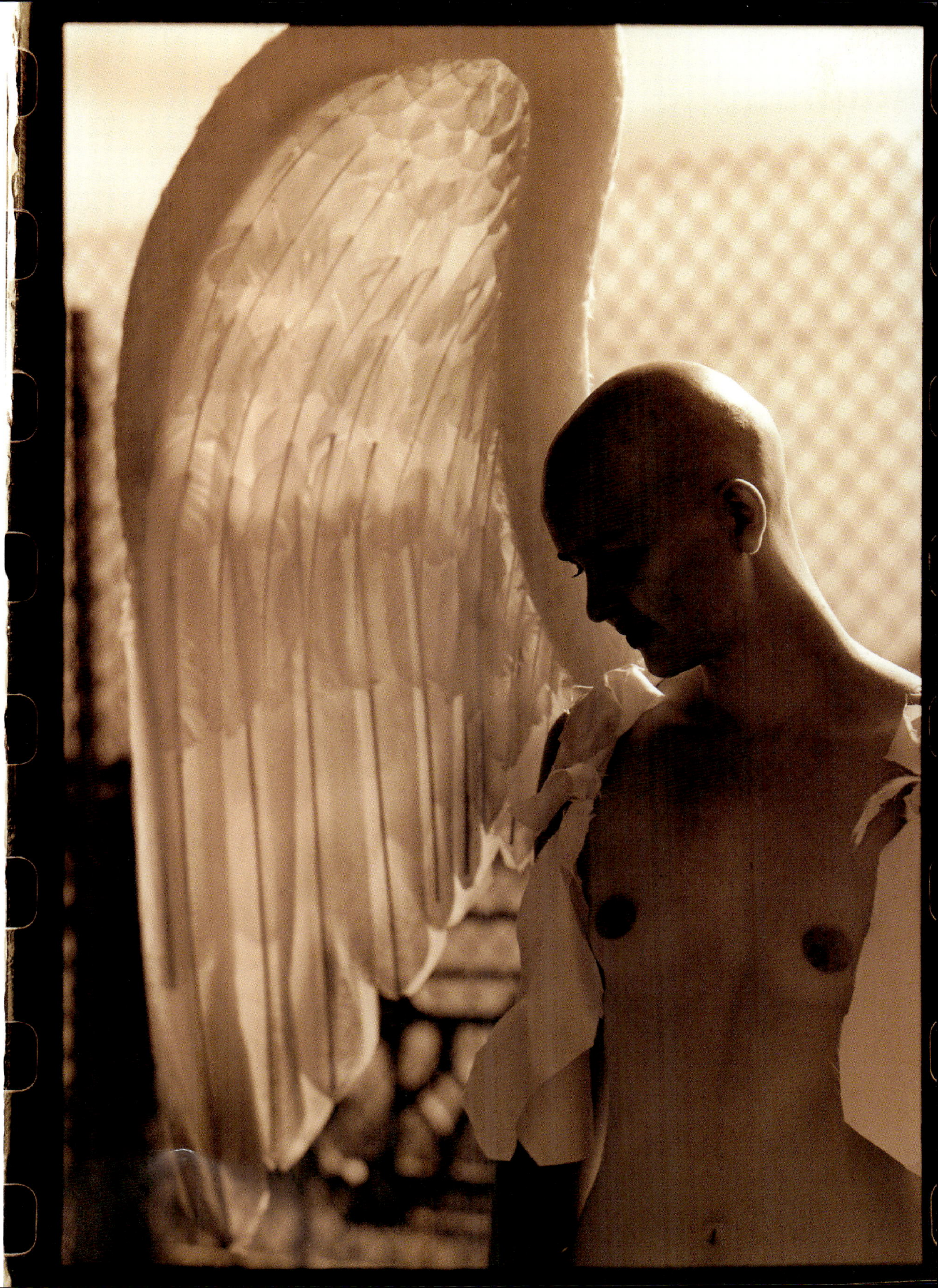

**pru**
australia

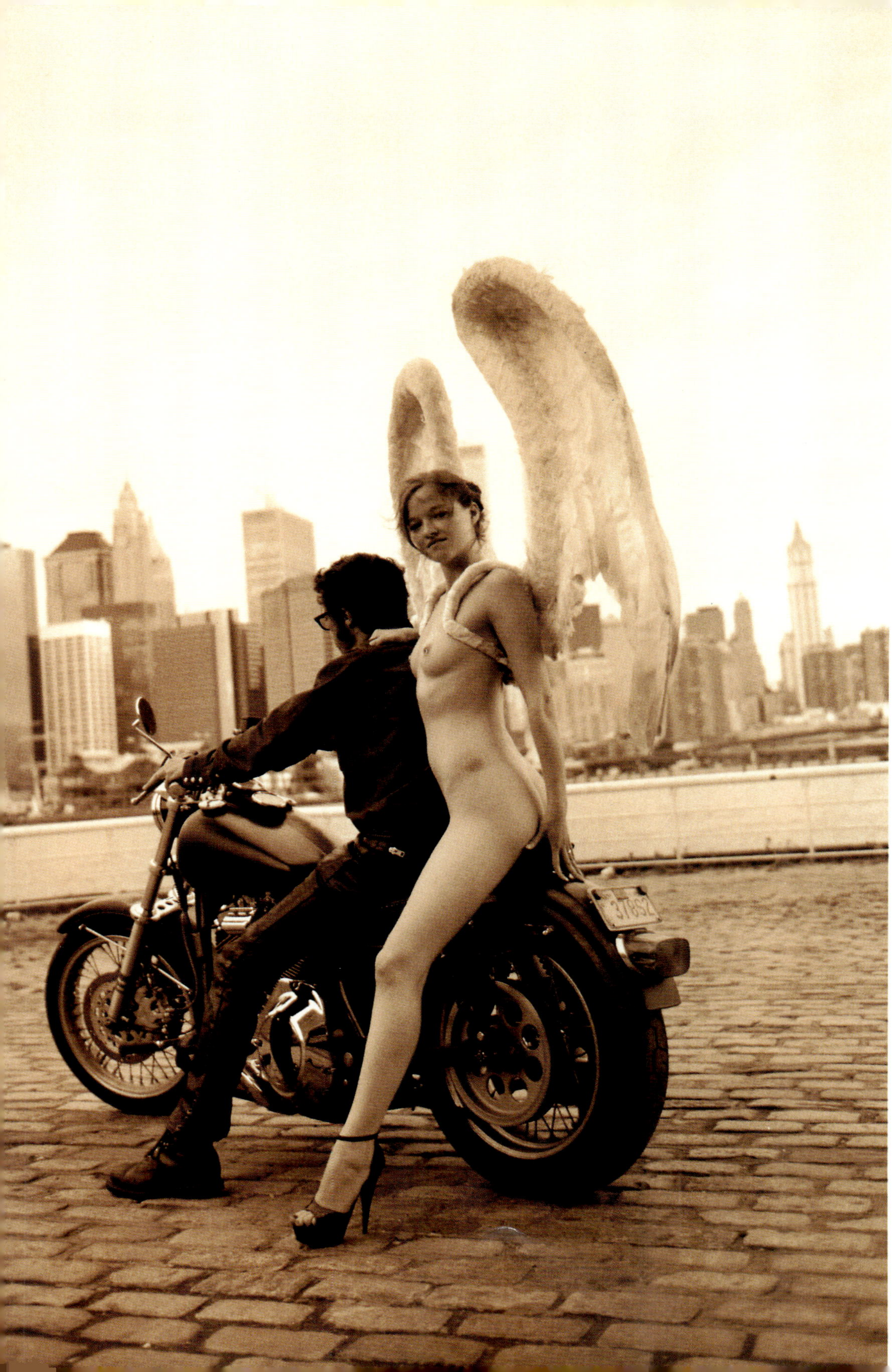

being able to do that
with tom
is all i need
to feel peace

**chrissie & tom**
usa & germany

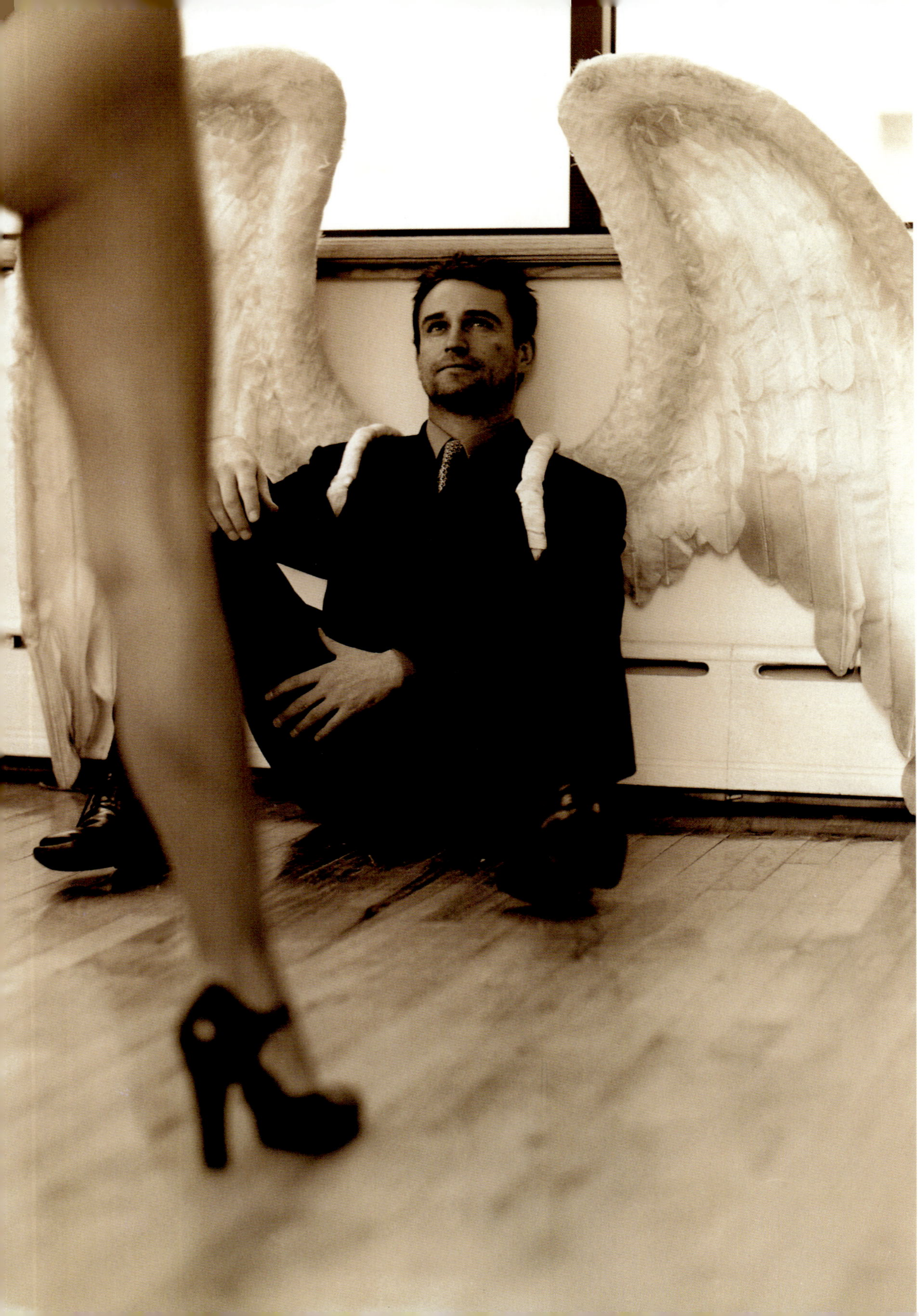

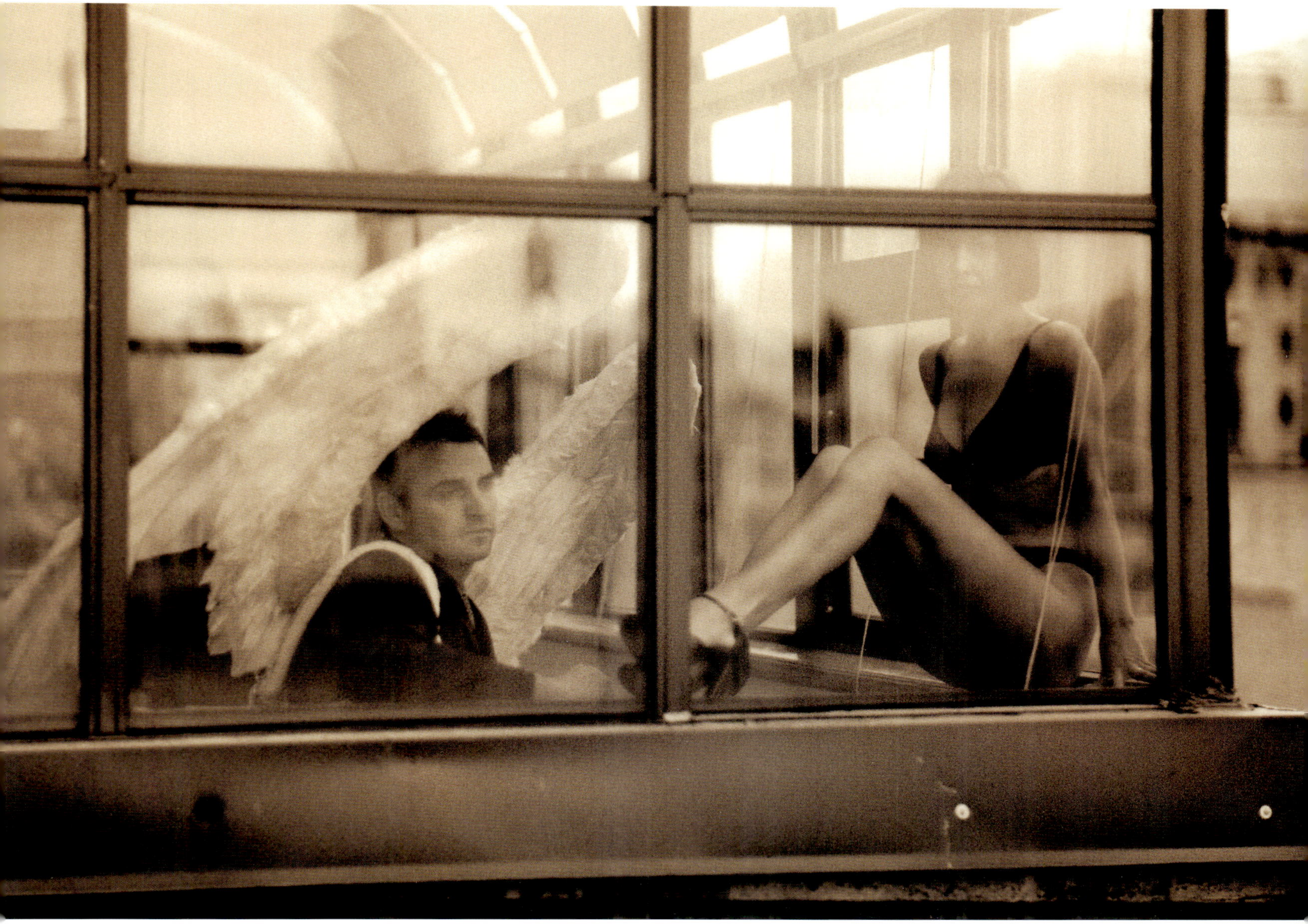

freedom is the universe of love

**emma & charles**
new zealand

come to me angel
once you appeared
outside my bedroom window
i saw myself out there
a strangely familiar self
evoked in pure presence
met in a state
of unification and peace

**rikke**
denmark

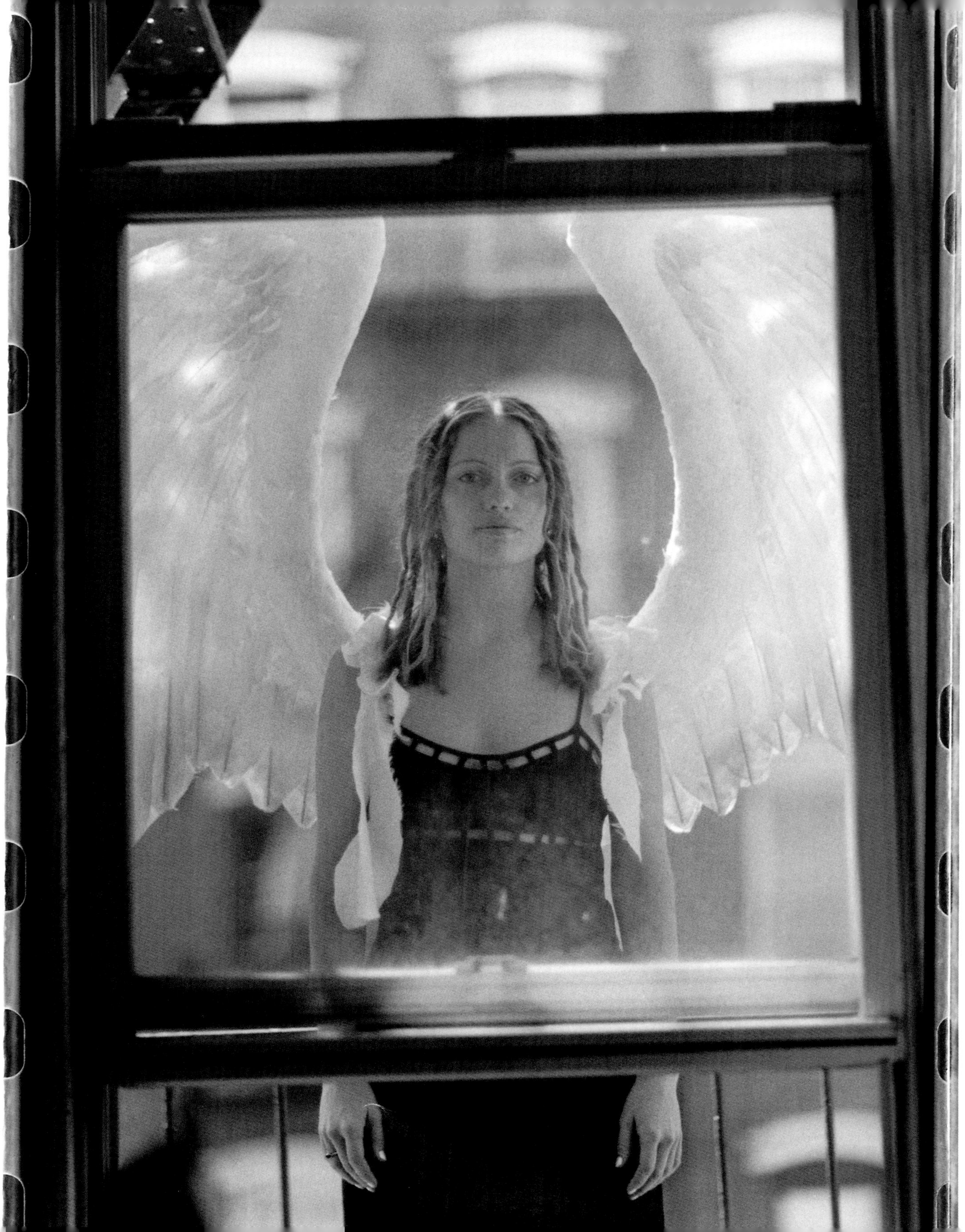

peace is a state of mind
that we all have to find sooner or later
because the world that we live in
does not offer it naturally

**lupino**
croatia

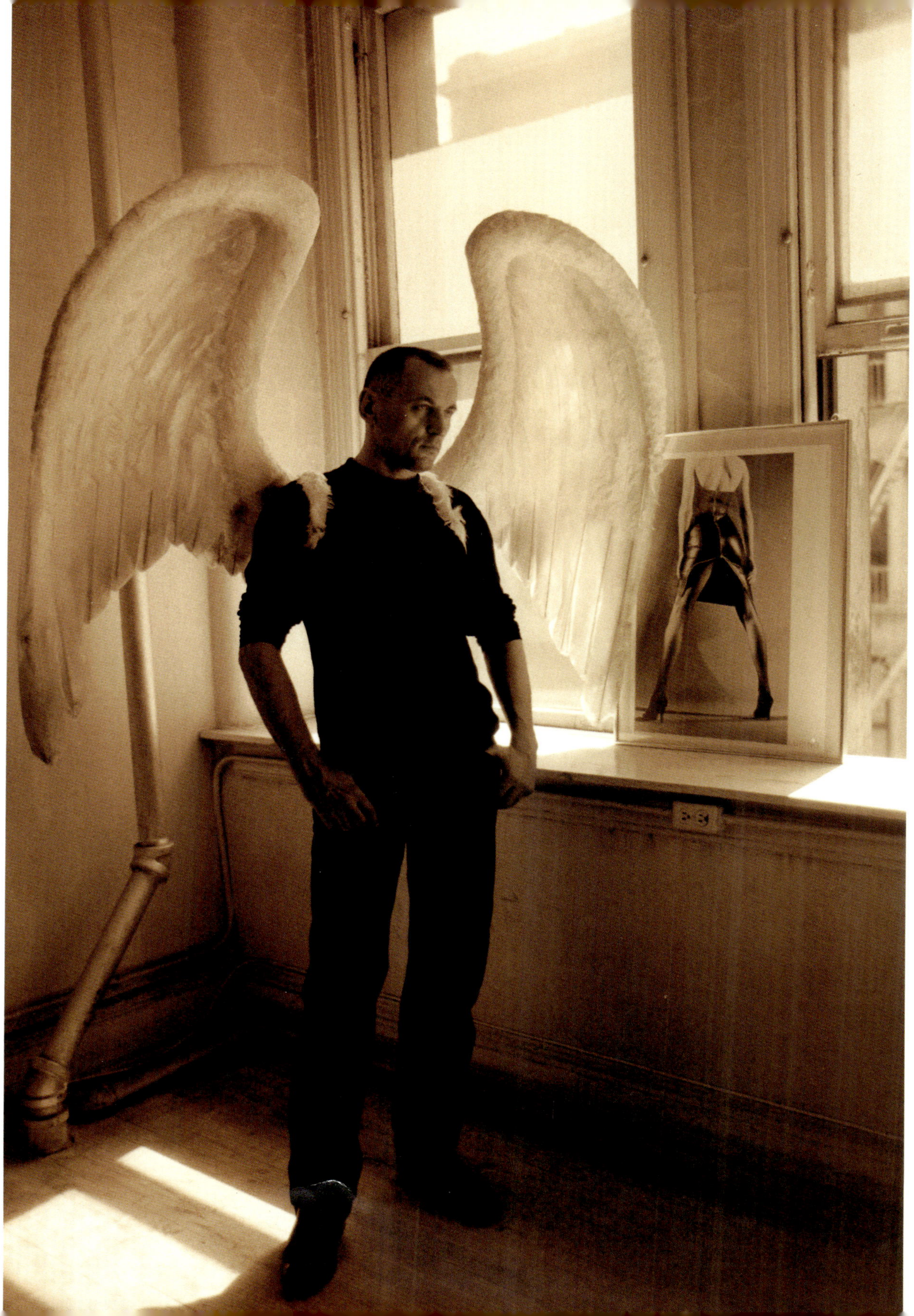

peace starts at one place
in your head
in my head

**emily**
sweden

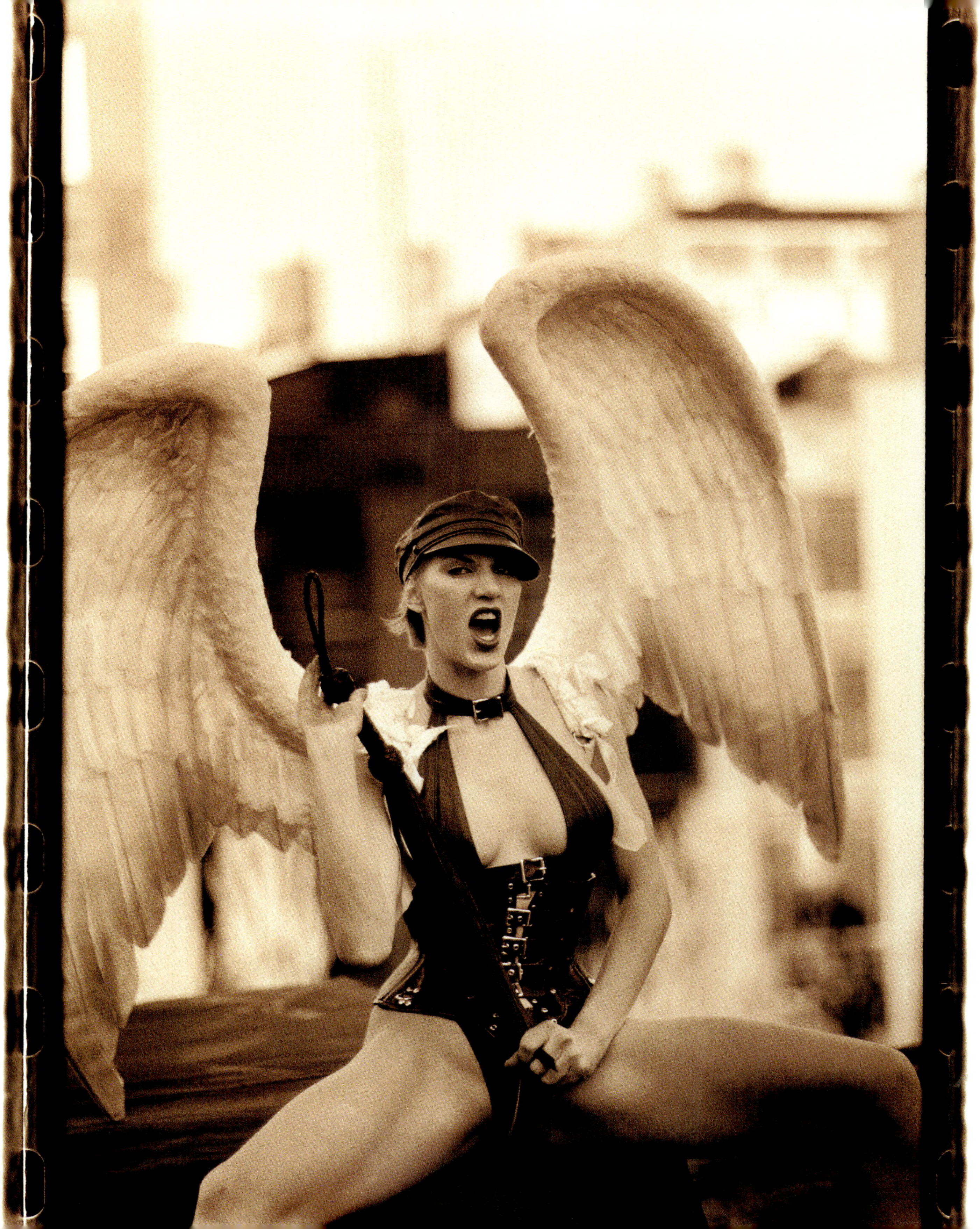

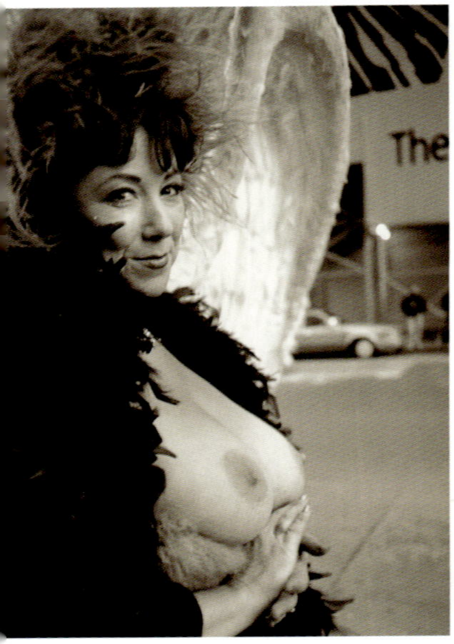
The

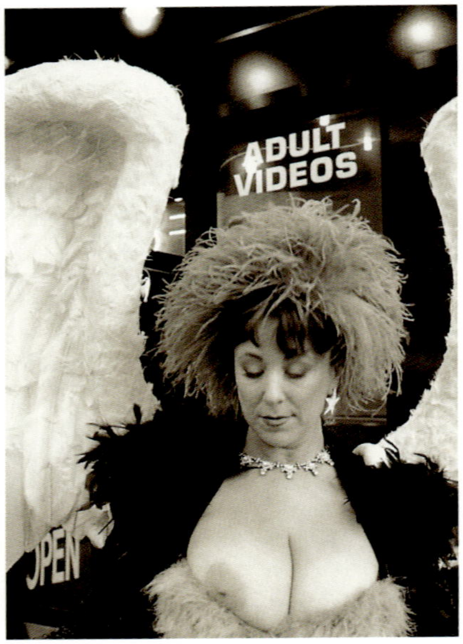
ADULT
VIDEOS
OPEN

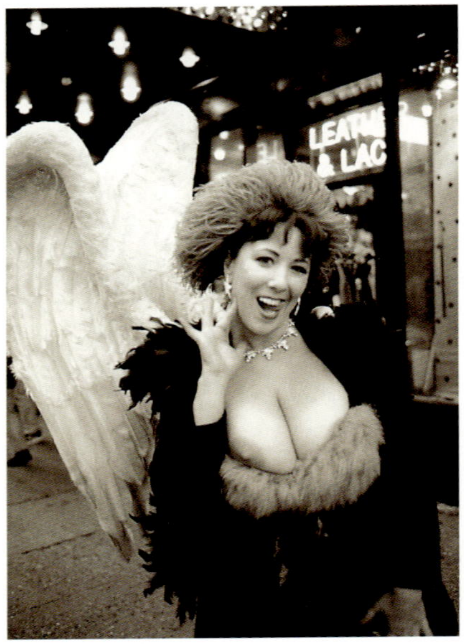

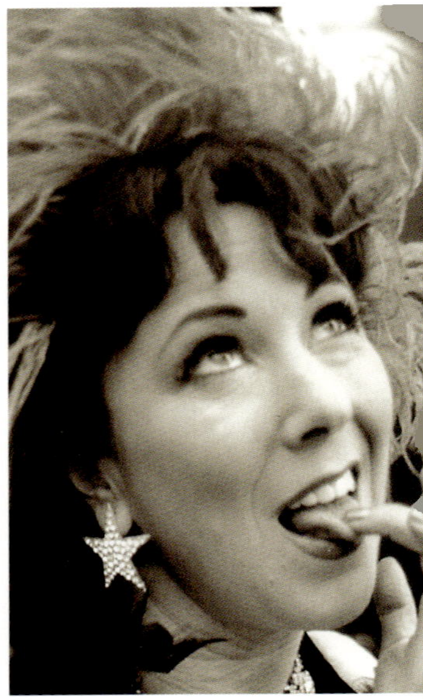

peace is erotic

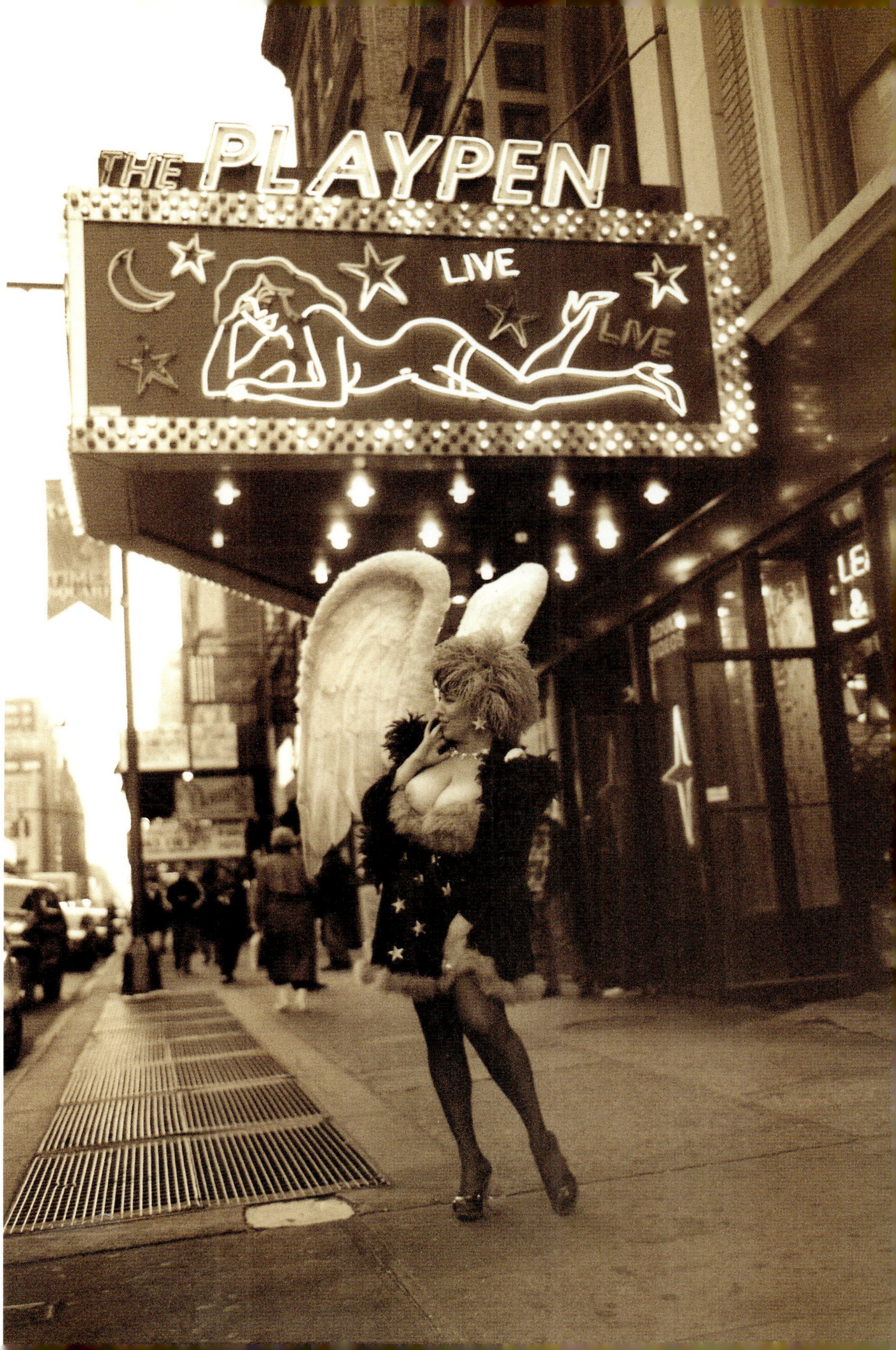


**annie sprinkle**

russia

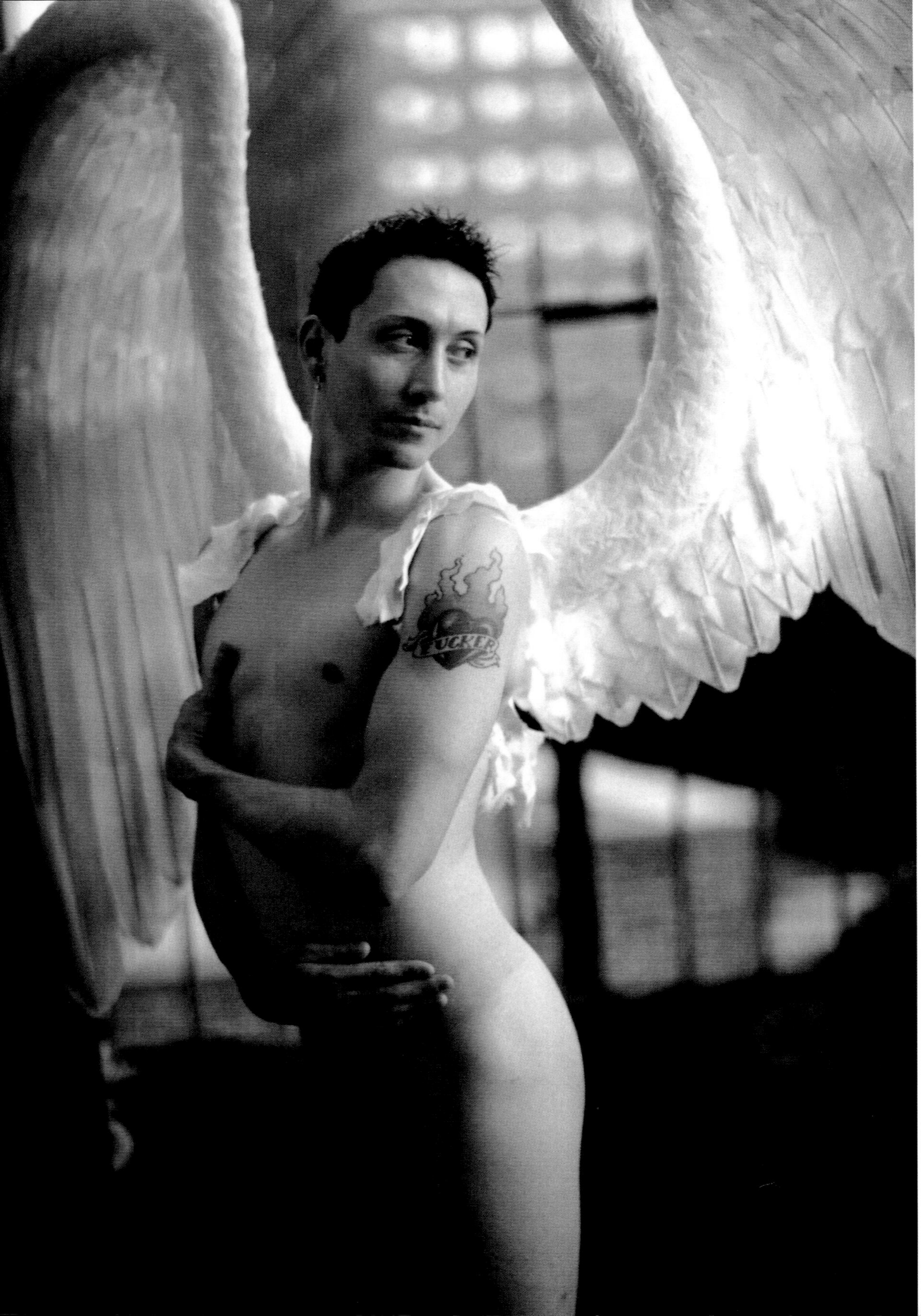

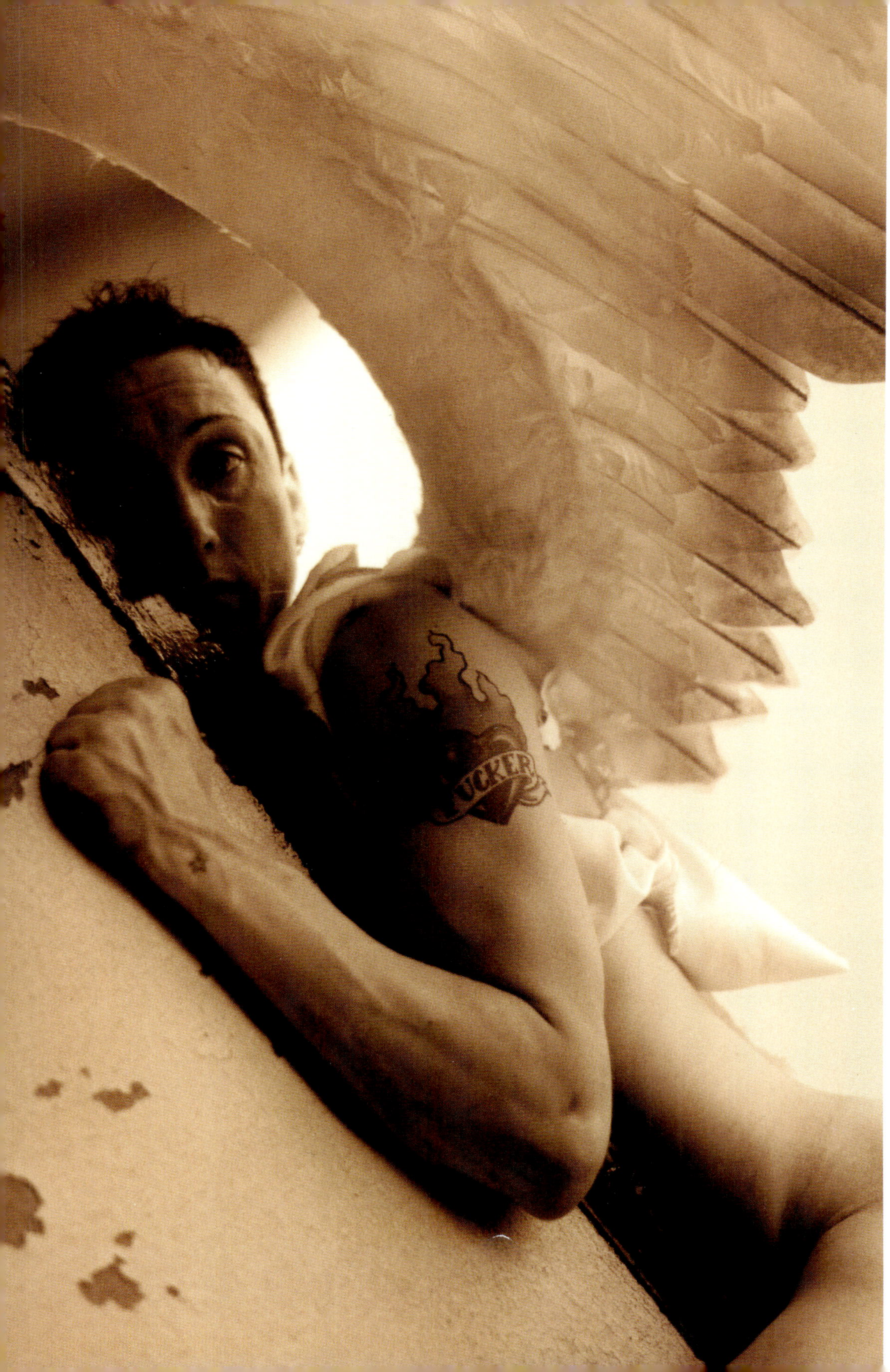

peace is
living as sinners and
feeling like saints
with no judges or juries
just the pure satisfaction
of experience

**michael**
hispanic

peace is making a new friend and
reclaiming a part of myself

**todd phillips**
scotland

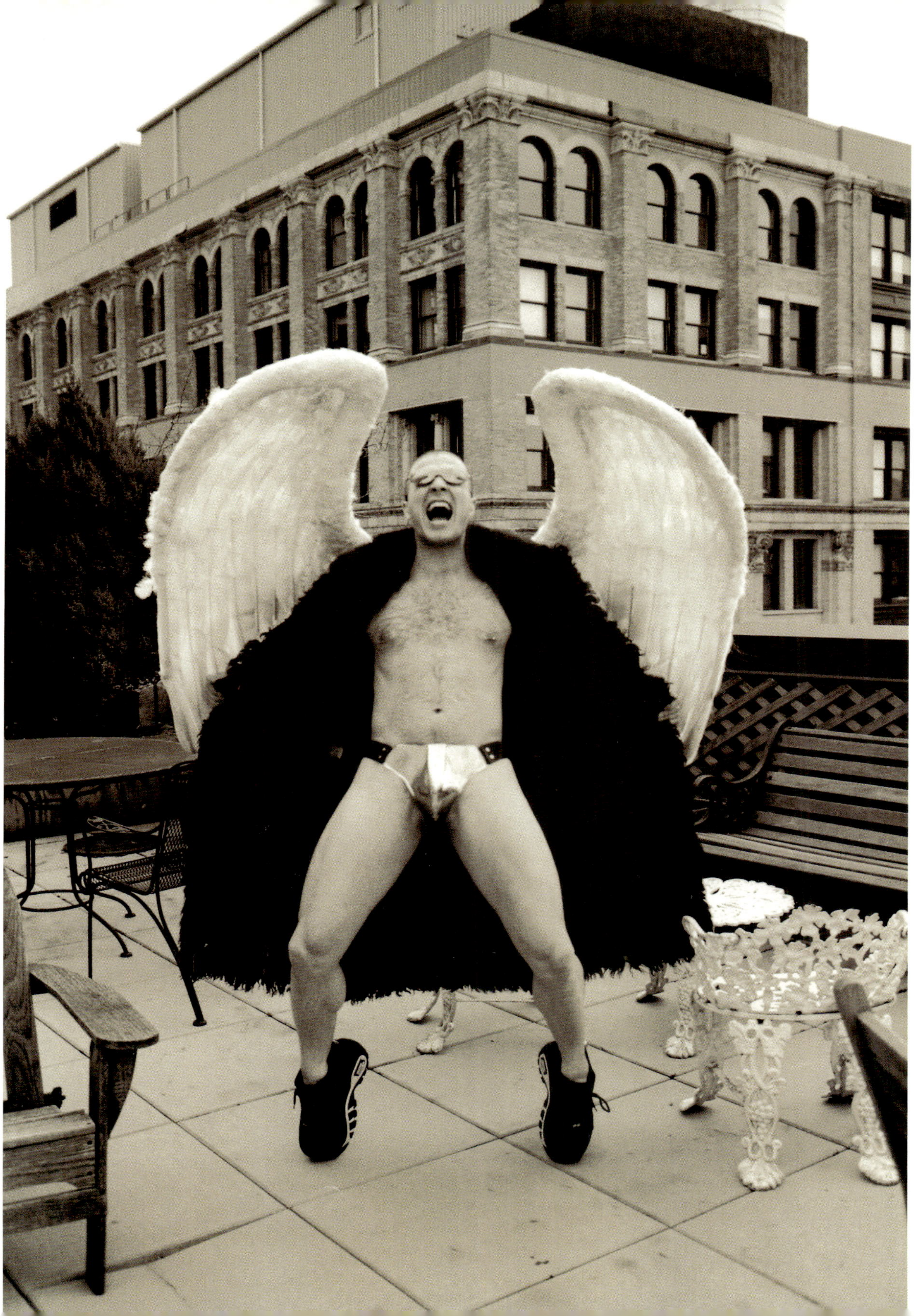

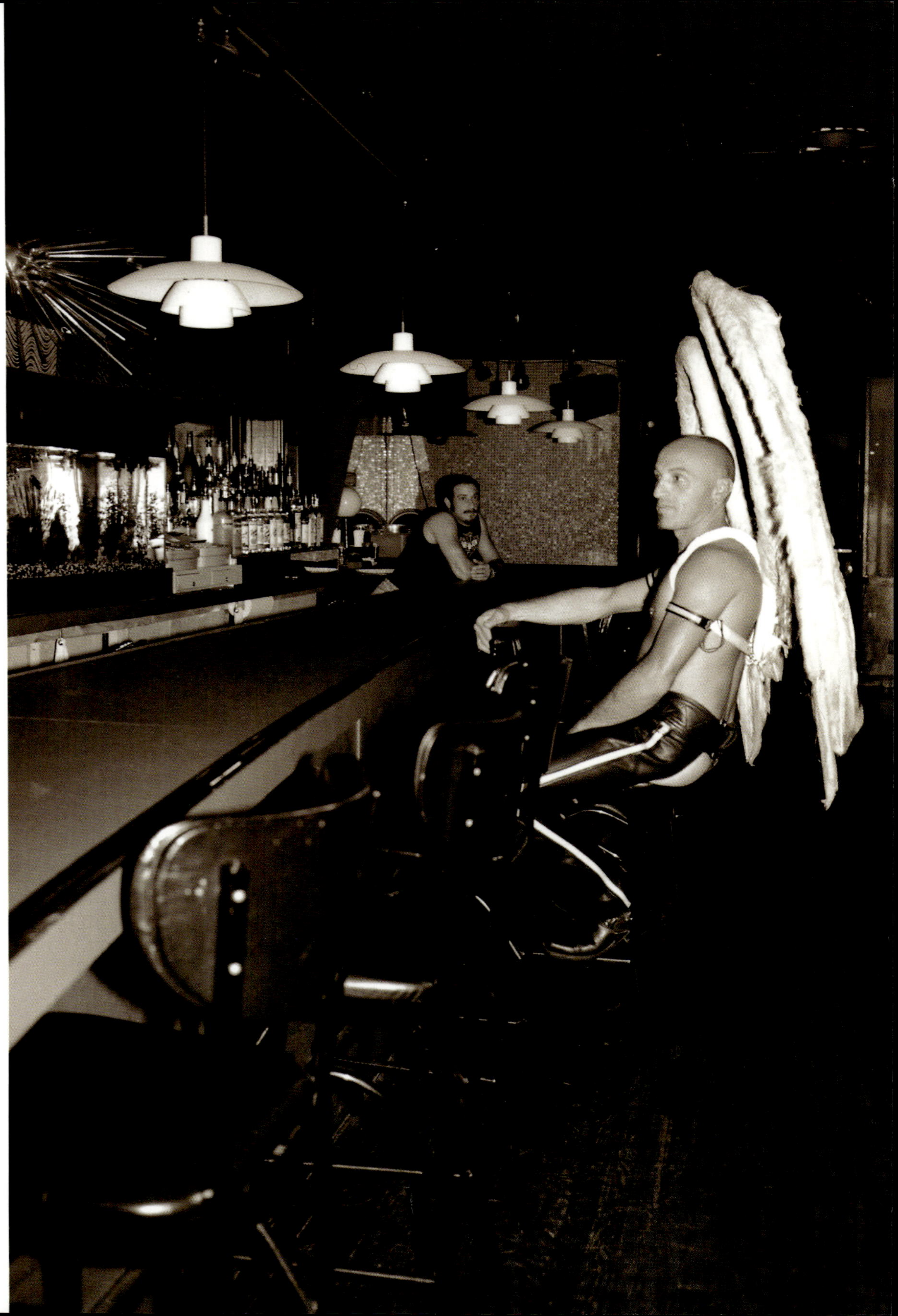

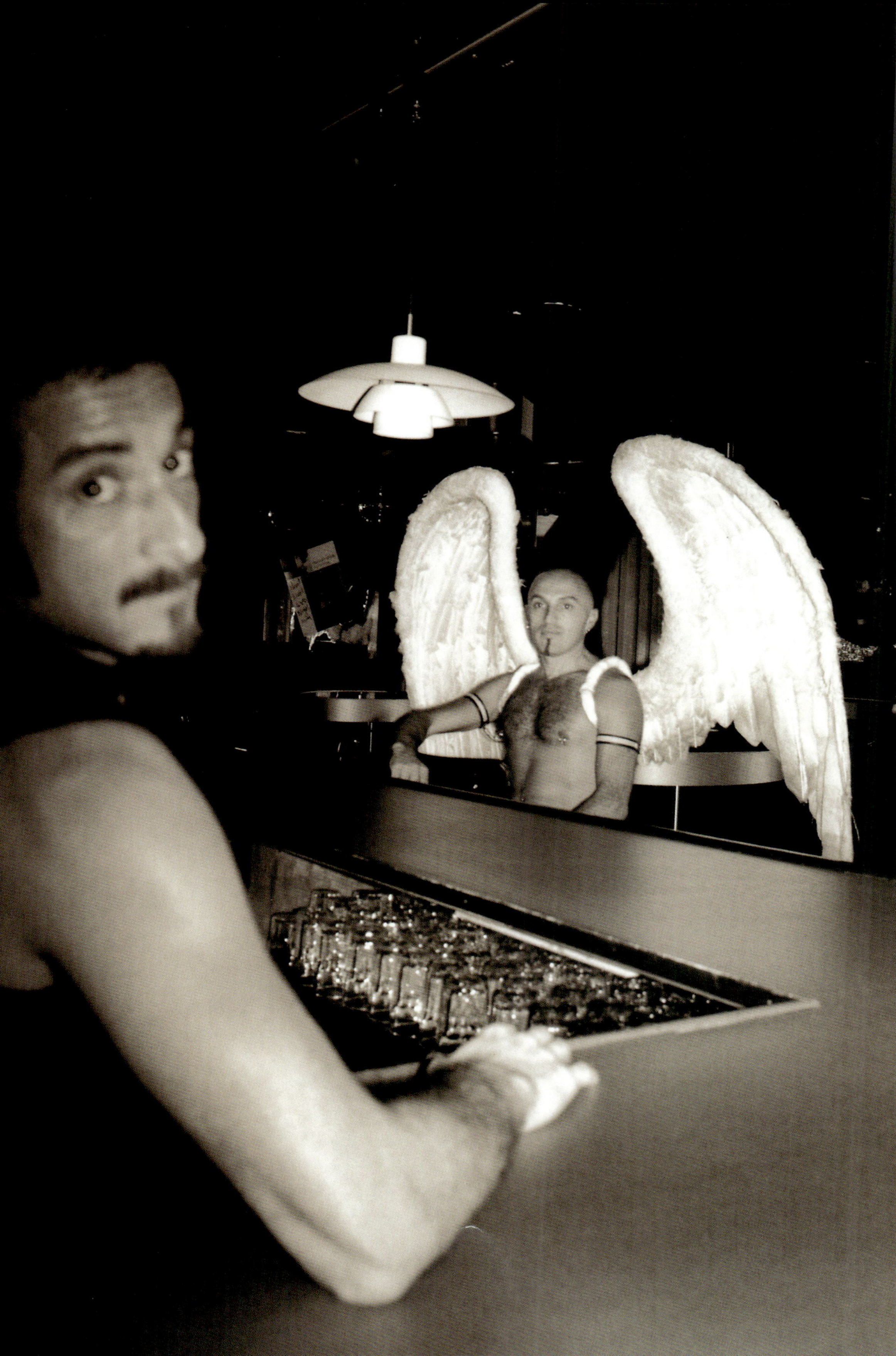

know and accept
yourself and
you will find peace

**george & cory**
malta

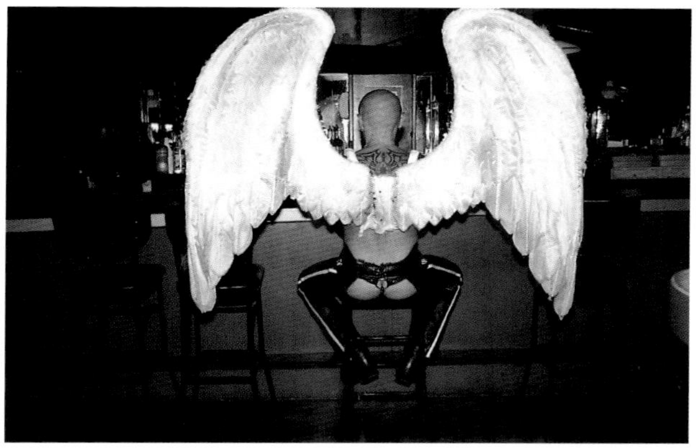

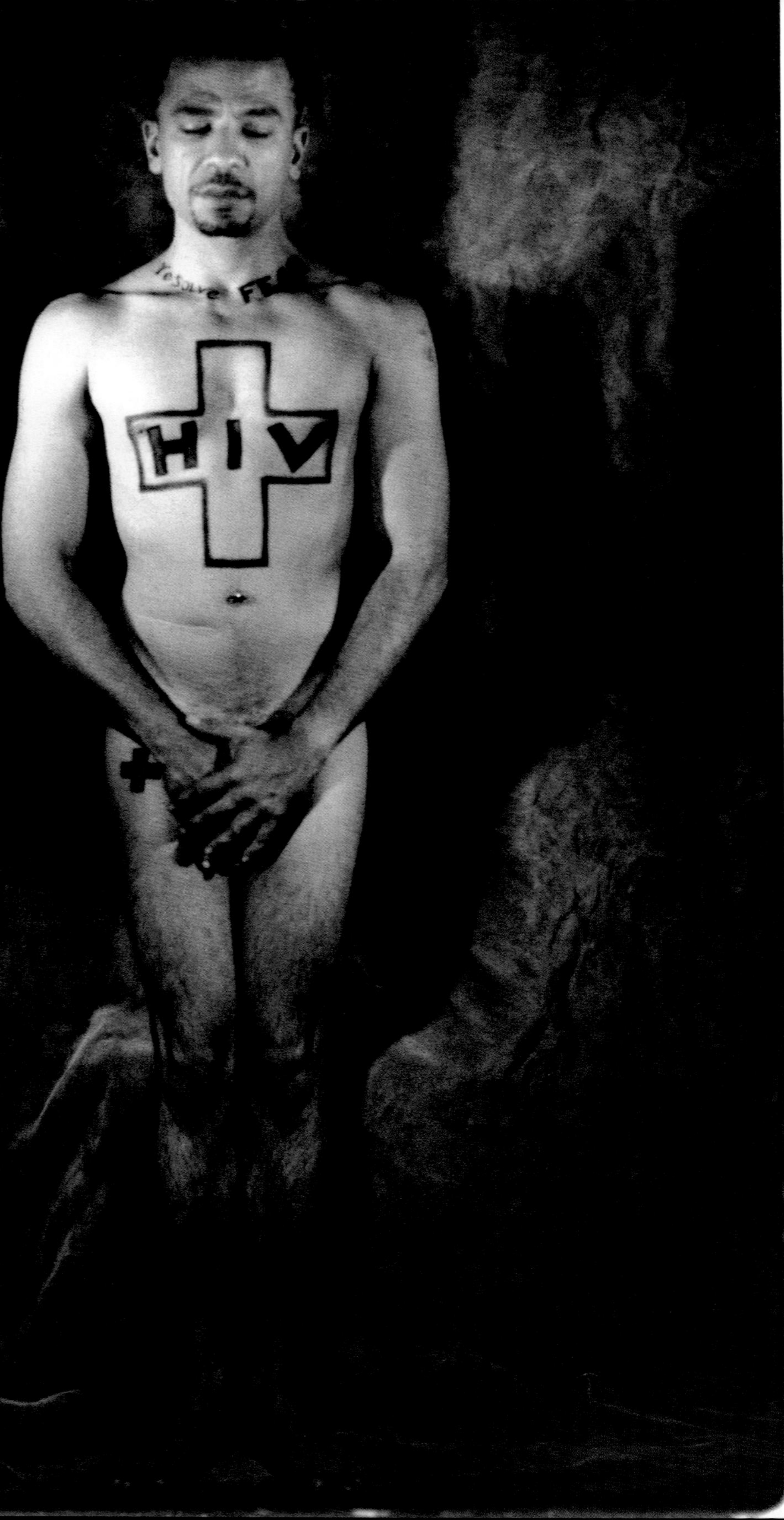


**arjan**
india

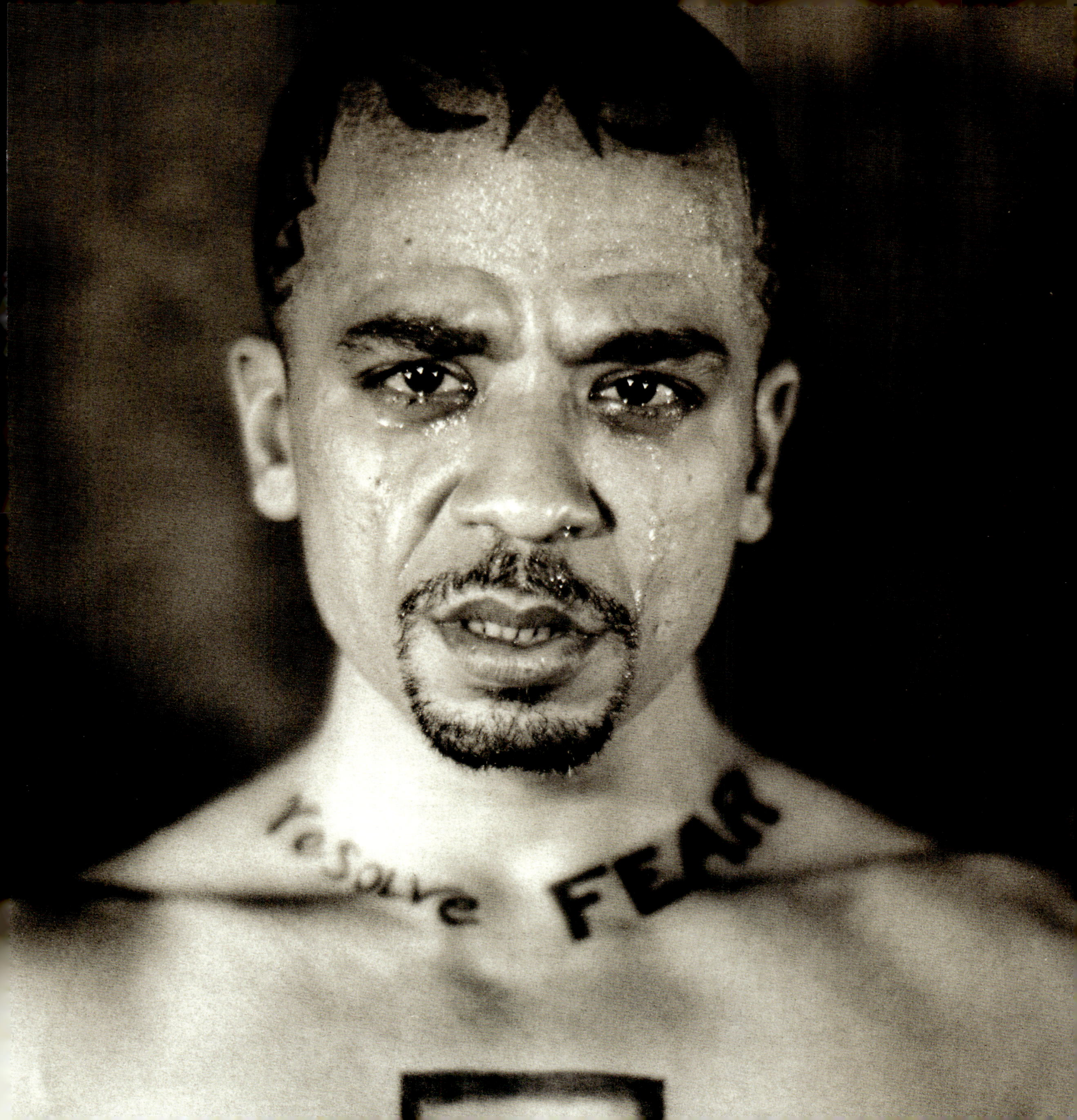
resolve FEAR

i flew back to new york
to search for my true path
i'm still looking . . .

**pru**
australia

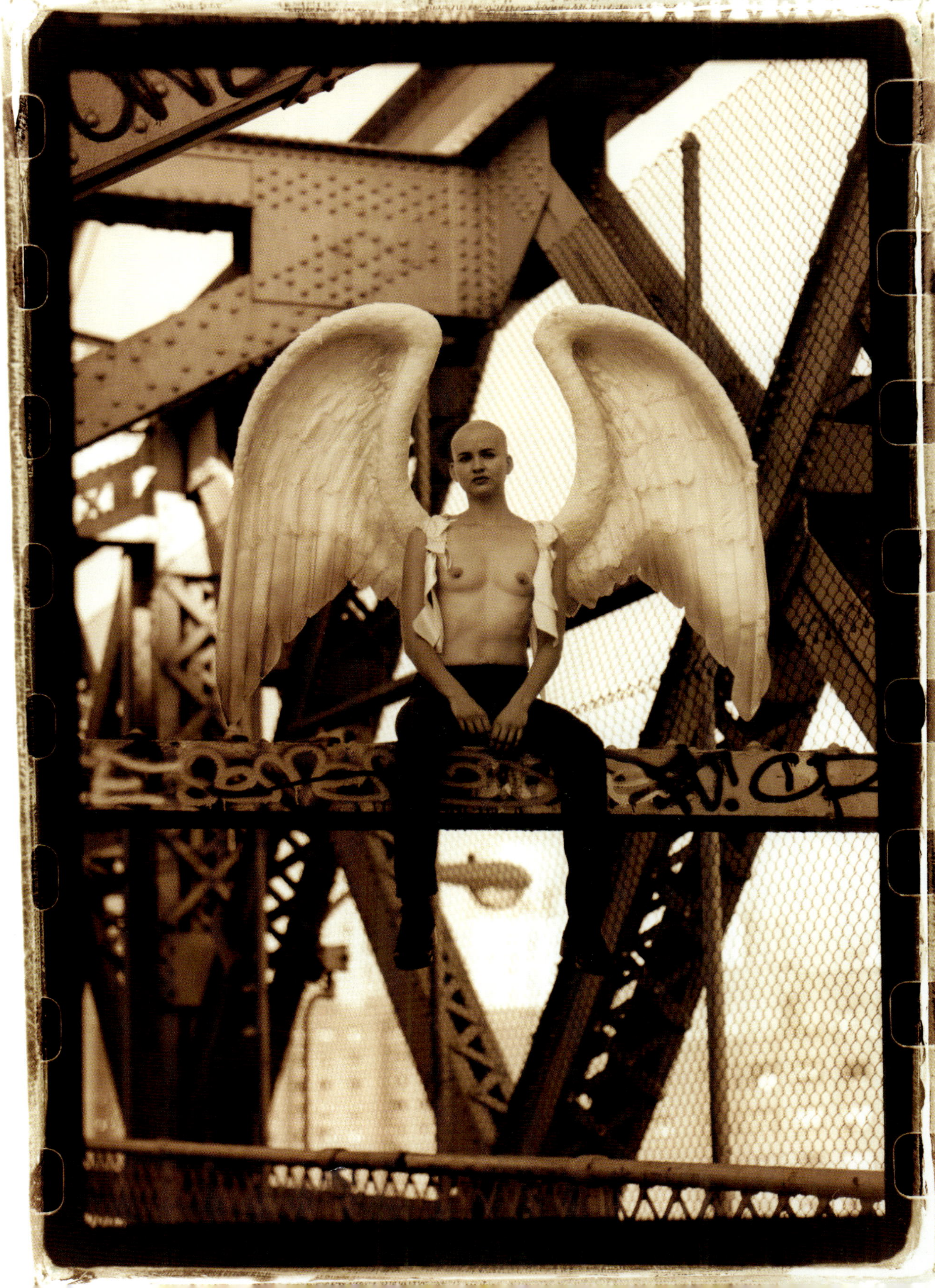

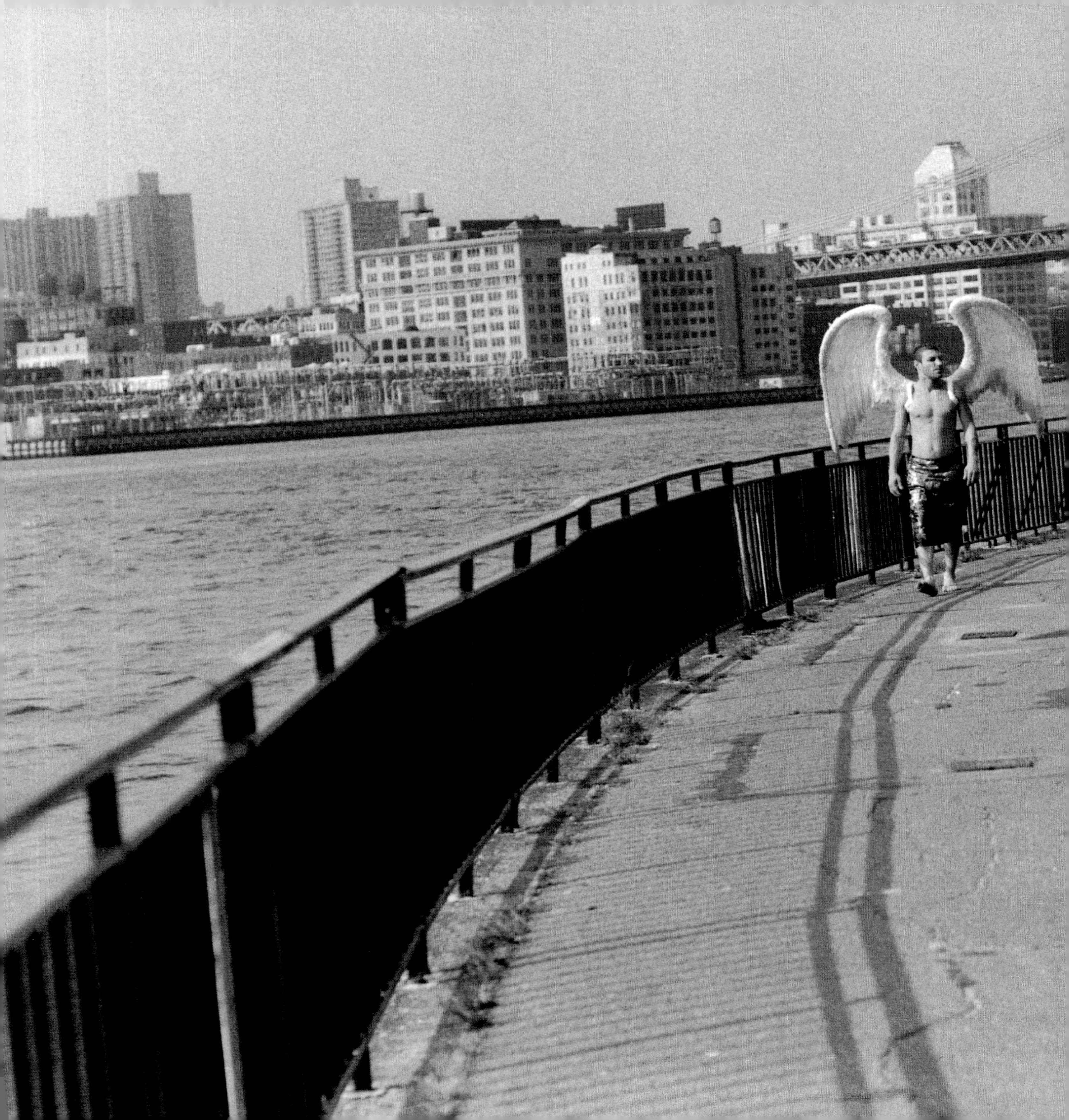

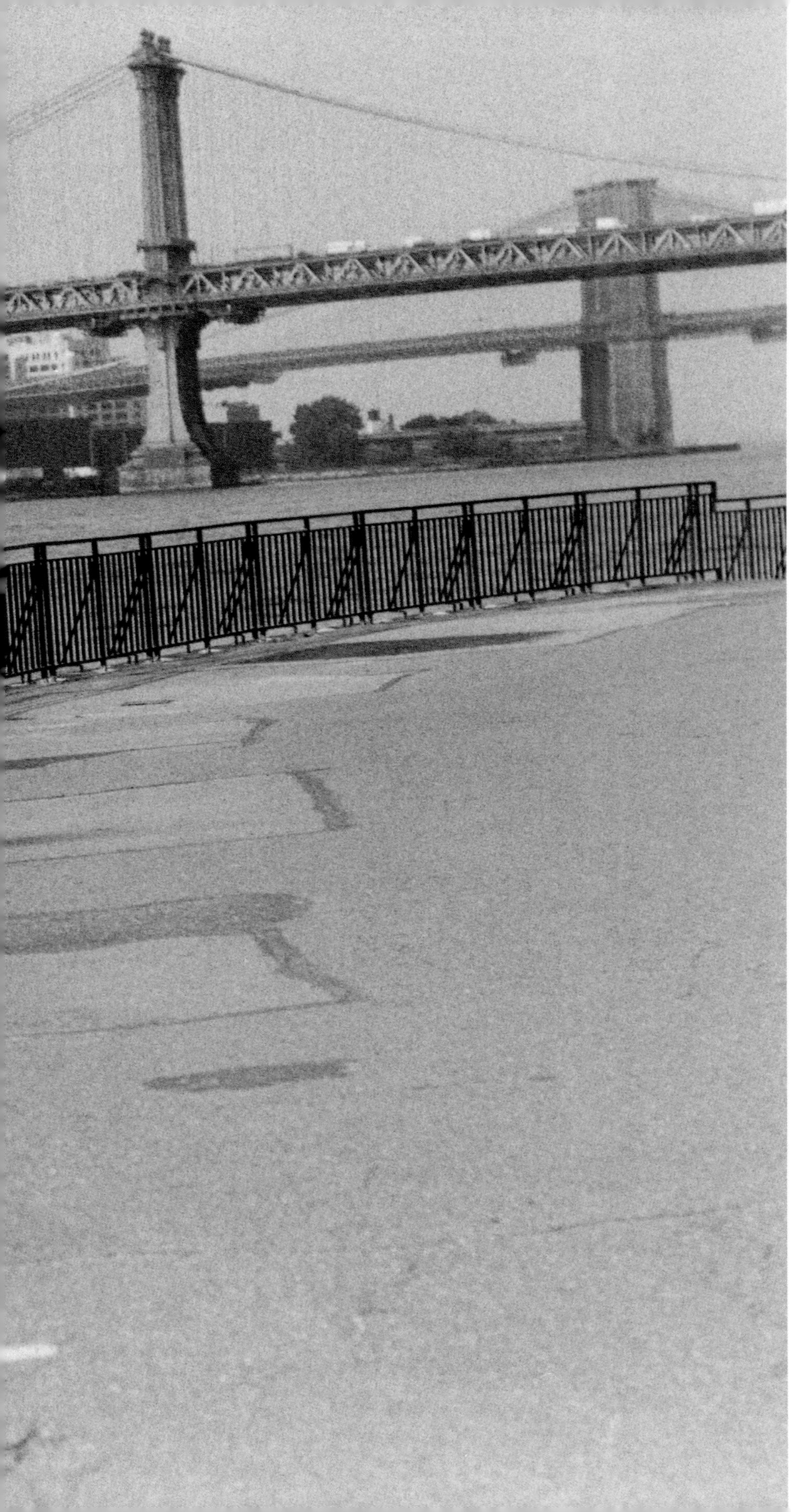

mankind must explore
the creation of the soul
and allow each individual
to experience true freedom

**swage**
portugal

peace is a way of thinking
a way of working
i think of the monks in tibet
it is said that through the meditation
and prayer of these monks
the whole world benefits

**brainhard**
norway

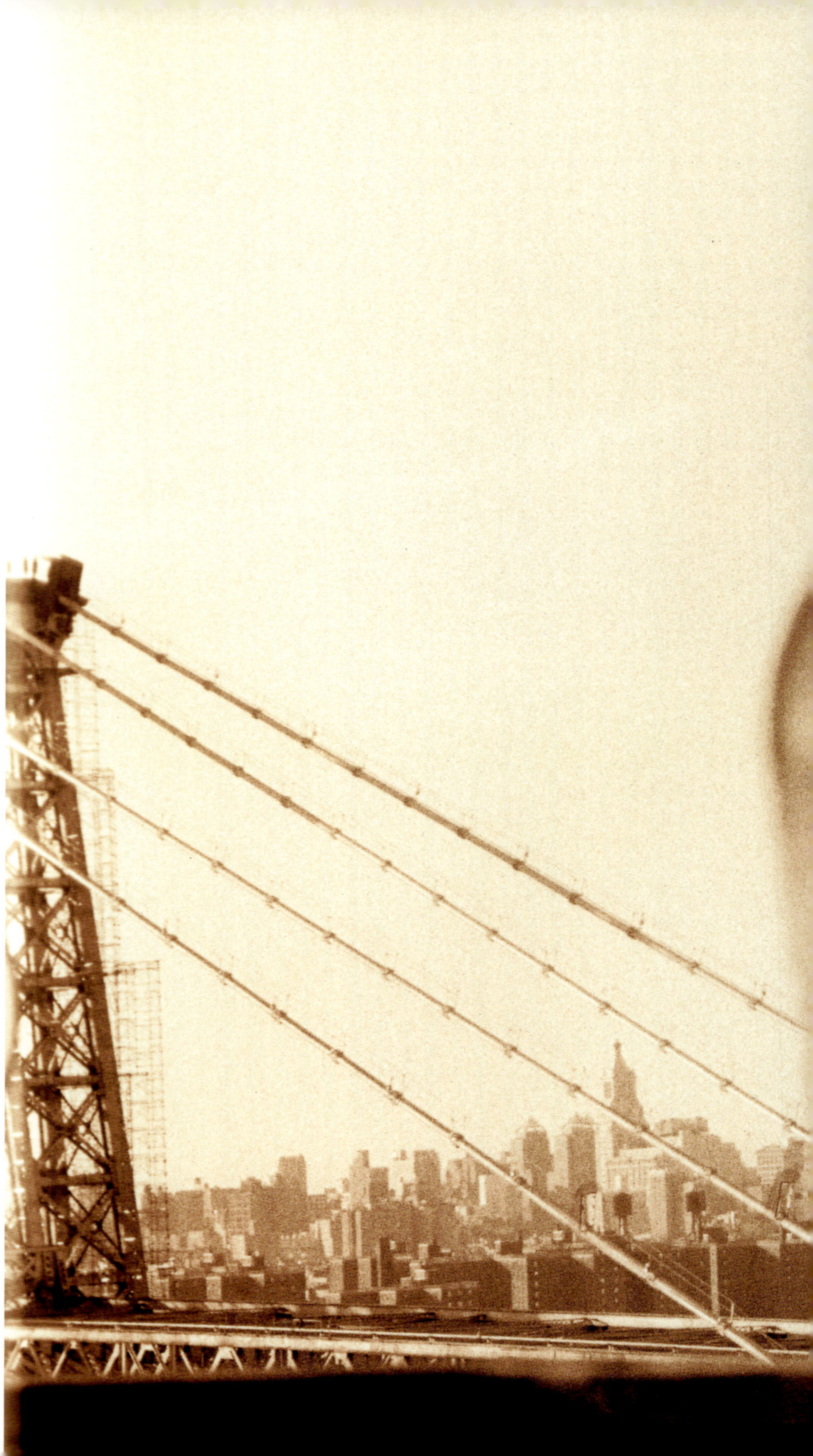

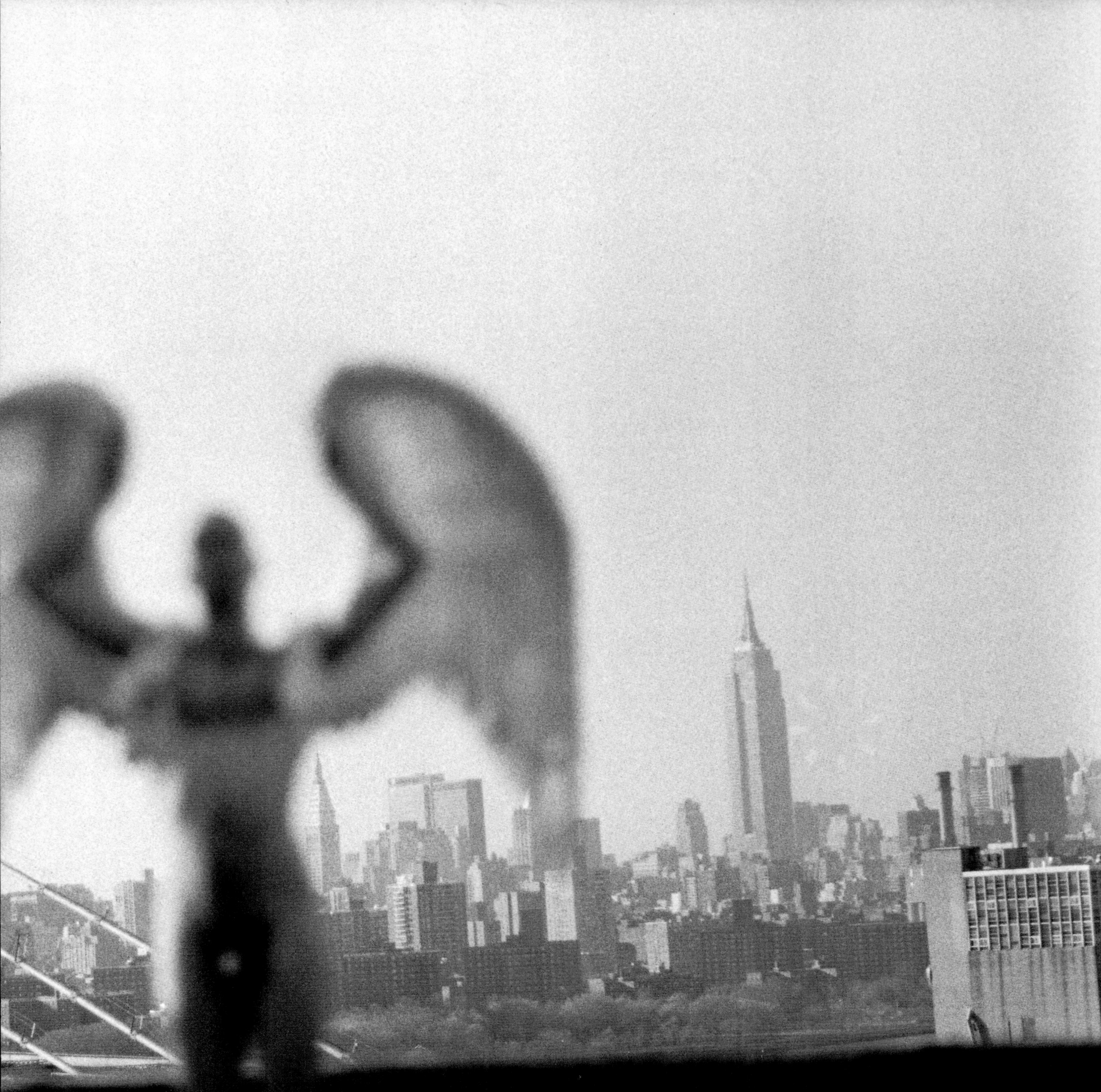

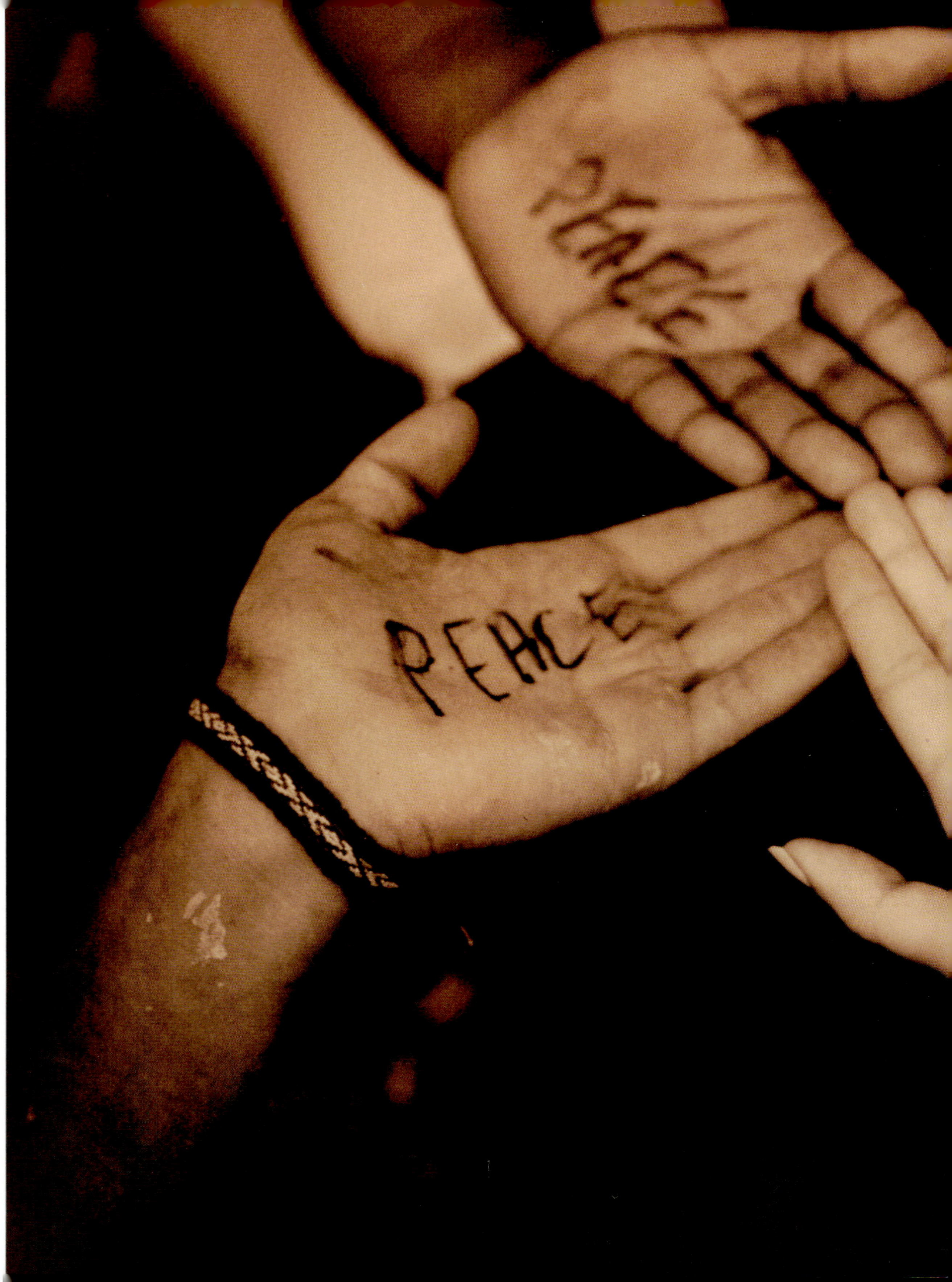
PEACE
PEACE

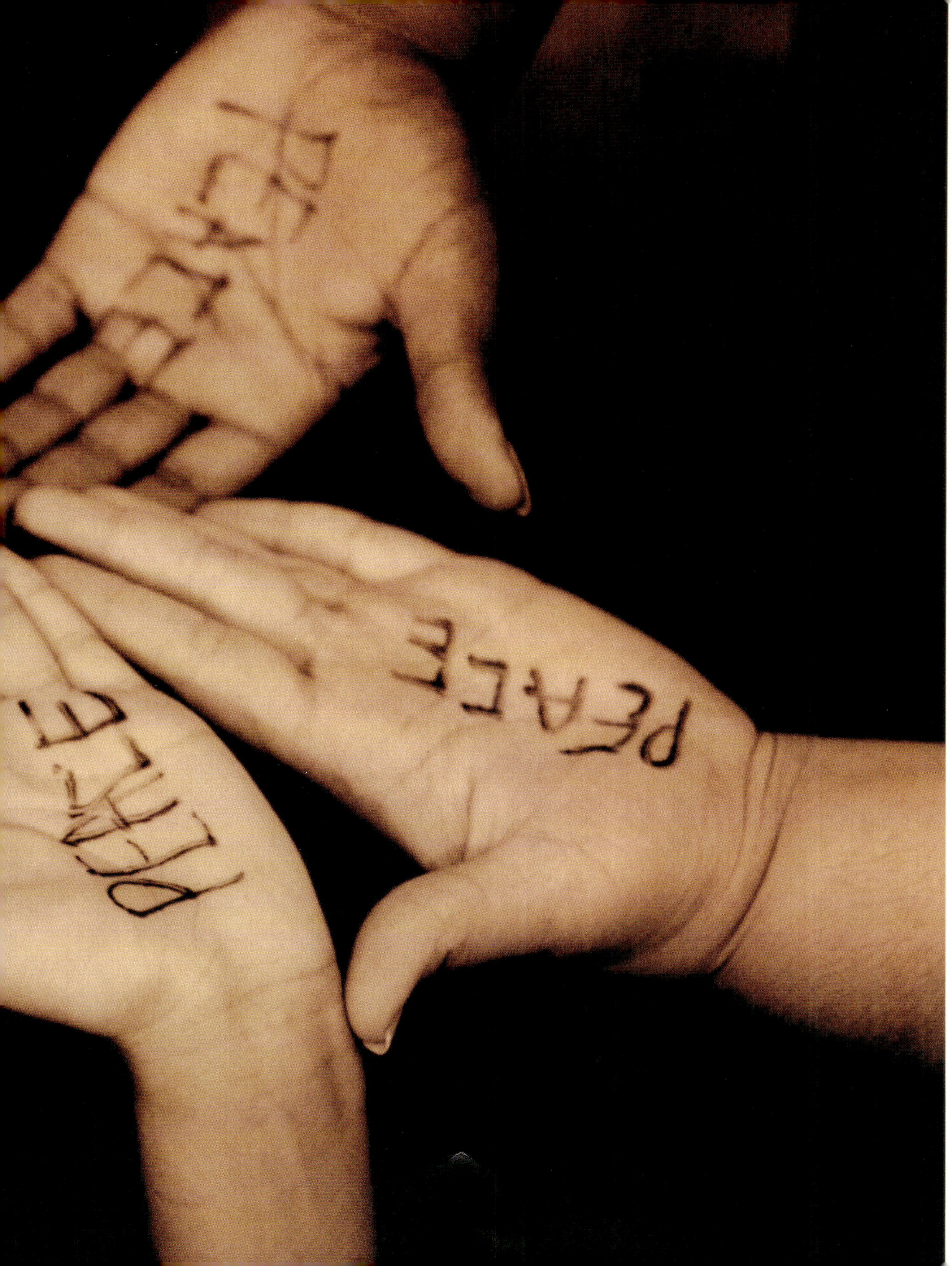
PEACE
PEACE
PEACE

**patti**
hungary

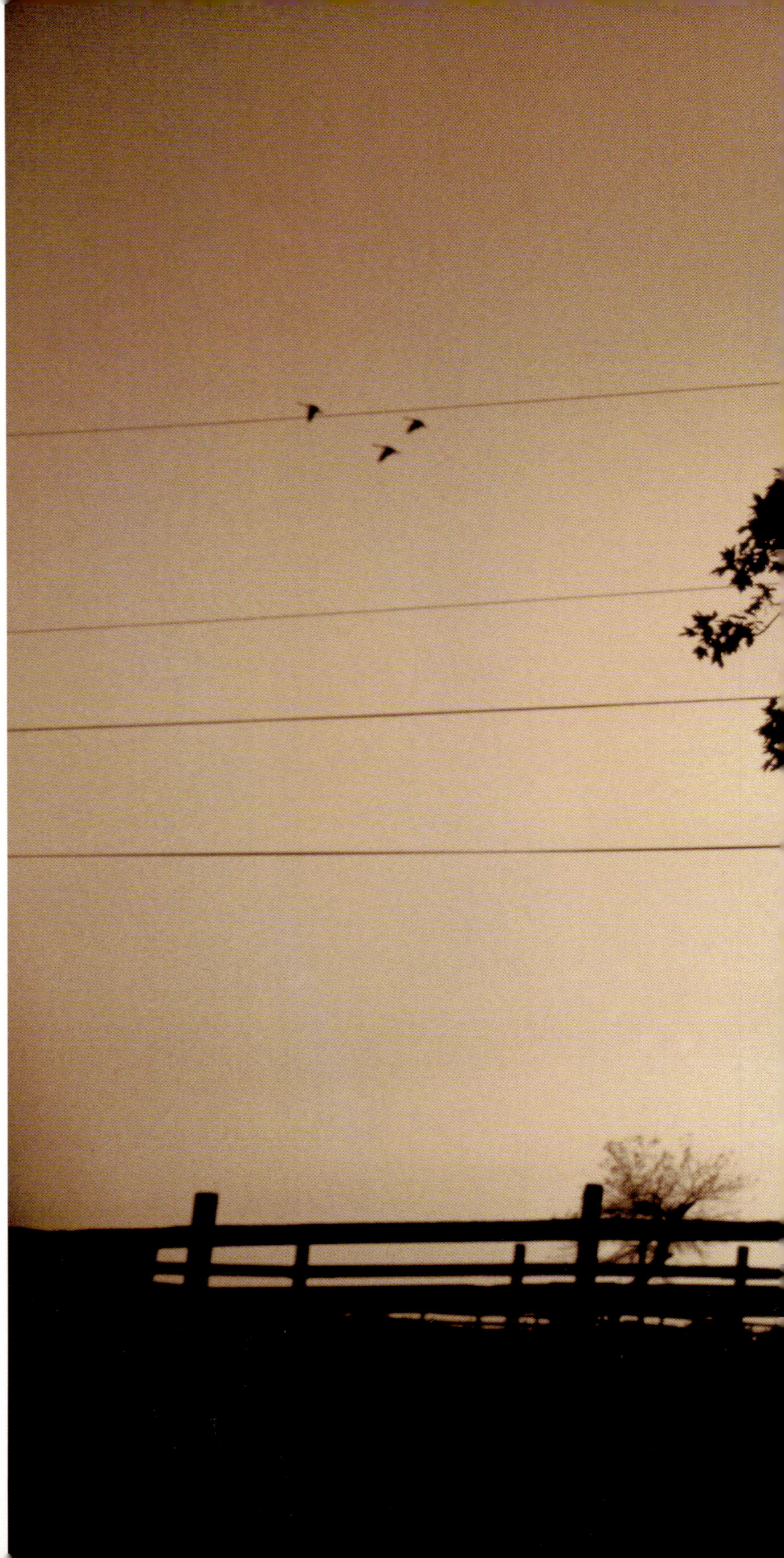

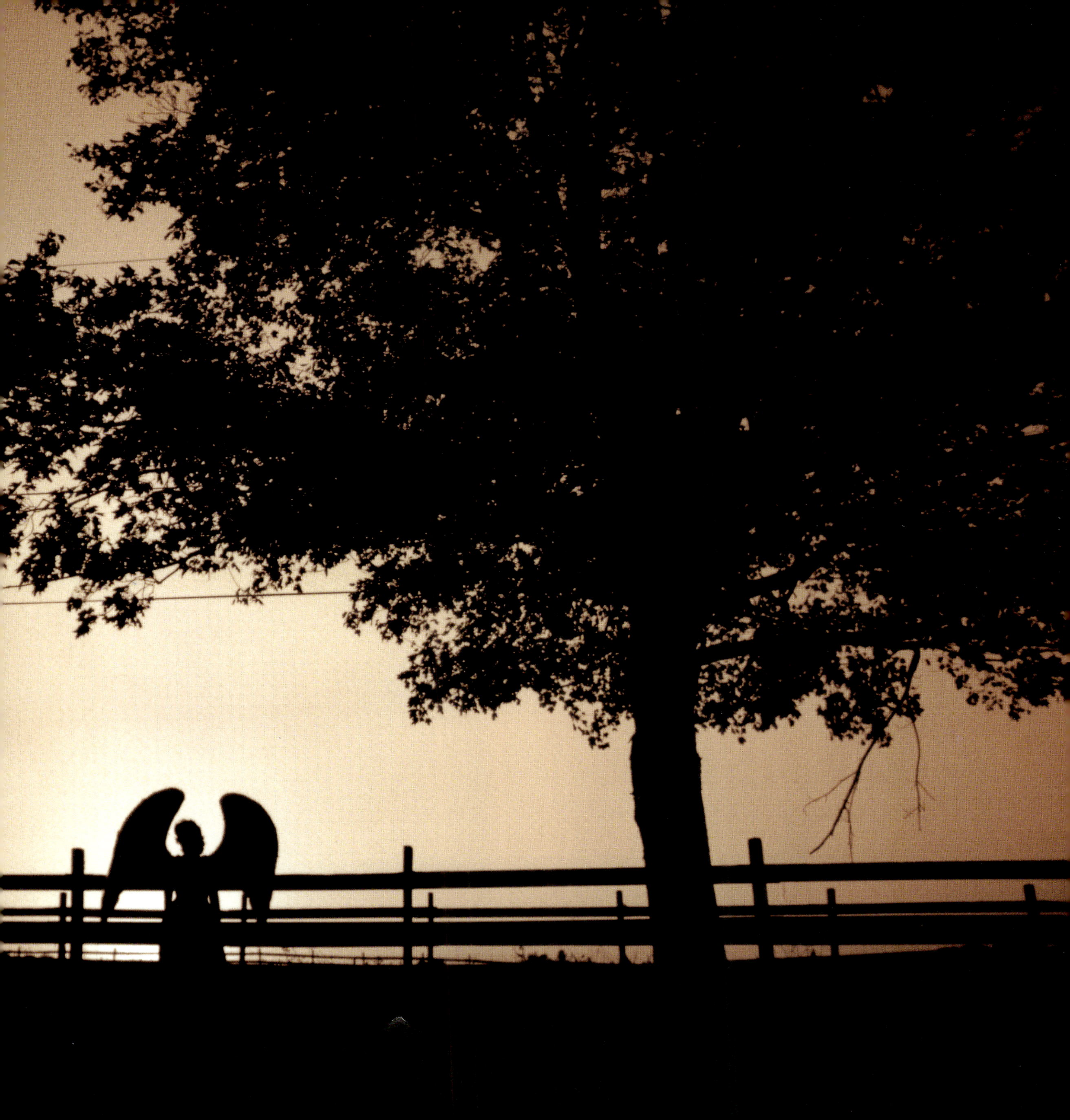

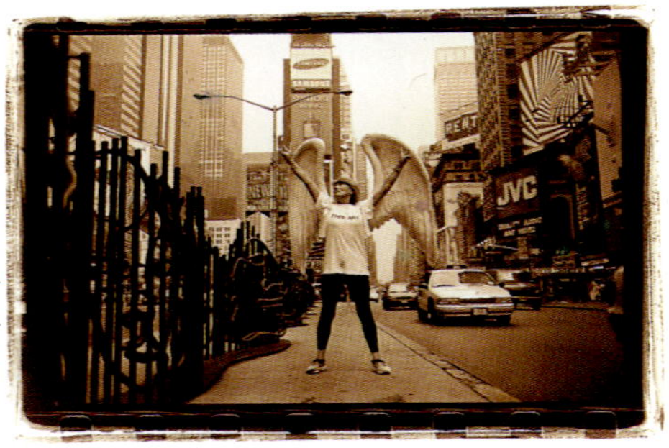




**panja jürgens**

## Acknowledgments

Troy: for the designing of the wings
Barbara Gentile: for the enlargements of the photos
Todd Phillips: for the documentary film »My Dream of Peace«
Edge Photolab NYC, Latent Image Photolab NYC, Quentin Crisp †, Annie Sprinkle, Leslie Barany, HR Giger, Rebecca Segeström, Monique Simard, Arjan Khiani, Charles H Favrod, Dr Thomas Druyen, Hayah, Saskia Middelburg, my children Jenny & Johnny

Raif Annome, Scott Sternick, Roger Kaufmann, Clayton Patterson, Carry Curran, Mikel Ortega, Kelly Gigante, Brian Winkowski, Pru Murphy, Arnold Mesches, Kevin, Emily Wetzel, Angela Arroyo, Cynthia Caralla, Otis Latimer, Ira Nahoun, Roberto Gracia, Brainhard Carey, Carlos Caballero, Rikke Ulk, Claudio Mazcarenhas, Zelda Kaplan, Roy Schatt, Flofox, Julius Bollax, Emanuel Xavier, Taylor Mead, Maki Kodaira, Carvassa Warden Nickens, Dimitris Yeros, Thomas N Hammond, Themba Sibeko, Moussa Sene Absa, Rose Edwards, Yuri Karpalow, Kelly Ann Brill, Daniel Jason, Stephan Lupino, Naz Shahrokh, Mariam Bonetti, Segal Yehudai, Robert Evollo, François Vaysettes, Florence Levy, Phillip ND Drennan, Neelam Cupta, Anil Cupta, Ria Cupta, Elena Oritz, Axel Stocks, Charry Sanders, Lida & Leeza Ahmady, Mijanon Montealegre, Yashine Hachani, Dalica Hachani, Mary Hawkins, Beverly A Chester, Little Hawk, Pony, Christopher Lindsay, Fritz Smitz, Evelyn McCue, Choi Chun Leung, Sahara, Stephanie Holley, Angel Rodriguez and his children, Peter Corbin, Robert Glass, Benita Howard, JP McCue, Monique Simard, Stephanie Ramenes, Swagi Warren, John G Lesko, David C Russel, Juan Jose Aviles, Bina Sharif, Norma Baloria, Lori Goldstone, Patricia Booream, Joe & Anna Adda, Sarah & Mason Plummer, Jerimiah Booream, Nancy H Weaver, Harry & Gloria Quick, William B, Andrew Ramos & Team, Eli Akleh, Michelle L Gabriel, Patricia A Gibbs Aleyne, Fatima Lim David, Katharina, Justin, Ninfa †, Felix, Victor and his son Kurt, Lucia Micelli, Grego Sim Lim Oh, George Calleja, Cory Jotso, Ismael Firado, Laurence Schad, Anthony Buzetta, Edwin Vasques, Bob Doukas, Glenora, David & Ivy Blackshire, Silvia Alloway, Diana & Iliana Hernandez Coppex, Chiara Young, Elsie Sannon, Muhsin Demirkan, Magdi H Edrees, Megan Rush, Nadja & Chiara Burghardt, Nasser Aou, Jordan Boettele, Emma Trask, Charles Bachelor, Dorris Chiannmonte, Uros Martir, Shaul, Barbara Patanovich, Mehdi A Rad, Branislav Matovic, Greg Gordan, Tashi Wansdi, Heru Ankh Ra Semahj, Victor Radilla, Adele Kiran, Maci D Alloul, Rebecca Veregara, Pat Storm †, Vilma & Oscar Villar, Christian Earl, Donald, Bobby Faust, Tom Shierlitz, Christina Stott, Ledama Ole Kantai, Rabbi Levi Shemtow, Thelma Blitz Knitz, William Akleh, John Akleh, Crazy Wolf, Sato Susumo, Jean

## Biography Panja Jürgens

| | |
|---|---|
| 1939 | Panja Jürgens born in Venne, Germany |
| 1979 | takes up photography during her first journey to Africa |
| 1982–1983 | photographic studies on birds in South Africa and on Bird Island, Seychelles |
| 1985 | stays in Tanzania with the Maasai |
| 1986–1987 | photographic series *Return to Paradise* |
| 1989 | starts working on the series *New York Drag Queens* |
| 1990 | photographic documentation on *New York Street People* |
| 1996 | World Calendar Award; publishes *Transformations. New York Drag Queens* |
| 1999 | documentary film by Todd Phillips about the project *Wings of Peace* |
| 1987–2001 | photographic documentation *Giger's Garden* |
| 2002 | article on "The soul is everything, says Aristotle," in: *Female - Male - Different*, Waxmann Verlag, Münster |

## Exhibitions

*Return to Paradise*
Nikon Galerie, Zürich; Galerie Pinx, Wien; Galerie Chalet Muri, Bern; Cinepress, Zürich; Nerlino Gallery, New York; Galerie Chalet Muri, Bern; Kunsthalle, Köln; Hyposwiss, Zürich; Museum HR Giger, Château St. Germain, Gruyères

*Street People*
Galerie Chalet Muri, Bern

*New York Drag Queens*
Museum für Photographie, Lausanne; Kulturabteilung Bayer AG, Leverkusen; Ludwig Forum für Internationale Kunst, Aachen; Jahrhunderthalle, Frankfurt am Main; Galerie Mangisch, Zürich

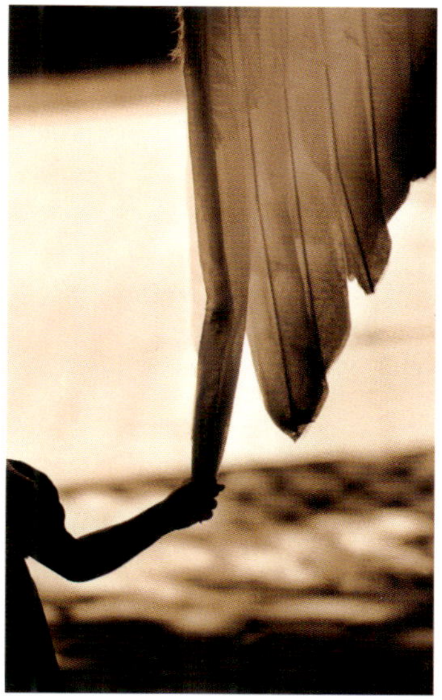

**ria**

india

Design: Herneid von dem Knesebeck
Project Manager: Monika Schaffrath
Typesetting: Satz und Repro Grieb, Munich
Separations: Karl Dörfel, Munich
Printed and bound in Germany by Passavia, Passau

ISBN 0-8109-6747-2

Published in 2002 by Knesebeck GmbH & Co. Verlags KG, Munich
www.knesebeck-verlag.de

Distributed in 2002 by Harry N. Abrams, Incorporated, New York


10 9 8 7 6 5 4 3 2 1

ABRAMS

Harry N. Abrams, Inc.
100 Fifth Avenue
New York, N.Y. 10011
www.abramsbooks.com

Knesebeck and Abrams are subsidiaries of

LA MARTINIÈRE
GROUPE